C000058000

Welcome to the 2... Small Hotels, Inns & Restaurants... some significant and refreshing changes. This new compact size remains highly visual and features easier to read entries, clearer maps and more informed text. Using less paper, the reduced weight also helps us to be more environmentally friendly as we distribute worldwide, currently stretching from Chile to China.

The Guide has been designed to help you make the right choice. Our Recommendations offer a breadth of variety and value as we understand that today's traveller often seeks out different experiences: a romantic anniversary break, a tranquil and informal environment, a contemporary city base or classic gourmet sophistication.

Our collection is made up of six Guides, representing over 1,300 annually inspected and recommended hotels, resorts, spas and meeting venues throughout 67 countries. You can read about the other guides on page 247 or see the whole collection online at www.johansens.com

This 2008 edition includes many new Recommendations as well as consummate favourites for you to try, and you can be certain that our team of Inspectors has been busy ensuring that only the best places are recommended and those that don't reach our exacting standards are not.

If you have a chance we would love to hear about your experience by completing a Guest Survey Report at the back of this Guide or online. Feedback is an influencing factor when we compile nominations for our Annual Awards for Excellence.

Above all, we hope you enjoy your stay and please remember to mention 'Condé Nast Johansens' when you make an enquiry or reservation.

Andrew Warren
Managing Director

BEYOND COMPARE...

Image from britainonview.com

Contents

Image from britainonview.com

About this Guide

To find a hotel by location:

· Use the **county maps** at the front of the Guide to obtain a page number for the area of the country you wish to search.

· Turn to the **indexes** which start on page 228.

· Alternatively, use the **maps** at the back of the Guide where each hotel is marked.

If you cannot find a suitable hotel you may decide to choose one of the properties within the *Condé Nast Johansens Recommended Hotels & Spas Guide*. These establishments are listed on pages 194–196.

Once you have made your choice please contact the hotel directly. Rates are per room, including VAT and breakfast (unless stated otherwise) and are correct at the time of going to press but you should always check with the hotel before you make your reservation. **When making a booking please mention that Condé Nast Johansens is your source of reference.**

Readers should be aware that by making a reservation with a hotel, either by telephone, e-mail or in writing, they are entering into a legal contract and must adhere to their terms, conditions and cancellation policies. A hotelier under certain circumstances is entitled to make a charge for accommodation when guests fail to arrive, even if notice of the cancellation is given.

Moray p178

Higland p173

Aberdeenshire p166

Argyll &
Bute p167

Fife
p172

SCOTLAND

Scottish Borders
p179

South
Ayrshire
p168

Dumfries & Galloway p169

N. IRELAND

IRELAND

Westmeath
p164

Kerry
p162

ENGLAND

WALES

SCOTLAND

N. IRELAND

IRELAND

WALES

ENGLAND

Northumberland p106

Cumbria p39

North Yorkshire p152

Lancashire p88

West Yorkshire p160

Merseyside p97

Conwy p183

Cheshire p31

Derbyshire p49

Lincolnshire p92

Gwynedd p185

Nottinghamshire p109

Shropshire p124

Leicestershire p90

Rutland p122

Norfolk p98

Powys p191

Worcestershire p147

Cambridgeshire p29

Pembrokeshire p189

Herefordshire p73

Bedfordshire p20

Suffolk p134

Carmarthenshire p182

Monmouthshire p188

Gloucestershire p64

Buckinghamshire p28

Hertfordshire p78

Essex p62

Vale of Glamorgan p192

Oxfordshire p112

London p95

Berkshire p21

Somerset p126

Wiltshire p140

Hampshire p70

Surrey p136

Kent p84

Devon p52

Dorset p60

West Sussex p138

East Sussex p137

Cornwall p32

Isle of Wight p80

Channel Islands

Guernsey p16

Jersey p18

7

Key to Symbols

⌂ [23]   Total number of bedrooms

⏚   Owner managed

CC   Credit cards not accepted

♧   Quiet location

♿   Wheelchair Access. We recommend that you contact the hotel to determine the level of accessibility for wheelchair users.

♜   Chef-patron

M [23]   Meeting/conference facilities with maximum number of delegates

⚦ [8]   Children welcome, with minimum age where applicable

🐕   Dogs welcome in rooms or kennels

🛏   At least 1 bedroom has a four-poster bed

📡   Cable/satellite TV in all bedrooms

💿   CD player in bedrooms

DVD/VCR   DVD/video player in bedrooms

📞   ISDN/modem point in all bedrooms

WiFi   Wireless Internet connection available in part or all rooms

🚭   Non-smoking bedrooms available

⬍   Lift available for guests' use

❄   Air conditioning in all bedrooms

🏋   Gym/fitness facilities on-site

SPA   A dedicated spa offering extensive health, beauty and fitness treatments together with water treatments

♨   Indoor swimming pool

♨   Outdoor swimming pool

🎾   Tennis court on-site

🚶   Walking – details of local walking routes and packed lunches can be provided and an overnight drying room for clothes is available.

🐟   Fishing on-site

🐟   Fishing can be arranged

⛳   Golf course on-site

⛳   Golf course nearby, which has an arrangement with the property allowing guests to play

🎯   Shooting on-site

🎯   Shooting can be arranged

♘   Horse riding can be arranged

H   Property has a helicopter landing pad

🔔   Licensed for wedding ceremonies

View of the lake at Sharrow Bay, Cumbria

the perfect end to every day.

Image from britainonview.com

Condé Nast Johansens

Condé Nast Johansens Ltd, 6-8 Old Bond Street, London W1S 4PH
Tel: +44 (0)20 7499 9080 Fax: +44 (0)20 7152 3565
E-mail: info@johansens.com
www.johansens.com

Publishing Director:	Patricia Greenwood
PA to Publishing Director:	Clare Freeman
Hotel Inspectors:	Jean Branham
	Peter Bridgham
	Geraldine Bromley
	Robert Bromley
	Audrey Fenton
	Henrietta Fergusson
	Pat Gillson
	Marie Iversen
	Pauline Mason
	John Morison
	John O'Neill
	Mary O'Neill
	Fiona Patrick
	Liza Reeves
	Leonora Sandwell
	Nevill Swanson
Production Manager:	Kevin Bradbrook
Production Editor:	Laura Kerry
Senior Designer:	Michael Tompsett
Copywriters:	Sophie Cliffe-Roberts
	Norman Flack
	Debra O'Sullivan
	Rozanne Paragon
	Leonora Sandwell
Marketing & Sales	
Promotions Executive:	Charlie Bibby
Client Services Director:	Fiona Patrick
PA to Managing Director:	Mairead Aitken
Managing Director:	Andrew Warren

Copyright © 2007 Condé Nast Johansens Ltd.
Condé Nast Johansens Ltd. is part of The Condé Nast Publications Ltd.
ISBN 978-1-903665-34-3
Printed in England by St Ives plc
Distributed in the UK and Europe by Portfolio, Greenford (bookstores).
In North America by Casemate Publishing, Pennsylvania (bookstores).
Front cover picture: Langar Hall, Nottinghamshire

'Life is to be enjoyed, let us do the hard work for you'.

Personal | Insurance | Solutions
Preferred insurance partner of Condé Nast Johansens

0800 230 0833
Johansens@jltgroup.com

Personal | Insurance | Solutions
Preferred insurance partner of Condé Nast Johansens

JARDINE LLOYD THOMPSON
Personal Risks

The Perfect Combination...

Condé Nast Johansens Gift Vouchers

Condé Nast Johansens Gift Vouchers make a unique and much valued present for birthdays, weddings, anniversaries, special occasions and as a corporate incentive.

Vouchers are available in denominations of £100, £50, €140, €70, $150, $75 and may be used as payment or part payment for your stay or a meal at any Condé Nast Johansens 2008 recommended property.

To order Gift Vouchers call +44 (0)207 152 3558 or purchase direct at www.johansens.com

Condé Nast Johansens Guides

As well as this Guide, Condé Nast Johansens also publish the following titles:

Recommended Hotels & Spas, Great Britain & Ireland 2008

Recommended Hotels & Spas, Europe & The Mediterranean 2008

Recommended Hotels, Inns, Resorts & Spas, The Americas, Atlantic, Caribbean & Pacific 2008

Luxury Spas Worldwide 2008

Recommended International Venues for Meetings & Special Events 2008

To purchase Guides please call FREEPHONE 0800 269 397 or visit our Bookshop at www.johansens.com

PENHALIGON'S
LONDON
Luxury Hotel Toiletries

Soothe, Relax and Rejuvenate Your Guests
with the Exclusive New Racquets Fragrance

  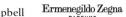

Image from britainonview.com

Channel Islands

For further information on the Channel Islands, please contact:

Visit Guernsey
PO Box 23, St Peter Port, Guernsey GY1 3AN
Tel: +44 (0)1481 723552
Internet: www.visitguernsey.com

Jersey Tourism
Liberation Square, St Helier, Jersey JE1 1BB
Tel: +44 (0)1534 448800
E-mail: info@jersey.com
Internet: www.jersey.com

Sark Tourism
The Visitors Centre, The Avenue, Sark, GY9 0SA
Tel: +44 (0)1481 832345
E-mail: contact@sark.com
Internet: www.sark.info

Herm Tourist Office
Administration Office, Herm Island, Guernsey GY1 3HR
Tel: +44 (0)1481 722377
E-mail: admin@herm-island.com
Internet: www.herm-island.com

or see **pages 197-200** for details of local historic houses, castles and gardens to visit during your stay.

For additional places to stay in the Channel Islands, turn to **pages 194-196** where a listing of our Recommended Hotels & Spas Guide can be found.

THE WHITE HOUSE

HERM ISLAND, GUERNSEY, CHANNEL ISLANDS GY1 3HR
Tel: 0845 365 2735 **International:** +44 (0)1481 722159 **Fax:** 01481 710066
Web: www.johansens.com/whitehouseherm **E-mail:** hotel@herm–island.com

Our inspector loved: This beautiful haven of total relaxation offers wonderful food and supreme hospitality - all in a unique private island setting.

Price Guide: (including dinner)
single £76–£104
double/twin £152–£192
crows nest £228

Awards/Recognition: 1 AA Rosette 2007-2008; Condé Nast Johansens Most Excellent Coastal Hotel 2005

Location: Via St Peter Port, Guernsey, 20-min ferry

Attractions: Swimming; Walks; Fantastic Beaches; Bird watching

Herm Island's magic will start working on you as soon as you arrive at the harbour. There are no cars so a tractor full of luggage chugs up from the jetty to the gleaming White House. Adrian and Pennie Heyworth are marvelous hosts and will be able to help even the most stressed arrival to relax. You will love exploring the island and will hardly notice the absence of TV's. You can picnic in sandy coves, walk the cliff tops, go in search of wildlife or just snooze by the pool. Most of the bedrooms have sea views, the remainder over the gardens. Plenty of flexibility for families including several charming cottages. Menus make the most of the daily catch - Guernsey lobster, scallops and crab.

LA SABLONNERIE

LITTLE SARK, SARK, CHANNEL ISLANDS GY9 0SD
Tel: 0845 365 1972 **International:** +44 (0)1481 832061 **Fax:** 01481 832408
Web: www.johansens.com/lasablonnerie **E-mail:** lasablonnerie@cwgsy.net

Our inspector loved: The total feeling of escapism from the real world - it is just such a wonderful place to recharge the batteries.

Price Guide: (including dinner)
single from £78
double/twin £156–£198

Location: Via St Peter Port, Guernsey, 45-min ferry

Attractions: George's boat trip around the island; Cycling, walking, swimming and bird watching; Champagne and lobsters; La Seigneurie Gardens

Owner and manager Elizabeth Perrée considers La Sablonnerie an oasis of good living and courtesy rather than a luxury hotel. It is an hotel of rare quality situated in a time warp of simplicity on a tiny, idyllic island where no motor cars are allowed and life ambles along at a peaceful unhurried pace. A vintage horse-drawn carriage collects guests from Sark's tiny harbour. Tranquil cosiness, friendliness and sophistication characterise this hotel with its low ceilings and 400-year-old oak beams. Elizabeth has extended and discreetly modernised the hotel with 22 bedrooms which are charmingly individual in style. The hotel has a reputation for superb cuisine. Many of the dishes are prepared from produce grown on its own farm and in its gardens, and enhanced by locally caught lobster and oysters.

CHÂTEAU LA CHAIRE

ROZEL BAY, JERSEY JE3 6AJ
Tel: 0845 365 2863 **International:** +44 (0)1534 863354 **Fax:** 01534 865137
Web: www.johansens.com/chateaulachaire **E-mail:** res@chateau-la-chaire.co.uk

Our inspector loved: The unique location in a romantic wooded valley close to the sea.

Price Guide: (inclusive of afternoon tea)
double (single occupancy) £89-£133
double £201-£288
suite £232-£330

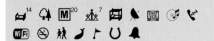

Awards/Recognition: 2 AA Rosettes 2007-2008

Location: A6, 1.5 miles; St Helier, 7 miles; Jersey Airport, 11 miles

Attractions: The Durrell Wildlife Conservation Trust; Jersey Pottery; Occupation Museum; Stunning Coastal Scenery

You can see that care and great attention to detail are important at this charming hotel. Built in 1843 as a rather grand elegant home today's owners have kept many original antiques and classical paintings to enhance the period charm. Nestled in a romantic spot high in a wooded valley close to the sea this is a great location from which to explore the island. The garden, currently awaiting restoration, will delight botanists. An excellent reputation follows the oak-panelled restaurant with a menu full of both Gallic and English influences whilst the sunny terrace seems a popular place for locals to catch up on news and chat during the islands many warm months.

Image from britainonview.com

England

For further information on England, please contact:

Cumbria Tourist Board
Tel: +44 (0)1539 822222
Web: www.golakes.co.uk

East of England Tourist Board
Tel: +44 (0)1284 727470
E-mail: info@eet.org.uk
Web: www.visiteastofengland.com

Heart of England Tourism
Tel: +44 (0)1905 761100
Web: www.visitheartofengland.com

Visit London
Tel: 0870 156 6366
Web: www.visitlondon.com

North East England Tourism Team
Tel: +44 (0)906 683 3000
Web: www.visitnortheastengland.com

North West Tourist Board
Tel: +44 (0)1942 821 222
Web: www.visitnorthwest.com

Tourism South East
Tel: +44 (0)23 8062 5400
Web: www.visitsoutheastengland.com

South West Tourism
Tel: 0870 442 0880
Web: www.visitsouthwest.co.uk

Yorkshire Tourist Board
Tel: +44 (0)1904 707961
Web: www.ytb.org.uk

English Heritage
Tel: +44 (0) 870 333 1181
Web: www.english-heritage.org.uk

Historic Houses Association
Tel: +44 (0)20 7259 5688
Web: www.hha.org.uk

The National Trust
Tel: 0870 458 4000
Web: www.nationaltrust.org.uk

or see **pages 197-200** for details of local historic houses, castles and gardens to visit during your stay.

For additional places to stay in England, turn to **pages 194-196** where a listing of our Recommended Hotels & Spas Guide can be found.

CORNFIELDS RESTAURANT & HOTEL

WILDEN ROAD, COLMWORTH, BEDFORDSHIRE MK44 2NJ
Tel: 0845 365 3246 **International:** +44 (0)1234 378990 **Fax:** 01234 376370
Web: www.johansens.com/cornfields **E-mail:** reservations@cornfieldsrestaurant.co.uk

Our inspector loved: The tempting comfort of the welcoming fire in the inglenook on a grey day.

Price Guide:
single £70–£90
double £120
suite £150
four poster £160

Location: A421, 2 miles; A1, 7 miles; Bedford, 7 miles

Attractions: Cambridge; Cecil Higgins Gallery in Bedford; Woburn; Grafham Water

Nestling in the undulating Bedfordshire countryside Cornfields Restaurant & Hotel is a haven for those in search of a peaceful retreat to unwind and indulge. The inn dates back to the 17th century and features original beams and an inglenook fireplace. King-size beds invite guests to retire in the spacious, individually appointed bedrooms.However, the property's true appeal lies in its cuisine and its owners' vision to create freshly cooked dishes using locally sourced produce. Starters such as stilton, walnut and bacon fritters with a redcurrant and port sauce are delicious and main courses available include British classics such as pork with mild grain mustard and caramelised apples. The smaller of the 2 dining rooms can be hired for private use and is ideal for exclusive dining or business meetings.

THE COTTAGE INN

MAIDENS GREEN, WINKFIELD, BERKSHIRE SL4 4SW
Tel: 0845 365 2435 **International:** +44 (0)1344 882242 **Fax:** 01344 890671
Web: www.johansens.com/cottageinn **E-mail:** cottage@btconnect.com

Our inspector loved: This tucked away excellent find of a superb restaurant with quiet bedrooms.

Price Guide: (including continental breakfast)
weekdays £87.50
friday/saturday £65–£87.50
sunday £65

Location: A330, 1 mile; M4/M3, 3 miles; Windsor, 3 miles; Heathrow, 12 miles

Attractions: Windsor; Ascot; Legoland; Wentworth Golf Course

Easily accessible down a country lane, and near to Ascot, Henley and Windsor, The Cottage Inn has a welcoming feel as soon as you arrive. Tables shaded by umbrellas offer alfresco dining in summer,whilst the restaurant with its friendly bar is as conducive to a romantic twosome as it is to a larger party. Two private dining areas, are available upon request and perfect for family and special occasions or small wedding parties. Menus are varied and delicious and come with generous portions and an excellent choice of wines and champagnes. Owners Bobby King and Jon Mee have run the inn for 19 years, and personally ensure that their high standards are maintained. Comfortable spacious bedrooms are located in the garden area of the cottage with their own entrance.

THE INN ON THE GREEN, RESTAURANT WITH ROOMS

THE OLD CRICKET COMMON, COOKHAM DEAN, BERKSHIRE SL6 9NZ
Tel: 0845 365 2547 **International:** +44 (0)1628 482638 **Fax:** 01628 487474
Web: www.johansens.com/innonthegreen **E-mail:** reception@theinnonthegreen.com

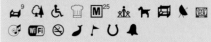

Our inspector loved: *The very pretty setting of this tucked away inn.*

Price Guide:
single £100-£130
double £120-£150
suite £150-£160

Awards/Recognition: 2 AA Rosettes 2006-2007

Location: A404, 4 miles; M40, 6 miles; Maidenhead, 6 miles; Heathrow Airport, 18 miles

Attractions: Windsor; Ascot; Henley; River Thames walks

Wind your way through the pituresque Thames Valley and you'll find this sophisticated 'restaurant with rooms' overlooking the village green. Ideal for both an intimate dinner and a gathering of friends or colleagues. Colours are warm, décor imaginative, and the nine bedrooms are thoughtfully furnished with antiques and modern facilities. Popular with locals for its atmosphere and modern European cooking, the chef sources locally and makes the best of the seasons. Downstairs is a rather cosy lounge bar and outside the Mediterranean-style terrace is just the spot for warm days. Local attractions include Windsor Castle, Legoland and the pretty riverside town of Marlow with its unique shops and restaurants. This boutique hotel is only 45 minutes from central London, making it a great escape for city dwellers.

THE ROYAL OAK RESTAURANT

PALEY STREET, MAIDENHEAD, BERKSHIRE SL6 3JN
Tel: 0845 365 2685 **International:** +44 (0)1628 620541
Web: www.johansens.com/royaloakpaley **E-mail:** royaloakmail@aol.com

Our inspector loved: The friendliness, excellent cuisine and atmosphere of this welcoming restaurant.

Price Guide:
starters from £4.95
mains from £8.50

Awards/Recognition: 1 AA Rosette 2006-2007

Location: A330, 0.5 miles; M4, 2 miles; Maidenhead, 3 miles; Heathrow Airport, 15 miles

Attractions: Ascot; Henley; Windsor; Legoland

The Royal Oak, owned by Nick Parkinson, has a friendly staff and a wonderful ambience with comfortable large sofas in the bar area and more formal seating in the airy restaurant. Renowned head chef, Dominic Chapman creates an imaginative seasonal menu both in the bar and restaurant concentrating on flavoursome British ingredients. Choose from, for example, smoked eel with beetroot and horseradish (delicious!) or buffalo Mozzarella with red peppers and basil for starters then middle white pork with mushy peas and braised onions or peppered haunch of venison. The pretty enclosed garden with smart garden furniture is an al fresco alternative on balmy days. The Royal Oak is also an excellent venue for private or business parties and a marquee can also be arranged for larger events.

The Leatherne Bottel Riverside Restaurant

THE BRIDLEWAY, GORING-ON-THAMES, BERKSHIRE RG8 0HS
Tel: 0845 365 2578 **International:** +44 (0)1491 872667 **Fax:** 01491 875308
Web: www.johansens.com/leathernebottel **E-mail:** leathernebottel@aol.com

Our inspector loved: *The magic of this wonderful restaurant in both winter and summer.*

Price Guide: (including VAT and service charge) Tuesday-Saturday lunch menu du jour £18.50 for 2 courses; £22.95 for 3 courses. á la carte - evenings - starters from £7.50 , mains £17.95 and puddings £7.25

Awards/Recognition: Condé Nast Johansens Most Excellent Restaurant 2006; 2 AA Rosettes 2006-2007

Location: A329, 5 miles; M4 J12, 9 miles; Wallingford, 6 miles; Heathrow, 47 miles

Attractions: Basildon Park (NT); Beale Wildlife Park; Walks along the River Thames; Reading

This is the type of restaurant you want to keep a secret. Nestled on the banks of the Thames, a haven of tranquility with the only distractions of ducks, swans and the occasional rowing eight. Chef, Julia Storey has been at The Leatherne Bottel for 10 years, and lovingly and passionately prepares meals from the finest of fresh ingredients such as herbs and salad leaves grown in the garden, fish, shellfish and caviar in the summer, and game in the winter. Freshly baked bread takes a creative twist using seasonal herbs and spices and the impressive wine list has been thoughtfully compiled through many hours of tastings and visits to vineyards. You'll also find some excellent armagnac and cognac. The creation of a lovely orangerie ensures this restaurant is as ideal in winter as in summer. Closed Sunday evenings and Monday

L'ORTOLAN RESTAURANT

CHURCH LANE, SHINFIELD, READING, BERKSHIRE RG2 9BY
Tel: 0845 365 1965 **International:** +44 (0)1189 888 500 **Fax:** 01189 889 338
Web: www.johansens.com/lortolan **E-mail:** info@lortolan.com

***Our inspector loved:** The contemporary sophistication of the dining experience - do try Chef's Table for budding chef's.*

Price Guide:
menu du jour lunch 3 course £24
menu gourmand £60 (lunch/dinner)
á la carte from £49

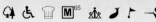

Awards/Recognition: 1 Star Michelin; 3 AA Rosettes 2007-2008

Location: A33, 2 miles; M4 J11, 3 miles; Reading, 6 miles; Heathrow Airport, 35 miles

Attractions: Reading; Oxford; Windsor; Ascot

Created from chef Alan Murchison's passion for fine food and dining, this Michelin-starred restaurant is certain to lift your taste buds. Sitting in its own pretty grounds L'ortolan is divided into different dinning areas that cleverly create individual stylish settings. Two new private dining rooms add an exciting choice of ambiance; the 'Winecellers' which is rather opulent and sophisticated and the festive 'Pommery' room with its central bubble effect glass table. Growing in demand is the Chefs table, where you can delight in watching culinary magic being spun, now an option at both lunch and dinner. Another great pairing is with Laurent Perrier to offer tasting menus featuring Grand Sciecle and other wines from this most prestigious of Champagne houses. Within easy reach of Reading, Oxford and London, this restaurant is worth taking a detour for.

STIRRUPS COUNTRY HOUSE HOTEL

MAIDENS GREEN, WINDSOR, BERKSHIRE RG42 6LD
Tel: 0845 365 2369 **International:** +44 (0)1344 882284 **Fax:** 01344 882300
Web: www.johansens.com/stirrups **E-mail:** reception@stirrupshotel.co.uk

Our inspector loved: *The refurbished contemporary bar and restaurant within this comfortable and well run hotel.*

Price Guide:
single from £120
double/twin from £130
suite from £150

Sitting in 10 acres of pretty grounds and in an enviable location close to the golf at Wentworth and the racing at Windsor and Ascot, you can see why this family owned country house is popular with those wishing for a few days break. At the heart of the hotel is Stirrups Bar and Restaurant which has recently undergone a modern redesign enhancing its older features of exposed brickwork, open fireplace and wooden beams. Passionate presentation of the imaginative menu is led by Head Chef, Jolyon Yates. Bedrooms are well sized and have been subtly decorated in natural woods and pastel colours. The hotel also proves popular for weddings, from a small gathering to a full blown party!

Location: A330, 250yds; M4 J8/9 M3 J3, 8 miles; Windsor, 6 miles; Heathrow, 18 miles

Attractions: Legoland; Windsor and Windsor Great Park; Thorpe Park; Ascot

CANTLEY HOUSE HOTEL

MILTON ROAD, WOKINGHAM, BERKSHIRE RG40 5QG
Tel: 0845 365 3223 **International:** +44 (0)118 978 9912 **Fax:** 0118 977 4294
Web: www.johansens.com/cantley **E-mail:** reservations@cantleyhotel.co.uk

Our inspector loved: The mix of traditional and contemporary in this comfortable country house hotel.

Price Guide:
single £119–£135
double/twin £155–£185
suite £195–£205

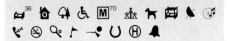

Location: A321, 0.20 miles; M4 jct 10, 5 miles; Wokingham, 0.75 miles; Heathrow, 25 miles

Attractions: Windsor; Legoland; Ascot Racecourse; Oxford

Cantley House Hotel is a spacious 36 bedroom Victorian Country House Hotel set in acres of Berkshire parkland. Formerly the home of the Marquis of Ormonde, the mansion was built with wonderful Victorian proportions & detail. The building has been restored over the years and in 2001 the Clocktower Wing was added to allow for 15 executive rooms and suites, many with patios leading onto the glorious landscaped grounds featuring a sunken garden, lavender walk and peaceful ponds. Miltons Restaurant serving modern English food is to be found in its own secluded 17th century courtyard and a generous touch is that their excellent wine list only has a standard per-bottle mark up – so a great bottle needn't cost the earth. Non-smoking throughout the hotel.

THE DINTON HERMIT

WATER LANE, FORD, AYLESBURY, BUCKINGHAMSHIRE HP17 8XH
Tel: 0845 365 2467 **International:** +44 (0)1296 747473 **Fax:** 01296 748819
Web: www.johansens.com/dintonhermit **E-mail:** dintonhermit@btconnect.com

Our inspector loved: Its cosy friendly bar and restaurant as well as the variety of pretty rooms.

Price Guide:
single from £80
double from £100
four-poster from £125

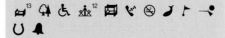

Location: A418, 2 miles; M40 J7 (northbound) J8 (southbound), 14 miles; Aylesbury, 6 miles; Heathrow, 35 miles

Attractions: Waddesdon Manor; Oxford; Bicester Village Shopping outlet; Vale of Aylesbury

An appealing inn with an intriguing name, taken from the reputed executioner of Charles I, who after performing the deed, allegedly hid in a cave nearby. 400 years old, Grade II listed and beautifully restored by owners Debbie and John Colinswood, you will be pleased to discover the inn's cosy bar, open fire and welcoming restaurant serving delicious modern British cuisine. Period named bedrooms have exposed wooden beams, four-poster beds and adjoining bathrooms. Bedrooms in the converted barn are contemporary and refreshing. Although you're surrounded by open views across fields and farmland, major motorway networks are easily accessible, making this the perfect stopover for a weekend walking break, corporate stay, wedding party, or dinner with friends. Golf and shooting breaks are available on request.

THE CROWN AND PUNCHBOWL

HIGH STREET, HORNINGSEA, CAMBRIDGE CB25 9JG
Tel: 0845 365 2893 **International:** +44 (0)1223 860 643 **Fax:** 01223 441 814
Web: www.johansens.com/crownandpunchbow **E-mail:** info@thecrownandpunchbowl.co.uk

Our inspector loved: The creative new menu - especially the fish dishes.

Price Guide:
single from £74.95
double from £94.95
2 night double £175
3 night double £250

Location: A14 jct 34, 0.9 miles; M11 jct 14, 5.5 miles

Attractions: Cambridge; Newmarket; Ely; Bury St. Edmunds

The Crown and Punchbowl is situated in a quiet village location, just 4 miles from the centre of celebrated Cambridge and minutes from the airport. The 400 year old inn has been carefully refurbished, successfully and unaffectedly blending simple, contemporary décor with original wood beams and flooring. The double guestrooms are decorated in a fresh, modern style with super bathrooms. The rural setting offers a tranquil retreat for business and leisure travellers alike. The restaurant and conservatory are equally ambient settings in which to enjoy the creative new à la carte menu, fine wine and ale. Blackboards promote numerous traditional British dishes, including homemade sausages, fresh locally sourced fish and other seasonally varying British favourites. A private room is available for parties of up to 24.

THE TICKELL ARMS, RESTAURANT

1 NORTH ROAD, WHITTLESFORD, CAMBRIDGESHIRE CB2 4NZ
Tel: 0845 365 2710 **International:** +44 (0)1223 833128 **Fax:** 01223 835907
Web: www.johansens.com/tickellarms **E-mail:** tickellarms@aol.com

Our inspector loved: The delightful peacocks and the elegant black swans on the small ornamental lake

Price Guide:
starters from £5.50
mains from £10.50

Location: A505, 1.5 mile; M11 jct 10, 2 miles

Attractions: The Imperial War Museum at Duxford; Cambridge; Newmarket Racecourse

Stylish, and just a little bit different, the Georgian Grade II listed Tickell Arms has quirky touches and antique furnishings including a nice long bar for you to lean on. The main dining area is traditionally decorated with dark polished tables and candlesticks, while the conservatory boasts stunning Bougainvillea in summer and leads onto the patio and award-winning garden where oriental ducks and glistening koi carp add further colour and entertainment. Dishes created by Chef Paul Leeves combine the best local produce, the à la carte has dishes such as sauté of foie gras, hand-dived Scottish sea scallops, Barbary duck breast and tarte tatin, and the al fresco with lighter salads and omelettes. Try the delicious fresh bread baked in an Aga.

BROXTON HALL

WHITCHURCH ROAD, BROXTON, CHESTER, CHESHIRE CH3 9JS
Tel: 0845 365 3208 **International:** +44 (0)1829 782321 **Fax:** 01829 782330
Web: www.johansens.com/broxtonhall **E-mail:** reservation@broxtonhall.co.uk

Our inspector loved: The cosy antique filled rooms and pretty landscaped garden.

Price Guide:
single £75
double/twin £85–£140

Location: A41, 100yds; A534, 400yds; M53 jct 12, 11 miles; Chester, 11 miles

Attractions: Historic Chester; Beeston and Cholmondeley Castles; Erddig (NT); Oulton Park Racing Circuit

A handsome black and white half-timbered building, Broxton Hall was built in 1671 by a local landowner, and the reception area reflects the character of the entire hotel, with its magnificent Jacobean fireplace, antique furnishings, oak panelled walls and carved mahogany staircase. On winter evenings the log fires glow, warming the grand rooms. Small but pleasant bedrooms are adorned with antiques, and the restaurant, with its dining awards, is great for tasting French and English dishes using local game and freshly caught fish. Breakfast in the sunny conservatory, then head out for a day to the North Wales coast, Snowdonia, golf, or horse-racing at Chester and Bangor-on-Dee.

THE BEECHES HOTEL & ELEMIS DAY SPA

60 CHARLESTOWN ROAD, CHARLESTOWN, CORNWALL PL25 3NN
Tel: 0845 365 2874 **International:** +44 (0)1726 73106
Web: www.johansens.com/thebeechescharlestown **E-mail:** info@thebeechescharlestown.co.uk

Our inspector loved: *The wonderful calming atmosphere and bedrooms with en suites to die for!*

Price Guide:
double £190-£275

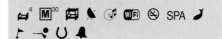

Location: A390, 0.5 miles; A30, 9 miles; Newquay Airport, 18 miles

Attractions: Eden Project; Charlestown Harbour; Cliff Top Walks; Tate Gallery, St Ives

Nestled in its own grounds just 500 metres from a small beach and the waters of St Austell Bay this hotel has a wonderful calm and relaxed atmosphere. The Beeches is like a home with beautiful designed bedrooms and large creative bathrooms. Guests enjoy a delicious breakfast spread each morning and during the day the fully licensed bistro produces dishes using fresh local ingredients. Try relaxing in the tranquil gardens with fresh scallops and king prawns accompanied by a bottle of crisp Chablis. Most spoiling is the on-site Premier Elimis Day Spa which also offers Ishi Choco – a range of luxury decedent face & body treatments designed by a world famous Italian chocolatier. Stroll down to see the beautifully maintained fleet of tall ships in Charlestown harbour and afterwards return to a signature High Tea.

CORMORANT HOTEL & RIVERSIDE RESTAURANT

GOLANT BY FOWEY, CORNWALL PL23 1LL
Tel: 0845 365 2875 **International:** +44 (0)1726 833426 **Fax:** 01726 833219
Web: www.johansens.com/cormorant **E-mail:** relax@cormoranthotel.co.uk

Our inspector loved: *The breathtaking location offering total peace and seclusion.*

Price Guide:
single £75-£160
double £90-£160

Location: B3269, 1.5 miles; A30, 11 miles; Exeter, 72 miles

Attractions: Eden Project; Lost Gardens of Heligan; Fowey Estuary; Lanhydrock House

Walk up to the front door, turn around and look out at a magical view of the upper reaches of the Fowey Estuary. A total refurbishment of this delightful small hotel under the new ownership and creative eye of Mary Tozer has worked wonders. Many of the crisp bedrooms have full-length windows leading on to balconies where you can sit and enjoy the changing tide and life on the river. The restaurant like the drawing room has big windows and delightful views and the menu has been composed using seasonal and local ingredients. On warm days you can enjoy a leisurely meal on the terrace or when things get cooler a wood burning stove transforms the restaurant.

Trevalsa Court Country House Hotel

SCHOOL HILL, MEVAGISSEY, ST AUSTELL, CORNWALL PL26 6TH
Tel: 0845 365 2765 **International:** +44 (0)1726 842468 **Fax:** 01726 844482
Web: www.johansens.com/trevalsa **E-mail:** stay@trevalsa-hotel.co.uk

Our inspector loved: Everthing from the moment of arriving.

Price Guide:
single £69–£118
double/twin £98–£170
suite £160–£220

Location: B3273, 0.5 miles; A390, 4.7 miles; A30, 15.5 miles; Newquay Airport, 20 miles

Attractions: Lost Gardens of Helligan; Eden Project; Lanhydrock Manor House; Tate Gallery in St Ives

Overlooking the sea and built in the 1930s, Trevalsa was discovered by the owners in 1999 when they set to work to lovingly restore the casual but elegant atmosphere of a country house. Blending traditional and modern styles, its oak-panelled hall and dining room, beautiful lounge and mullioned windows reflect another era, whilst the bedrooms are simply and classically furnished. All principal bedrooms have splendid sea views. The hotel's beautiful gardens are above the sheltered Polstreath Beach and access to its sloping sands and coves for swimming and fishing is directly available from the garden. A footpath also leads to the harbour and typically Cornish streets of Mevagissey. Trevalsa Court's location makes it an excellent base for touring all parts of Cornwall.

THE OLD COASTGUARD HOTEL

MOUSEHOLE, PENZANCE, CORNWALL TR19 6PR
Tel: 0845 365 2610 **International:** +44 (0)1736 731222 **Fax:** 01736 731720
Web: www.johansens.com/oldcoastguard **E-mail:** bookings@oldcoastguardhotel.co.uk

Our inspector loved: *Everything about this first class welcoming hotel.*

Price Guide:
single £50–£125
double £90–£160
premium double £120–£190

Awards/Recognition: 2 AA Rosettes 2007-2008

Location: B3315, 1.23 miles; A30, 2.67 miles; Penzance, 3.3 miles; Lands End, 10.9 miles

Attractions: Coastal walk to Lamorna Cove; Minack Theatre in Porthcurno; Cape Cornwall; St Michaels Mount

Described by Dylan Thomas as "the most beautiful village in England", Mousehole is remarkably unspoilt and with a charm of its own. Within this vibrant community and nestled between rolling headlands is the charming Old Coastguard Hotel. Here the lush sub-tropical gardens lead down to the sea, beach and rock pools. Many of the hotel rooms have panoramic views over Mounts Bay. Cool, contemporary furnishings of cream and black create a relaxed and refreshing ambience. While away the hours watching little fishing boats and yachts drift across the coastline from one of many bedroom balconies or explore endless Cornish coastal paths and bridleways, hidden coves and villages. Delectable daily changing menus feature locally sourced dishes and fresh fish from nearby Newlyn fish market.

-IN-VALE COUNTRY HOUSE HOTEL

...IIAN, ST AGNES, CORNWALL TR5 0QD
Tel: 0845 365 2306 **International:** +44 (0)1872 552202 **Fax:** 01872 552700
Web: www.johansens.com/roseinvalecountryhouse **E-mail:** reception@rose-in-vale-hotel.co.uk

Our inspector loved: The new wonderfully presented Rose Suite with a superb bathroom.

Price Guide:
single from £80
double/twin from £135
suite £260

Awards/Recognition: 1 AA Rosette 2007-2008

Location: A3075, 1.4 miles; A30, 2.3 miles; Newquay Airport, 15 miles

Attractions: Local Beaches; Eden Project; Lost Gardens of Heligan; Various National Trust Gardens

This Georgian manor house is tucked away in its own secluded Cornish wooded valley. The hotel is a family concern, owned and run by James and Sara Evans. The stunning north Cornish coast provides the perfect backdrop for this intimate and homely country house hotel. The hotel has a lovely cosy feel to it with comfortable furnishings and roaring log fires in winter months. Bedrooms and Suites are well appointed. The newly refurbished Rose Suite, is wonderful with super king size four-poster bed, double spa bath, double monsoon shower and sitting room, it is perfect for special occasions. New for 2008 will be the Garden Suite, which will lead the way in environmental technology. Take a dip in the (solar) heated swimming pool or hot tub or enjoy a hearty Cornish cream tea in the lovely gardens. In the evening you can enjoy an aperitif in the bar before going to eat in the Valley Restaurant. The hotel was awarded a rosette for fine dining in 2007.

HIGHLAND COURT LODGE

BISCOVEY ROAD, BISCOVEY, NEAR ST AUSTELL, CORNWALL PL24 2HW
Tel: 0845 365 1852 **International:** +44 (0)1726 813320 **Fax:** 01726 813320
Web: www.johansens.com/highlandcourt **E-mail:** enquiries@highlandcourt.co.uk

Our inspector loved: *This beautifully presented small lodge that must be seen to be appreciated.*

Price Guide:
single from £95
double £130–£190
suite from £220

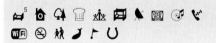

Location: Just off A390; A391, 1.15 miles; A30, 9.24 miles; St Austell, 3.6 miles

Attractions: Eden Project; Lost Gardens of Helegan; National Maritime Museum, Falmouth; St Ives

Embrace your inner child with a supervised tree climb at this award-winning Cornish retreat, then soothe aching muscles with an indulgent soak amongst aromatherapy candles or an in-house holistic therapy, designed to uplift the body and soul. Beautifully presented bedrooms have fresh flowers and Egyptian cotton sheets, and you can fully appreciate views of St Austell Bay and Carlyon Bay Golf Course from adjoining private patios. In winter, a cosy fire in the lounge gets you in the mood for an evening drink, a good book or a chat amongst friends. Local catch of the day inspires menus packed with fresh, organic produce and scrumptious desserts. Nearby, the Cornish Riviera with its magnificent coastal path beckons, and the Eden Project is just a mile away.

TREDETHY HOUSE

HELLAND BRIDGE, BODMIN CORNWALL PL30 4QS
Tel: 0845 365 2758 **International:** +44 (0)1208 841262 **Fax:** 01208 841707
Web: www.johansens.com/tredethyhouse **E-mail:** info@tredethyhouse.co.uk

Our inspector loved: *Firstly location, followed by welcome, comfort and peace - Quite superb.*

Price Guide:
single from £105
double from £125
luxury double from £165

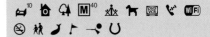

Location: Just off B3266; A30, 3 miles; Bodmin, 5 miles

Attractions: Eden Project; Bodmin Moor; Padstow; Lost Gardens of Heligan

Tredethy House is a peaceful country house in a romantic setting surrounded by 7 acres of glorious grounds. Relax by the fire with a favourite book in winter, stroll or sunbathe in the garden and enjoy the peace and quite in the summer when everywhere else around has become too crowded. Owned and run by Marco and Cristina Mombelli, Tredethy House offers excellent hospitality in a relaxed and unpretentious atmosphere. Impressively environmentally conscious about all they use, from household items to food. Breakfast is cooked by the owners using the best organic and local produce with a minimum of food miles. The bedrooms in the front of the house are all very spacious and offer breathtaking views. At the back of the house are well appointed standard size rooms and a big family suite overlooking the courtyards. The excellent location is convenient for just about any destination in Cornwall.

NENT HALL COUNTRY HOUSE HOTEL

ALSTON, CUMBRIA CA9 3LQ
Tel: 0845 365 2081 **International:** +44 (0)1434 381584 **Fax:** 01434 382668
Web: www.johansens.com/nenthall **E-mail:** info@nenthall.com

Our inspector loved: *This country house hotel near to Englands highest market town.*

Price Guide:
single £75–£120
double/twin £109–£200
suite £225

Location: On the A689; A68, 15 miles ; A1 M Jct 58, 40 miles; Alston, 2 miles

Attractions: Hadrians Wall; The Lake District; Nenthead Mines; South Teesdale Railway; Hexham

Nestling within the Nent Valley just over a mile east of Alston, the highest market town in England, Nent Hall was built in 1738 by a local mine owner and recently restored to its former glory. Bedrooms include feature rooms and suites,with either traditional four-poster or brass beds. The 5-room tower suite is available for special occasions. The East Wing offers family, twin and wheelchair accessible accommodation. All rooms are non-smoking and include a DVD player with films available from an extensive library. You can dine in the Coach House Bar or in the more formal surroundings of the Valley View restaurant. Both have excellent menus and incorporate local fare complimented by an extensive wine list. A marquee is available for special occasions.

THE PHEASANT

BASSENTHWAITE LAKE, NR COCKERMOUTH, CUMBRIA CA13 9YE
Tel: 0845 365 2643 **International:** +44 (0)17687 76234 **Fax:** 017687 76002
Web: www.johansens.com/pheasantcumbria **E-mail:** info@the-pheasant.co.uk

Our inspector loved: The comfort and Olde World ambience and charm of this traditional inn.

Price Guide:
single £80–£100
double/twin £140–£190

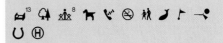

Awards/Recognition: 1 AA Rosette 2007-2008

Location: A66, 0.5 mile; M6 jct 40, 25 miles; Keswick, 6 miles; Cockermouth, 6 miles

Attractions: Bassenthwaite Lake; Lake District National Park; Wordsworth House

This 500 year old hotel is rightly proud of its heritage – it has remained truly British in the classical sense. There is a charm and peacefulness about the place and set in 40 acres of gardens and woodlands just a few yards from Bassenthwaite Lake makes it ideal for exploring this beautiful unspoilt northern part of the Lake District. The bar is testament to a bygone era with traditional wood-panelling and highly polished walls. The beamed dining room serves delicious traditional Cumbrian specialties as well as delicate fine dishes which are influenced by the seasons and local produce. Several lounges invite you to curl up with a good book and relax. Charming bedrooms combine light colours and textures with antiques and personal touches.

CROSBY LODGE COUNTRY HOUSE HOTEL

HIGH CROSBY, CROSBY-ON-EDEN, CARLISLE, CUMBRIA CA6 4QZ
Tel: 0845 365 3253 **International:** +44 (0)1228 573618 **Fax:** 01228 573428
Web: www.johansens.com/crosbylodge **E-mail:** info@crosbylodge.co.uk

Our inspector loved: *Philippa Sedwick's wine warehouse in the courtyard, selling quality wines and home-made produce.*

Price Guide:
single £90–£100
double £150–£190

Location: A689, 0.5 mile; M6 jct 44, 3.5 miles; Carlisle, 4.5 miles

Attractions: Hadrians Wall; Historic City of Carlisle; Scottish Borders; Lake District

Crosby Lodge is a Grade II listed mansion skillfully converted into a country hotel amidst pastoral countryside close to the Scottish Lowlands, Hadrian's Wall and the Lake District. Spacious interiors are elegantly furnished and reflect the superb comfort and service created by Michael and Patricia Sedgwick. Most of the bedrooms have antique and half-testers beds. The 2 bedrooms situated in the converted stables are ideal if you want to take your dog. In The Lodge restaurant, the head chef and his team create dishes from traditional English recipes - and also continental cuisine, matched by an extensive wine list. Tables are set with cut glass and silver cutlery, complementing the surroundings. Crosby Lodge makes a superb venue for weddings, parties, business and social events. Closed 24 December to 16 January.

WEST VALE COUNTRY HOUSE & RESTAURANT

FAR SAWREY, HAWKSHEAD, AMBLESIDE, CUMBRIA LA22 0LQ
Tel: 0845 365 2795 **International:** +44 (0)1539 442 817 **Fax:** 01539 445 302
Web: www.johansens.com/westvale **E-mail:** enquiries@westvalecountryhouse.co.uk

Our inspector loved: The delicious dinner cooked by Glynn, the owner.

Price Guide:
single £80-£98
double £110-£140
suite £153-£164

Awards/Recognition: 2 AA Rosettes 2007-2008

Location: On the B5285; M6 jct 36, 16 miles; Hawkshead, 2 miles; Windermere Ferry, 1 mile

Attractions: Windermere; Hawkshead with Beatrix Potter; Langdale; Grizdale Forest

In the heart of the Lake District National Park this late 19th century former Victorian gentleman's residence is on the edge of a tranquil village, well associated with Beatrix Potter who wrote her much loved stories at "Hilltop," just a few minutes' walk away. Carefully restored with captivating views of Grizedale Forest and The Old Man of Coniston, the AA and Visit Britain 5 Star West Vale exudes the grace of a bygone age with traditional touches such as a complimentary decanter of sherry awaiting you in your bedroom. The bedrooms are well appointed and fresh fruit and complimentary slippers are provided in the de luxe rooms. Excellent classical cuisine is served in the award winning restaurant where fresh local fresh produce is used whenever possible. Special breaks available. Closed January.

THE WHEATSHEAF @ BRIGSTEER

BRIGSTEER, KENDAL, CUMBRIA LA8 8AN
Tel: 0845 365 2734 **International:** +44 (0)15395 68254 **Fax:** 015395 68948
Web: www.johansens.com/brigsteer **E-mail:** wheatsheaf@brigsteer.gb.com

Our inspector loved: This delightful village inn, specialising in traditional English cuisine with a modern twist.

Price Guide:
single £75
double £85

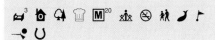

Location: A591, 2 miles; M6 jct 36, 6 miles; Kendal, 3 miles

Attractions: Sizergh Castle; Gateway to The lakes; Morecombe Bay; Damson growing region of the Lyth Valley

A totally non-smoking inn with 3 excellent double bedrooms. The raison d'être of the Wheatsheaf is great food expertly prepared. Its renowned restaurant offers an impressive seasonal à la carte menu, with an emphasis on locally sourced produce, game and meat, including rare breeds, fresh fish and seafood, delivered daily. Tucked away in the Lakeland village of Brigsteer, at the foot of Scout Scar, with stunning panoramic views, and on the edge of a damson-growing region of Lyth Valley. Morecombe Bay is located one side and the Old Man of Conniston on the other. Parts of the inn date back to 1762; it began life as 3 cottages plus a "shoe-ing" room for horses, then became an alehouse and was licensed in the early 1800s.

DALE HEAD HALL LAKESIDE HOTEL

THIRLMERE, KESWICK, CUMBRIA CA12 4TN
Tel: 0845 365 3258 **International:** +44 (0)17687 72478 **Fax:** 017687 71070
Web: www.johansens.com/daleheadhall **E-mail:** onthelakeside@daleheadhall.co.uk

Our inspector loved: The feeling of total
peace and quiet - the only house on Lake
Thirlmere.

Price Guide: (including dinner)
single £130–£155
double £210–£320

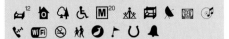

Awards/Recognition: 2 AA Rosettes 2007-2008

Location: A591, 0.25 miles; M6 jct 40, 14 miles;
Keswick, 4 miles; Windermere, 14 miles

Attractions: Lake District National Park;
Worsdsworth Country; Helvellyn; Castlerigg Stone
Circle

The key handed to you upon arrival at Dale Head Hall isn't simply the key to a room – it's the key to complete relaxation. This is the boast of the Hill family, caring owners of this fine hotel that stands alone on the shores of Lake Thirlmere. A bird watcher's paradise, the setting is nothing less than idyllic, and inside, the furnishings and atmosphere are warm and welcoming. Some of the rooms are in the Elizabethan house, while others are in the Victorian extension; all have stunning lake and mountain views as do both lounges. You can enjoy superb food from the finest, freshest seasonal local produce, complemented by an extensive international wine list in the award winning restaurant. The hotel also has it's own boat on the Lake.

HIPPING HALL

COWAN BRIDGE, KIRKBY LONSDALE, CUMBRIA LA6 2JJ
Tel: 0845 365 1859 **International:** +44 (0)15242 71187 **Fax:** 015242 72452
Web: www.johansens.com/hippinghall **E-mail:** info@hippinghall.com

Our inspector loved: *The delicious dinner in the 15th-century banqueting hall.*

Price Guide: (including dinner)
single from £150
double £200–£290

Location: A65, 100yds; Kikby Lonsdale, 2 miles; M6 Jct 36, 8 miles

Attractions: Lake District; Yorkshire Dales; Eden Valley; Trough of Bowland

New owners in 2005 and sensitive restoration, has regenerated 300 year old Hipping Hall and rediscovered its old English charm. The use of bold fabrics and striking colours create vibrant interiors with an atmosphere of stylish elegance. Dinner is served in the magnificent 15th-century oak beamed banqueting hall, where you can experience the unique modern cuisine of Head Chef, Jason Birkbeck whose excellent reputation is based on dishes using the finest locally sourced ingredients.These include roast breast of quail, ballotine of reared Lincolnshire rabbit, roast short loin of Kittridding and fillet of line caught Sea Bass. The beautifully designed bedrooms are light and airy. All have handmade beds, exposed beams and either large walk-in showers or baths; many overlook the pretty gardens.

TEMPLE SOWERBY HOUSE HOTEL AND RESTAURANT

TEMPLE SOWERBY, PENRITH, CUMBRIA CA10 1RZ
Tel: 0845 365 2389 **International:** +44 (0)17683 61578 **Fax:** 017683 61958
Web: www.johansens.com/templesowerby **E-mail:** stay@templesowerby.com

Our inspector loved: *Dining in the garden restaurant overlooking the secluded walled garden.*

Price Guide:
single £90–£120
double £120–£160

Awards/Recognition: 2 AA Rosettes 2006-2007

Location: Just off A66; M6 jct 40, 7 miles; Penrith, 7 miles

Attractions: The Northern Lakes & Fellside Villages; Settle to Carlisle Railway; Dalemain Historic House & Gardens; Lilliput Lane Visitor Centre

Set in a lovely old walled garden, this delightful country hotel provides a welcoming and relaxing stay, an ideal base for exploring this area of outstanding natural beauty. Situated in the Eden Valley, a short drive from Ullswater yet handy for a Scotland 'stopover'. Individually-styled bedrooms include superior rooms with aqua-spa baths or hydro-therapy showers, and classic rooms (including 2 ground floor) with new contemporary bathrooms. Dine in the Conservatory Restaurant from seasonally inspired menus using the best of local produce. Enjoy drinks on the Terrace with views across the garden or, on winter evenings, by a blazing fire in one of the elegant reception rooms. Feature breaks include Wine Weekends and Easter. The A66 Temple Sowerby By-Pass opens in Autumn 2007, returning the hotel to a peaceful village setting.

Fayrer Garden House Hotel

LYTH VALLEY ROAD, BOWNESS-ON-WINDERMERE, CUMBRIA LA23 3JP
Tel: 0845 365 3292 **International:** +44 (0)15394 88195 **Fax:** 015394 45986
Web: www.johansens.com/fayrergarden **E-mail:** lakescene@fayrergarden.com

Our inspector loved: The new redesigned bedrooms with views over the gardens and Lake Windermere.

Price Guide: (including 5-course dinner)
single £81–£140
standard £142–£200
lake view £206–£300

Awards/Recognition: 2 AA Rosettes 2007-2008

Location: A5074, 0.25 miles; A591, 8 miles; M6 jct 36, 16 miles; Windermere, 2.5 miles

Attractions: Lake Windermere; Lake District National Park and Visitor Centre; Beatrix Potter; Blackwell Arts and Crafts House

A lovely Victorian house in spacious gardens and grounds. Its hard to find such wonderful views over Lake Windermere at such excellent value for money. The garden is full of gorgeous colours and a terrace enviably positioned to catch all the afternoon sun. Menus change daily and use local produce such as fish, game and poultry – whatever is in season. The wine list is excellent and again, very reasonably priced. Many of the bedrooms benefit from the views, some with four-posters and some leading directly onto the garden. There is much to entertain you nearby, with the Windermere Steamboat Museum, boating from Bowness Pier, golf at Windermere Golf Club and The Beatrix Potter attraction all available.

LINTHWAITE HOUSE HOTEL

CROOK ROAD, BOWNESS-ON-WINDERMERE, CUMBRIA LA23 3JA
Tel: 0845 365 2031 **International:** +44 (0)15394 88600 **Fax:** 015394 88601
Web: www.johansens.com/linthwaitehouse **E-mail:** stay@linthwaite.com

Our inspector loved: The unstuffy ambiance of this hotel with spectacular views of Lake Windermere.

Price Guide:
single £120-£150
double £145-£300
suite £265-£320

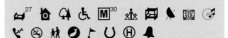

At the heart of the Lake District situated in 14 acres of garden and woodland is Linthwaite House overlooking Lake Windermere and Belle Isle. The hotel combines stylish originality with the best of traditional hospitality. Most bedrooms have lake or garden views whilst the restaurant offers excellent cuisine with the best of fresh, local produce accompanied by a fine selection of wines. There is a 9 hole putting green within the grounds and a par 3 practice hole. You can if you wish, fish for brown trout in the hotel tarn. Fell walks begin at the front door, and you can follow in the footsteps of Wordsworth and Beatrix Potter to explore the spectacular scenery.

Awards/Recognition: Condé Nast Johansens Most Excellent Country House 2007; 3 AA Rosettes 2007-2008; Condé Nast Traveller Gold List 2006

Location: B5284, 0.25 miles; Windermere, 2 miles; A591, 2 miles; M6 Jct 36, 14 miles

Attractions: Windermere; Beatrix Potter Museums & Dove Cottage; Lake District National Park;

DANNAH FARM COUNTRY HOUSE

BOWMAN'S LANE, SHOTTLE, NEAR BELPER, DERBYSHIRE DE56 2DR
Tel: 0845 365 3262 **International:** +44 (0)1773 550273/550630 **Fax:** 01773 550590
Web: www.johansens.com/dannah **E-mail:** slack@dannah.co.uk

Our inspector loved: The diverse selection of rooms, all highly individual and very special. Fun too.

Price Guide:
double (single occupancy) from £75
double/twin £140–£190
suite £195–£225

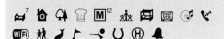

Location: A517, 2 miles; M1, 16 miles; A50, 18 miles; East Midlands Airport, 20 miles

Attractions: Peak District; Chatsworth House; Haddon Hall; Crich Tramway Museum

Experience the joys of rural living with the comforts of home at this unique 18th-century Georgian farmhouse. Brimming with character, its bedrooms overlook rolling pastures and pretty gardens and are beautifully furnished. All are different, some with four-poster beds, private sitting rooms, wet rooms and double spa-baths. Aromas of freshly baked bread waft from the kitchen to whet your appetite for breakfast, cooked to order using free range eggs and locally sourced produce. Newly completed, the Spa facilities situated in "The Leisure Cabin", can be booked for exclusive use with any of the rooms. These private facilities are tucked out of sight and feature a huge Canadian Spa hot- tub set on a private terrace, a sauna, steam shower and luxurious sitting room, overlooking farmland into the distance. Dannah has been awarded "Highly Commended, 5 Yellow Star", from the AA, putting it in the top 10% of guest accommodation in the country.

THE WIND IN THE WILLOWS

DERBYSHIRE LEVEL, GLOSSOP, DERBYSHIRE SK13 7PT
Tel: 0845 365 2743 **International:** +44 (0)1457 868001 **Fax:** 01457 853354
Web: www.johansens.com/windinthewillows **E-mail:** info@windinthewillows.co.uk

Our inspector loved: Ian Wilkinson's desire to maintain the essence of this early Victorian country house.

Price Guide:
single from £75
double from £135

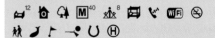

This charming and homely country house is true to its Victorian heritage and has been sympathetically refurbished with this in mind. Oak-panelling, traditional furnishings, open fires and personal touches are all part of the welcoming atmosphere created by Ian Wilkinson and his family. Bedrooms, with their splendid views, are decorated with antique furniture and some with solid Victorian tester beds and roll-top baths. Unspoilt views of the Peak District National Park and heather-clad Pennine hills surround you, and you can satisfy appetites created by the fresh air with traditional cuisine made from local farm and farmers' markets produce. Next to the grounds is a 9-hole golf course, where you can play amidst beautiful scenery, and many activities can be arranged locally, including sailing, horse riding, fly fishing and pot holing.

Location: Situated within High Peak; A57, 1 miles; A624, 2 miles; Manchster Airport, 14 miles

Attractions: Pennine Way; Kinder Scout(Hayfield); Ladybower and Derwent Reservoirs (WWII Bouncing Bombs); Chatsworth House

THE CROWN INN

RIGGS LANE, MARSTON MONTGOMERY, DERBYSHIRE DE6 2FF
Tel: 0845 365 3608 **International:** +44 (0)1889 590 541
Web: www.johansens.com/crowninn **E-mail:** info@thecrowninn-derbyshire.co.uk

Our inspector loved: Its location set in the delightful unspoilt South Derbyshire countryside, yet everything close-by.

Price Guide:
double from £60
twin from £75
family rooms from £85

Awards/Recognition: 1 AA Rosette 2006-2007

Location: A 515, 2 miles; A52, 5 miles; A50, 2 miles; East Midlands Airport, 24 miles

Attractions: Uttoxeter Race Course; Peak District; Chatsworth House; Sudbury Hall (NT)

A pretty inn standing at the southern edge of the Peak District, an area of outstanding natural beauty, in the small delightful hamlet of Marston Montgomery. The inn has been completely refurbished and updated yet retains its original charm and character. The restaurant has a strong local reputation as a popular and intimate venue for both lunch and dinner, serving simple British dishes and using largely local produce. An excellent range of beer is to be found in the cosy bar whilst the elevated patio and garden area provides a beautiful space in which to enjoy long summer days and mild evenings. The seven guestrooms are unfussy and individually decorated. Winner of Best Pub/ Bistro category in the Derbyshire Food Awards, 2006. Closed Christmas Day and New Years Day.

YEOLDON HOUSE HOTEL

DURRANT LANE, NORTHAM, NR BIDEFORD EX39 2RL
Tel: 0845 365 2837 **International:** +44 (0)1237 474400 **Fax:** 01237 476618
Web: www.johansens.com/yeoldon **E-mail:** yeoldonhouse@aol.com

Our inspector loved: The welcome and relaxed atmosphere.

Price Guide:
single £72.50–£77.50
double/twin £110–£125

Location: Just off A386; A39, 0.5 mile; M5 jct 31, 43 miles; Barnstaple, 9.2 miles

Attractions: Lundy; Clovelly; Rosemoor RHS Gardens; Exmoor

Set in 2 acres of tranquil gardens, with beautiful views over the River Torridge, Yeoldon House Hotel is a wonderful place to unwind, offering high standards of food and service and warm hospitality in a relaxed atmosphere. Imaginative meals are served in the award winning Soyer's Restaurant, named after the famous Victorian Chef, Alexis Soyer. All 10 bedrooms are individually decorated and are all en suite. Choose from the elegant four-poster, a delightful split level room or "The Crow's Nest" tucked up under the eaves, its balcony offering a stunning view. Situated on the North Devon Coast Path and with some excellent 3 day breaks available throughout the year Yeoldon House, would make an excellent base for exploring the delights of North Devon.

PENHAVEN COUNTRY HOUSE HOTEL

RECTORY LANE, PARKHAM, NR BIDEFORD, DEVON EX39 5PL
Tel: 0845 365 3745 **International:** +44 (0)1237 451 711 **Fax:** 01237 451 878
Web: www.johansens.com/penhaven **E-mail:** info@penhaven.co.uk

Our inspector loved: *This tucked away little haven.*

Price Guide:
single £63-£83
double £126-£166

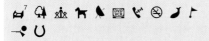

Awards/Recognition: 1 AA Rosette 2007-2008

Location: A39, 1.6 miles; A361, 17 miles; M5 jct 27, 50 miles; Barnstaple, 16 miles

Attractions: Clovelly; North Devon Coastal Paths; Exmoor; Lynton/Lynmouth

Penhaven is a perfect base for exploring the delightful sights of North Devon with its stunning beaches and spectacular scenery though you needn't go far as the house comes with 10 acres of idyllic gardens and woodland, home to plenty of wildlife including a family of badgers who occasionally venture up to the house in search of food. Attention to detail is important to Geoff and Lorraine Baker who have just completed a refurbishment of the ground floor. Background neutrals emphasise the vibrant textures of the wallpaper and fabrics and the resulting impact is one of style, individuality and country quirkiness. Upstairs comfortable bedrooms are light and airy and for those wanting a little more privacy there are rooms in the cottages. Inspired by local ingredients the intimate Woodlands restaurant has deservedly won an AA rosette for the last ten consecutive years.

MILL END

DARTMOOR NATIONAL PARK, CHAGFORD, DEVON TQ13 8JN
Tel: 0845 365 2062 **International:** +44 (0)1647 432282 **Fax:** 01647 433106
Web: www.johansens.com/millend **E-mail:** info@millendhotel.com

Our inspector loved: This little gem tucked away within the fringes of Dartmoor.

Price Guide:
single £90–£125
double/twin £90–£175
suite £175–£220

Gleaming white under slate grey tiles, Mill End is an idyllic hideaway in Dartmoor's National Park, surrounded by a beautiful English garden with colourful borders that run down to the River Teign. Built in the mid 1700s as a flour mill, you will find little corner nooks, paintings and old photographs that imbue a feeling of seclusion, enhanced by the smell of wood smoke and polished wood. The delightful bedrooms feature lovely fabrics and attractive local hand-crafted furniture. The elegant dining room offers you the delightful cuisine of Head Chef, Christophe Ferraro and his young team who's menus include; crab risotto with chilli and lemon grass froth followed by slow roasted fillet of beef with truffle potato and marrow soufflé and a carpaccio of pineapple with coconut ice cream and warm malibu jelly.

Awards/Recognition: 2 AA Rosettes 2006-2007

Location: On the A382; A30, 3.66 miles; M5 jct 31, 19 miles; Newton Aboot, 16 miles

Attractions: Chagford; Castle Drogo; Rosemoor Gardens; Eden Project

THE NEW INN

COLEFORD, NEAR CREDITON, DEVON EX17 5BZ
Tel: 0845 365 2607 **International:** +44 (0)1363 84242 **Fax:** 01363 85044
Web: www.johansens.com/newinncoleford **E-mail:** enquiries@thenewinncoleford.co.uk

Our inspector loved: This charming tucked away thatched inn offering all one could wish for.

Price Guide:
single £60–£70
double £75–£85

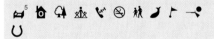

Location: A377, 1.2 miles; M5 jct 29, 23 miles; Exeter, 13 miles

Attractions: Exeter Cathedral; Dartmoor; Exmoor; Barnstaple

You will appreciate an escape to this 13th-century thatched inn, where you can wander the secluded valley and listen to a hypnotic babbling brook in the gardens. You will receive a warm welcome by owners Melissa and Simon Renshaw, and not to forget Captain, their talkative parrot! This highly rated Grade II listed, cob built inn has spacious, comfortable bedrooms, and the cosy warmth of a log fire in the lounge in winter. 3 full-time chefs create memorable dishes such as spicy lamb in a honey and citrus sauce or salmon escalope with brandy sultanas and fish valoute. There is also a good choice of speciality dishes, grills and puddings. Traditional ales are served in the bars and the selection of wines has won awards.

COMBE HOUSE

GITTISHAM, HONITON, NEAR EXETER, DEVON EX14 3AD
Tel: 0845 365 3241 **International:** +44 (0)1404 540400 **Fax:** 01404 46004
Web: www.johansens.com/combehousegittisham **E-mail:** stay@thishotel.com

Our inspector loved: The feeling of not wanting to leave, then the thought of returning again soon.

Price Guide:
single £139
double/twin £168–£275
suite £315–£450

Awards/Recognition: 2 AA Rosettes 2007-2008

Location: M5 jct 28/29, 11 miles; A303/A30, 2 miles; Honiton railway Station, 4 miles; Exeter Airport, 10 miles

Attractions: South West Coastal Path – Sidmouth to Lyme Regis; Dartmoor; Exeter Cathedral; Powderham Castle

Hidden in 3500 acres Combe House is simply magical. In 10 years Ken and Ruth have created a very special experience and they seem to tirelessly pursue the desire to find new ways to delight their Guests. For instance many of the bedrooms have recently been refurbished with a stunning combination of contemporary furnishings, fine antiques and fresh flowers. The two Master Chefs of Great Britain have recently earned a 'Rising' Michelin Star. They love to weave their culinary magic drawing on the West Country's bounteous larder and Combe's own kitchen garden. Ken maintains a predominantly old world cellar in which wines have been through a rigorous 'blind tasting' and been selected for taste rather than name or vintage. Deservedly they were named Devon's Restaurant of the Year – Taste of the West.

HOME FARM HOTEL

WILMINGTON, NR HONITON, DEVON EX14 9JR
Tel: 0845 365 1874 **International:** +44 (0)1404 831278 **Fax:** 01404 831411
Web: www.johansens.com/homefarm **E-mail:** info@thatchedhotel.co.uk

Our inspector loved: The superbly refurbished en suites and cuisine.

Price Guide:
single from £60
double from £90
junior suite from £125

Awards/Recognition: 1 AA Rosette 2006-2007

Location: On the A35; A30, 3 miles; Honiton, 3 miles; Exeter Airport, 15-min drive

Attractions: Seaton Tram Way; Otter Nurseries; Killerton House; Wilmington Hayes Gardens and Waterfowl Collection

Surrounded by 4 acres of grounds, abundant with shrubs and flower borders this former 16th-century whitewashed, thatched farmhouse makes a charming and romantic retreat. Situated 3 miles from Honiton, gateway to the West Country. You will receive a warm welcome from the owners Steve and Marilyn Lundy, who have refurbished the interior. The bedrooms situated in the main building and across a cobbled courtyard, feature widescreen TV's, complimentary wireless Internet and well appointed bathrooms. Relax on a Chesterfield in the lounge bar with an apéritif before enjoying Chef Lee Villiers' imaginative and beautifully presented cuisine in the restaurant. Among his memorable creations are Devon ruby beef topped with local blue cheese butter and roasted duck breast served on bubble and squeak, accompanied by a vanilla and honey sauce.

HEDDON'S GATE HOTEL

MARTINHOE, PARRACOMBE, BARNSTAPLE, DEVON EX31 4PZ
Tel: 0845 365 1834 International: +44 (0)1598 763481
Web: www.johansens.com/heddonsgate **E-mail:** hotel@heddonsgate.co.uk

Our inspector loved: *The enthusiasm of Eddie and Anne and magnificant location.*

Price Guide: (including dinner)
single £95–£107
double/twin £160–£184
exclusive use from £1670

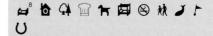

Location: A39, 2.5 miles; M5 jct 27, 45 miles; Barnstaple, 12 miles; Exeter, 39 miles

Attractions: Heddon Valley; Lynton & Lynmouth; Arlington Court (NT); Marwood Hill Gardens

Owners Anne and Eddie Eyles love of Heddon Gate is matched by the warmth of their welcome. Built in the 1890's as a Swiss style lodge it will take you on a journey through different eras of décor and styles, from Grandma's Room, with a Victorian feel and four-poster bed, to the Indian Room, a homage to the colonial era. Enjoy leisurely breakfasts and daily dinner menus, where Anne and Eddie source and prepare their ingredients with the utmost care. And what more could you ask for than a complimentary traditional afternoon tea of homemade savouries, scones and cakes! The house is superbly located on the slopes of the Heddon Valley, and the natural beauty of Exmoor's coast, moorland and wildlife make it a walker's paradise.

KINGSTON H...

STAVERTON, NEAR TOTNES, DEVO...
Tel: 0845 365 1937 **International:** +44 (0)1803 762 235 **Fax:** 01...
Web: www.johansens.com/kingstonhouse **E-mail:** info@kingston-estate.co.uk

Our inspector loved: This beautiful country house offering total peace and seclusion.

Price Guide:
single £105–£115
double £180
suite £190–£200

Location: A384, 2 miles; A38, 5.5 miles; M5 jct 31, 24 miles; Totnes, 4 miles

Attractions: Exeter; Dartmoor National Park; River Dart; Dartmouth

Offering some of the dreamiest accommodation in the country, the Kingston Estate nestles amongst rolling hills and valleys, bounded by Dartmoor and the sea. Kingston House and its superb self-catering cottages have been restored by the Corfields without losing a drop of 18th-century charm. In the main house 3 striking period suites are reached by one of the finest examples of a marquetry staircase in England. The bedrooms have original panelling and shutters, fine plasterwork and profusion of wall paintings. Soak up the atmosphere of crackling log fires in winter, summer drinks on the terrace, and candlelight glittering on sparkling crystal in the elegant dining room. Here you are as welcome as if it were Elizabeth and Michael Corfields' own private house party. Plenty of flexible space for weddings, meetings and gatherings.

THE BRIDGE HOUSE HOTEL

PROUT BRIDGE, BEAMINSTER, DORSET DT8 3AY

Tel: 0845 365 2408 **International:** +44 (0)1308 862200 **Fax:** 01308 863700
Web: www.johansens.com/bridgehousebeam **E-mail:** enquiries@bridge-house.co.uk

Our inspector loved: *The continuing improvements, and the owners' commitment to guests' pleasure.*

Price Guide:
single from £62
double/twin £116–£180

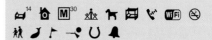

Awards/Recognition: 1 AA Rosettes 2006-2007

Location: On the A3066; A356, 7 miles; M5 jct 25, 22 miles; Exeter, 42 miles

Attractions: Jurassic Coast; Abbotsbury; Chesil Beach; Lyme Regis

This beautiful old West Dorset retreat partly dates back to the 13th century but today its attentive staff create a memorable experience. The bedrooms, some with stone fireplaces and garden views, are spacious. The gardens, surrounded by an ancient stone wall, are a suntrap, ideal for lunches or candle-lit dinners. The oldest room is a quiet bar with a quaint, atmosphere and an impressive range of drinks. A large inglenook fireplace in the lounge is the perfect place to enjoy a drink before dinner or earlier an afternoon tea. Seasonal menus include daily à la carte specials of delicious fresh organic cuisine such as the acclaimed medallions of pork served with fresh figs and stilton sauce. A healthy breakfast is served in the conservatory overlooking the gardens that are floodlit at night.

THE GRANGE AT OBORNE

OBORNE, NR SHERBORNE, DORSET DT9 4LA
Tel: 0845 365 2506 **International:** +44 (0)1935 813463 **Fax:** 01935 817464
Web: www.johansens.com/grangesherborne **E-mail:** reception@thegrange.co.uk

Our inspector loved: This lovely hotel continues to delight.

Price Guide:
single from £90
double from £105
four-poster from £150

Location: A30, 0.25 mile; M27 lct 2, 45 miles; Sherborne, 1.5 miles; Bristol, 54 miles

Attractions: Montacute House; Cerne Abbas; Shaftesbury; Stourhead

This 200-year-old house nestles peacefully in formal gardens, just 1.5 miles from historic Sherborne. Guests are welcomed by owners Jennifer Matthews and Jon Fletcher, and can relax in each of the 18 well-appointed and spacious bedrooms. Dinner is served in a most pleasant atmosphere, overlooking the attractive floodlit gardens. The restaurant specialises in both international and traditional cuisine. For those planning an event or occasion the hotel can provide a service for up to 120 guests, and is also suited to conferences and business meetings. This quiet haven is a most ideal escape from city life, and visitors will be able to unwind with horse riding, fishing or simply taking in the local scenery.

THE SWAN INN

THE ENDWAY, GREAT EASTON, DUNMOW, ESSEX CM6 2HG
Tel: 0845 365 2864 **International:** +44 (0)1371 870359
Web: www.johansens.com/swangreateaston **E-mail:** theswangreateaston@tiscali.co.uk

Our inspector loved: The friendly enthusiasm and welcome.

Price Guide:
single £50
double from £80

Location: Just off the B184; A120, 4 miles; M11 jct 8, 10 miles; Stansted Airport, 7 miles

Attractions: Saffron Walden, Audley End House; Cambridge; Thaxted

A charming privately owned 15th-century freehouse that retains a wealth of original features including a heavily oak-beamed lounge bar and large inglenook fireplace. The restaurant has a glowing reputation for food, and you can be assured that everything, even the chutneys and dips, are homemade. Our inspector describes The Swan as "a little bit of tradition livened up by a young and professional team" and with its warm and friendly atmosphere coupled with the attractive setting, this is a comfortable and unpretentious place to stay. There are 4 delightful and welcoming bedrooms featuring traditional beams and pretty bedding with views of the undulating countryside.

THE CROWN HOUSE

GREAT CHESTERFORD, SAFFRON WALDEN, ESSEX CB10 1NY
Tel: 0845 365 2453 **International:** +44 (0)1799 530515 / 530257 **Fax:** 01799 530683
Web: www.johansens.com/crownhouse **E-mail:** reservations@crownhousehotel.com

Our inspector loved: *The lovely Oriel window - one of only two surviving in the County.*

Price Guide:
single £65–£89.50
double/twin £84.50–£145

Awards/Recognition: 1 AA Rosette 2007-2008

Location: On the B1383; M11 jct 10, 5 miles; Stansted Airport, 19 miles

Attractions: Audley End House (NT); Imperial War Museum at Duxford; Cambridge; Newmarket Racecourse

Conveniently located for the famous university city of Cambridge, as well as the historic market town of Saffron Walden, this impressive former coaching inn is also steeped in history and dates back beyond the Tudor times. A classical hotel though the warm service is very much one of a privately run establishment. The comfortable guest rooms retain their characteristic traditional charm and some feature handsome four-poster beds. The restaurant places an emphasis on seasonal flavours and local ingredients which you'll enjoyed in the charming and intimate ambience of the oak-panelled dining room. There is a roaring log fire in the lounge on cool nights and on warm day you can enjoy lazing around in the beautiful nurtured gardens.

BIBURY COURT

BIBURY COURT, BIBURY, GLOUCESTERSHIRE GL7 5NT
Tel: 0845 365 3035 **International:** +44 (0)1285 740337 **Fax:** 01285 740660
Web: www.johansens.com/biburycourt **E-mail:** info@biburycourt.com

Our inspector loved: The amazing building in beautiful, relaxing grounds.

Price Guide:
single from £125
double from £150
suite £230

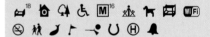

Awards/Recognition: 2 AA Rosettes 2006-2007

Location: Just off B4425; A40, 8.5 miles; Cirencester, 7 miles; Cheltenham, 22 miles

Attractions: Stow-on-the-Wold; Bourton-on-the-Water; Arlington Row; Hidcote Manor Gardens

Charles II and during the reign of George III, the Prince Regent, are said to have visited here. Dating from Tudor times, the main house was built in 1663 by Sir Thomas Sackville. Following generations of illustrious owners, it became a hotel in 1968. Set in 6 acres on the outskirts of Bibury, which William Morris called "the most beautiful village in England" Bibury Court is run as a country house focusing on good food and wine in informal and pleasurable surroundings. You can enjoy log fires in the cooler months and there are some lovely panelled rooms to explore, with fine detail and antique furniture. Many of the bedrooms have four-posters, all have private bathrooms and for those who like greater privacy there is the Sackville suite.

LYPIATT HOUSE

LYPIATT ROAD, CHELTENHAM, GLOUCESTERSHIRE GL50 2QW
Tel: 0845 365 2051 **International:** +44 (0)1242 224994 **Fax:** 01242 224996
Web: www.johansens.com/lypiatt **E-mail:** stay@lypiatt.co.uk

Our inspector loved: *The immaculate tastefully decorated bedrooms and great location.*

Price Guide:
single £70–£90
double/twin £80–£110

Location: On the A40; M5 jct 11, 2.6 miles

Attractions: Cotswolds; Cheltenham Racecourse; Rococo Gardens, Painswick; Moreton-in-Marsh

Staying at this hotel in the fashionable Montpellier district gives you a great location for exploring Cheltenham's main shopping areas, theatres and interesting corners. Lypiatt House has a stunning contemporary décor and a homely atmosphere, all of which set off its Victorian style perfectly. In the sunny drawing room large windows and warm colours give a spacious, light ambience The bedrooms are also generously sized and nicely done while a substantial full English breakfast will ensure you're set up for the day. The 'honesty' bar is a welcome touch and allows you to concoct a drink to your own standards before heading out to dinner. With no restaurant on site yet a plethora of good eateries nearby the team will be happy to make reservations for you.

CHARLTON KINGS HOTEL

CHARLTON KINGS, CHELTENHAM, GLOUCESTERSHIRE GL52 6UU
Tel: 0845 365 3230 **International:** +44 (0)1242 231061 **Fax:** 01242 241900
Web: www.johansens.com/charltonkings **E-mail:** enquiries@charltonkingshotel.co.uk

Our inspector loved: The friendly welcome, relaxed atmosphere and well-appointed bedrooms.

Price Guide:
single £65–£85
double £85–£125
family £125–£160

Location: on the A40; Cheltenham, 2.5 miles

Attractions: Cotswolds; Sudeley Castle; Chipping Campden; Cheltenham Racecourse

A warm welcome, comfort and friendliness are hallmarks of this well appointed hotel, surrounded by the Cotswold Hills. Enthusiastic and experienced staff have a great knowledge of the area so they will be pleased to help you plan visits to places of interest, local events and entertainment. Standard bedrooms are very comfortable, superior rooms are much larger, perfect for when you're planning a longer stay or a special occasion. The restaurant offers varied dishes, and vegetarians or vegans are happily accommodated. Cheltenham Spa is famous for its architecture, festivals and racing, and there's plenty on offer in the way of theatres, restaurants and shops. If you long for peace and solitude however, follow the footpath running alongside the Hotel and explore miles of beautiful Cotswold countryside.

THE FLEECE HOTEL

MARKET PLACE, CIRENCESTER, GLOUCESTERSHIRE GL7 2NZ
Tel: 0845 365 2857 **International:** +44 (0)1285 658507 **Fax:** 01285 651017
Web: www.johansens.com/fleecehotel **E-mail:** relax@fleecehotel.co.uk

Our inspector loved: The great location right in the centre of this lovely market town.

Price Guide:
single £86-£115

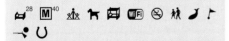

Location: A429, 2 miles; A417, 2 miles; M4 jct 15, 10 miles; Cheltenham, 15 miles

Attractions: Cotswolds; Longleat House; Oxford; Bath

In the heart of the market town of Cirencester you'll find this charming and historic coaching inn where an emphasis is placed firmly on comfort and informality. The relaxed and friendly atmosphere is enhanced by the warmth and character that stems from the building that dates back to the mid-17th century. Bedrooms are pretty and retain many original features. Whilst being pursued by Cromwell and disguised as a man-servant Charles II hid here over 350 years ago and hence the eponym of the popular 1651 Brasserie and Bar. Light meals include English favourites and the main menu has an emphasis for Mediterranean flavours. The outside terrace is a buzzy meeting place in warm weather.

NEW INN AT COLN

COLN ST-ALDWYNS, NR CIRENCESTER, GLOUCESTERSHIRE GL7 5AN
Tel: 0845 365 3754 **International:** +44 (0)1285 750651 **Fax:** 01285 750657
Web: www.johansens.com/newinnatcoln **E-mail:** info@thenewinnatcoln.co.uk

Our inspector loved: The newly decorated bedrooms and restaurant. A great mix of original features and contemporary touches.

Price Guide:
single £75–£120
double £120–£180
suite from £180

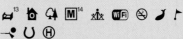

Location: A417, 3 miles; A429, 8 miles; M4/M5, 20 miles; Cheltenham, 23 miles

Attractions: Cirencester; Burford; Bibury; Stow on the Wold

Now under new ownership this quaint inn hidden beneath a bright carpet of green creeper has recently undergone an extensive refurbishment. Original features, including oak beams in the bedrooms and an open fire, mix well with contemporary facilities including flat screen TVs and sleek furniture. In the summer you can enjoy a glass of Pimms on the large south-facing terrace or take a stroll in the orchard. The British menu, including fish and chip and rhubard and custard, is simplicity at its best. Located in the heart of the Cotswolds between Burford and Cirencester, there is plenty to keep you entertained, including fishing, golf, boating, antique shopping, and of course Cheltenham Racecourse only 23 miles away.

LOWER BROOK HOUSE

BLOCKLEY, NR MORETON-IN-MARSH, GLOUCESTERSHIRE GL56 9DS
Tel: 0845 365 2045 **International:** +44 (0)1386 700286 **Fax:** 01386 701400
Web: www.johansens.com/lowerbrookhouse **E-mail:** info@lowerbrookhouse.com

Our inspector loved: *The super stylish bedrooms and Anna's lovely home-cooked food.*

Price Guide:
single £80–£175
double £95–£175

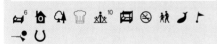

Location: On the B4479; A44, 1.5 miles; Broadway, 8.5 miles

Attractions: Hidcote Manor and Gardens; Snowshill Manor; Sudeley Castle; Broadway Tower

Blockley is a village within a designated Area of Outstanding Natural Beauty and perhaps one of the Cotswold's best kept secrets. Characterised by wisteria covered cottages, dovecotes, and a meandering babbling brook this lovely 17th-century house stands serenely at its heart. The brook once provided power for 12 mills, 6 of which now give their names to the hotel's charming guest rooms. Owners, Julian and Anna, have taken every care to ensure you feel totally at ease in this idyllic setting. The large, deep open fireplace in the relaxing lounge is a favorite spot for a social chat or just to curl up with a good book. Homemade biscuits in your room, big fluffy bathrobes, sumptuous breakfasts and imaginative dinner menus make this a place you'd like to keep all to yourself.

THE MILL AT GORDLETON

SILVER STREET, HORDLE, NR LYMINGTON, NEW FOREST, HAMPSHIRE SO41 6DJ
Tel: 0845 365 2597 **International:** +44 (0)1590 682219 **Fax:** 01590 683073
Web: www.johansens.com/themillatgordleton **E-mail:** info@themillatgordleton.co.uk

Our inspector loved: *The delightful new private dining or small meeting room with its swish Bang and Olufsen technology.*

Price Guide:
single from £85
double/Twin £130
suite from £150

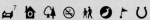

Awards/Recognition: Condé Nast Johansens Most Excellent Value for money 2005

Location: A337, 2 miles; M27 jct 1, 12 miles; Lymington, 3 miles; Southampton, 23 miles

Attractions: New Forest; Lymington and Harbour; Exbury Gardens; Beaulieu and Bucklers Hard

Tucked away between the New Forest National Park and the sea lies this idyllic ivy-clad 17th-century rural hideaway owned and run by Liz Cottingham. Immaculately restored to its former glory, the Mill was the winner of Condé Nast Johansens Most Excellent Value for Money Award 2005. The landscaped gardens exude rustic charm, and visitors weary of their hectic urban lifestyles will certainly relax here to the sound of the mill pond with its charming sluice gates and well fed ducks. The restaurant has a most welcoming atmosphere serving an excellent choice of imaginative dishes. On warm sunny days you can sit outside but be sure to book well in advance! The bedrooms have been refurbished in a most stylish way with delightful bathrooms.

The Nurse's Cottage Restaurant with Rooms

STATION ROAD, SWAY, LYMINGTON, HAMPSHIRE SO41 6BA
Tel: 0845 365 2609 **International:** +44 (0)1590 683402
Web: www.johansens.com/nursescottage **E-mail:** nurses.cottage@lineone.net

Our inspector loved: The exceptional level of attention to guest comfort - Tony Barnfield has a remarkable ability to anticipate your every requirement.

Price Guide: (including dinner)
single £85
double/twin £160–£180

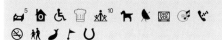

Location: A337, 3.5 miles; M27 jct 1, 11 miles; Lymington, 4 miles; Bournemouth, 13 miles

Attractions: New Forest National Park; ArtSway Gallery ; Beaulieu National Motor Museum; Exbury Gardens and Bucklers Hard

The motto 'good things come in small packages' is certainly true of this charming little hotel, where the cosy, ground-floor bedrooms are named after Sway's successive District Nurses, who lived here until 1983. Chef/Proprietor Tony Barnfield's innovative pampering of guests cannot fail to impress: extras in the bedroom include a blank videotape/dvd, Beaulieu chocolates, biscuits and fruit bowl and, in a small fridge, Hildon mineral water, fresh organic milk, fruit juices and snacks. Jason Noble's kitchen brigade caters for guests in the smart Conservatory Restaurant, open to non-residents for breakfast and dinner. The seasonally-changing menu includes such British classics as steak and kidney pudding alongside fruity tenderloin of pork, one of several house specialities. Over 60 bins comprise the award-winning Wine List and the numerous other accolades range from Best Breakfast in Britain to Excellence in Commitment to the Interests of Disabled People.

LANGRISH HOUSE

LANGRISH, NEAR PETERSFIELD, HAMPSHIRE GU32 1RN
Tel: 0845 365 1986 **International:** +44 (0)1730 266941 **Fax:** 01730 260543
Web: www.johansens.com/langrishhouse **E-mail:** frontdesk@langrishhouse.co.uk

Our inspector loved: This fine old family home in the peace and tranquility of the Hampshire countryside.

Price Guide:
single £72–£90
double £104–£140
suite £145–£155

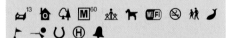

Awards/Recognition: 1 AA Rosette 2007-2008

Location: A272, 0.5 miles; Petersfield, 3 miles; Portsmouth, 15 miles; Heathrow, 53 miles

Attractions: Uppark; Hinton Ampner; Portsmouth Dockyard and HMS Victory; Goodwood

Capture the full traditional country house experience here at Langrish House. Extended by the present owners forbears in 1842 it opened as a hotel in 1979 and remains very much a family home, expertly run by Nigel and Robina Talbot-Ponsonby. Family portraits, antiques and heirlooms grace the rooms, and 14 acres of mature grounds include a picturesque lake. Individually decorated bedrooms with thoughtful touches give you ample opportunity to soak up the peace and quiet. Frederick's Restaurant affords glorious views of the lawns and rambling countryside, whilst its menus feature fresh regional produce, such good food has won the house AA recognition. Langrish House is an ideal venue for wedding receptions and business conferences offering dining facilities for up to 100 people.

AYLESTONE COURT

AYLESTONE HILL, HEREFORD, HEREFORDSHIRE HR1 1HS
Tel: 0845 365 3022 **International:** +44 (0)1432 341891 **Fax:** 01432 267691
Web: www.johansens.com/aylestonecourt **E-mail:** enquiries@aylestonecourthotel.com

Our inspector loved: *The lovely Orangery opening onto a patio area and walled garden.*

Price Guide:
single from £75
double from £95
family from £120

Location: On the A4103; Hereford Town Centre, 1 mile

Attractions: Hay on Wye; Ludlow; Ross-on-Wye; Ledbury

This handsome Georgian town house has been restored and extended to create an elegant and attractive environment, combining original features and contemporary comforts. The 9 non-smoking bedrooms are individually designed and include tea and coffee making facilities. Dinner can be taken in AC's Restaurant, which also provides a cosy, relaxing bar. Breakfast meetings can be arranged upon request, and morning coffee and lunch are also served. Two delightful rooms are licensed for civil weddings and can hold a maximum of 60 people for buffets and the walled garden and patio areas provide the perfect backdrop for photographs. Two conference areas are suitable for corporate events and special packages are available. Aylestone Court is conveniently located for Hereford's town centre as well as its train station.

MOCCAS COURT

MOCCAS, HEREFORDSHIRE HR2 9LH

Tel: 0845 365 2071 **International:** +44 (0)1981 500 019 **Fax:** 01981 500 095
Web: www.johansens.com/moccas **E-mail:** info@moccas-court.co.uk

Our inspector loved: A truly unique property and a real treat if you want to stay somewhere different.

Price Guide:
double/twin £140-£195
dinner £35

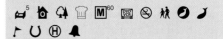

Location: B4352, 1 mile; A438, 4.34 miles; A49, 10.47 miles; Hereford, 10.8 miles

Attractions: Hay on Wye; Mappa Mundi, Hereford Cathedral; Ludlow; The Black and White Trail

Moccas Court sits proudly above terraced banks over the River Wye and affords exceptional long sweeping views across its grounds and deer park. You can expect an exceptional experience when staying with Ben and Mimi Chester-Masters; personal touches, elegance and the warm atmosphere of a private English country house. Beautiful large bedrooms are classically styled and touches include fresh flowers, antiquities and bathroom candles. At 7.30pm guests meet in the library for drinks before moving through to the gorgeous Round dining room, designed by Robert Adam and with its exquisite hand-painted wallpaper enhanced at night by soft candlelight. Ben uses his 18 years of experience and natural culinary talent to create classical yet unpretentious menus inspired by seasonal ingredients. He sources everything on the day and uses largely home grown and reared ingredients. This is a very special place indeed. Closed in January and February.

THE CHASE HOTEL

GLOUCESTER ROAD, ROSS-ON-WYE, HEREFORDSHIRE HR9 5LH
Tel: 0845 365 3741 **International:** +44 (0)1989 763161 **Fax:** 01989 768330
Web: www.johansens.com/chasehotel **E-mail:** res@chasehotel.co.uk

Our inspector loved: *Harry's restaurant with its original Georgian features*

Price Guide:
single £85–£179
double/twin £99–£179
four poster £169–£179

Awards/Recognition: 1 AA Rosette 2006-2007

Location: Town Centre, 3-min walk; A40, 0.25 mile; M50 jct 4, 1 mile; Hereford, 16 miles

Attractions: Forest of Dean; Wye Valley and River Wye; Hereford Cathedral; Gloucester Cathedral;

A Georgian house that sits proudly within 11 acres of grounds and landscaped gardens in the picturesque countryside of Herefordshire. The owners have retained many of the original features, including an impressive staircase and in Harry's Restaurant the ornate plaster covings have been made a striking feature against the more contemporary, pale silk drapes and cream and tan colour scheme. Comfortable bedrooms each have their own character and the four-posters in the original Georgian house have wonderful high ceilings. In such a beautiful setting, with versatile meeting rooms and so many outdoor pursuits close at hand The Chase knows how to organise private and company events. Team building could include white water rafting, hill walking, ballooning and caving. Though for the less energetic there is antiquing and gentle river walks.

WILTON COURT HOTEL

WILTON, ROSS-ON-WYE, HEREFORDSHIRE HR9 6AQ
Tel: 0845 365 2809 **International:** +44 (0)1989 562569 **Fax:** 01989 768460
Web: www.johansens.com/wiltoncourthotel **E-mail:** info@wiltoncourthotel.com

Our inspector loved: The beautifully decorated bedrooms and idyllic location overlooking the river.

Price Guide:
single £70–£110
double £90–£130
suite £120–£150

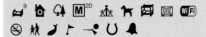

Awards/Recognition: 2 AA Rosettes 2007-2008

Location: Off the B4260; A40, 0.5 miles; Ross on Wye, 1 miles

Attractions: The Forest of Dean; Hereford Cathedral; Hay-on-Wye; Tintern Abbey

You can see how much care and personal effort has been put into making this an enchanting hotel by it's owners Helen and Roger Wynn, both previously trained under the auspicious eye of renowned luxury hotels. Leaded windows, stone mullions, walled gardens with mature shrubs and sloping lawns down to the banks of River Wye make this a delight. Bedrooms all have views and having recently been refurbished offer plenty of charm. The cosy bar with its fire in winter has been cleverly styled using artifacts from the Wynn's many travels. The bright conservatory Mulberry Restaurant has 2 AA Rosettes and weather permitting you can eat al fresco. Sporting enthusiasts will be in their element with local activities including canoeing, fishing on the River Wye, walking, horse riding, claypigeon shooting, ballooning, tennis, cycling and golf.

GLEWSTONE COURT

NEAR ROSS-ON-WYE, HEREFORDSHIRE HR9 6AW
Tel: 0845 365 1782 **International:** +44 (0)1989 770367 **Fax:** 01989 770282
Web: www.johansens.com/glewstonecourt **E-mail:** glewstone@aol.com

Our inspector loved: *A lovely house in a beautifully peaceful setting with great food.*

Price Guide: (closed for Christmas)
single £55-£80-£95
double £95-£115-£135

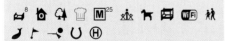

Location: A40, 1 mile; M50, 3 miles; Hereford, 14 miles

Attractions: Wye Valley, area of outstanding natural beauty; Royal Forest of Dean; Brecon Beacons; Hereford Cathedral and the Mappa Mundi

Refreshing and unstuffy, Glewstone Court's eclectic antiques, works of art and bric-a-brac epitomise the relaxed, hospitable owners, Christine and Bill Reeve-Tucker. The comfortable atmosphere permeates the bedrooms where you'll find a hospitality tray with delicious homemade biscuits, and soft bathrobes. A finalist for the Restaurant of the Year and Breakfast of the Year in the "Flavours of Herefordshire", Christine's food is innovative and prepared from good, fresh local ingredients; organic and free-range whenever possible. Herefordshire is marvellous walking country and although you're secluded here, you're still only 3 miles from Ross-on-Wye. Alternatively, relax by the log fires, or on fine days, laze in the garden. Places of interest nearby include Hay-on-Wye, the Welsh Marches, Hereford Cathedral with the Mappa Mundi, and the Brecon Beacons.

REDCOATS FARMHOUSE HOTEL AND RESTAURANT

REDCOATS GREEN, NEAR HITCHIN, HERTFORDSHIRE SG4 7JR
Tel: 0845 365 2143 **International:** +44 (0)1438 729500 **Fax:** 01438 723322
Web: www.johansens.com/redcoatsfarmhouse **E-mail:** sales@redcoats.co.uk

Our inspector loved: The warm and friendly character and the fun artwork.

Price Guide: (weekend breaks available)
single £76–£115
double £111–£125
suite £145

Dating back to 1450 Redcoats farmhouse has clung fiercely to its traditional warmth and family atmosphere. Bedrooms are individually decorated with rich fabrics and chaise longues encourage you to put your feet up and relax. If you want to be pampered opt for Bobbie's Room - complete with sitting room, and Jacuzzi. Gastronomes will be delighted with the offerings in Redcoats' dining rooms, from fresh native oysters and smoked haddock rarebit to rack of lamb. Sweet tooths never fear as brandy snaps, zabagliones and ice creams are all homemade but it's well worth saving room for the cheeseboard. Conferences can be held on-site for up to 15 delegates whilst corporate awaydays can be arranged with clay-pigeon shooting, archery and reverse steer driving, for outdoor fun.

Location: B656, 0.5 miles; A1(M) jct 8, 1 mile; Stevenage, 3 miles; Hitchin, 3 miles

Attractions: Knebworth House; Hatfield House; St. Albans; Woburn

The White House and Lion & Lamb Bar & Restaurant

SMITHS GREEN, DUNMOW ROAD, TAKELEY, BISHOP'S STORTFORD, HERTFORDSHIRE CM22 6NR
Tel: 0845 365 2736 **International:** +44 (0)1279 870257 **Fax:** 01279 870423
Web: www.johansens.com/whitehousestansted **E-mail:** info@whitehousestansted.co.uk

Our inspector loved: The quiet dappled garden surrounding the house.

Price Guide:
single from £60
double from £75

Location: Just off B1256; M11 jct 8, 3 miles; Great Dunmow, 4.4 miles; Bishops Stortford, 5.3 miles

Attractions: Cambridge; Newmarket Racecourse; Constable Country; Audley End House

Situated in an acre of gardens this 15th-century Grade II listed country manor house offers excellent accommodation. Recently refurbished, the comfortable bedrooms have state-of-the-art bathrooms and double aspect windows creating a light and airy feel. First-class dining is available at The Lion & Lamb; free transport is offered for the 2-minute drive. Open fires in the traditional restaurant provide warmth on chilly days, whilst soft lighting and beautiful old blackened oak beams create an intimate atmosphere. Service is professional but relaxed, with an emphasis on superb food, prepared with fresh ingredients and fish from Billingsgate, and accompanied by fine wines. A most unusual country-style room with its own terrace and garden is available for functions and meetings for up to 25 people.

WINTERBOURNE COUNTRY HOUSE

BONCHURCH VILLAGE ROAD, BONCHURCH, ISLE OF WIGHT PO38 1RQ
Tel: 0845 365 2813 **International:** +44 (0)1983 852 535 **Fax:** 01983 857 529
Web: www.johansens.com/winterbourne **E-mail:** info@winterbournehouse.co.uk

Our inspector loved: Its quiet and private coastal setting with pheasants in the garden and magnificent views.

Price Guide:
single from £65
double/twin £100–£190

Location: A3055, 1 mile; Ventnor, 2 miles; Cowes (Southampton) Ferry Terminal, 17 miles; Fishbourne (Portsmouth) Ferry Terminal, 18miles

Attractions: Walking on St Boniface Down; Isle of Wight Glass; Carisbrooke Castle; Osborne House

Obviously the perfect antidote to writers' block, Charles Dickens worked on "David Copperfield," while staying here in July 1849 and wrote to his wife, "I have taken a most delightful and beautiful house - cool, airy, everything delicious" You'll still find a house of charm and character, with many of the original features. The lawns sweep down to the bay and in summer the gardens blaze with colour. There's a secluded swimming pool, sun terrace, gently flowing stream and via a private path you reach the shingle and sand beach. Winterbourne has several lovely restaurants close by and as they only provide breakfast you will be happily advised on where to dine, though a pre-dinner drink on the terrace is highly recommended.

THE PRIORY BAY HOTEL

PRIORY DRIVE, SEAVIEW, ISLE OF WIGHT PO34 5BU
Tel: 0845 365 2649 **International:** +44 (0)1983 613146 **Fax:** 01983 616539
Web: www.johansens.com/priorybayiow **E-mail:** enquiries@priorybay.co.uk

Our inspector loved: *Probably the best six hole golf course in Britain!*

Price Guide:
single from £70
double £120-£270
suite £250-£375

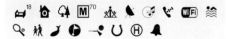

Awards/Recognition: 1 AA Rosette 2006-2007

Location: A3055, 2 miles; Ryde, 3.5 miles; Cowes (Southampton) Ferry Terminal, 10.6 miles; Fishbourne (Portsmouth) Ferry Terminal, 6.1 miles

Attractions: Ventnor Botanic Garden; Osborne House; Carisbrooke Castle; Sailing at Seaview and Bembridge

For centuries this beautiful site has been used by Medieval monks, Tudor farmers and Georgian gentry, and now thanks to its current owners you can experience the buildings as a splendid hotel. A carved, arched stone entrance leads to delightful, flower-filled gardens and thatched tithe barns, and inside, public rooms are framed by tall windows and heavy curtains. Each of the 18 comfortable bedrooms has views over the grounds, and all are individually furnished. The two dining rooms and terraces serve up delicious modern European cuisine and freshly caught seafood, including tuna and sea bass. For those who want to stretch their legs, the outdoor pool, adjoining 6-hole golf course, tennis courts and neighbouring woodlands are certain to keep all active and entertained. Coastal paths also pass by the gate.

RYLSTONE MANOR

RYLSTONE GARDENS, SHANKLIN, ISLE OF WIGHT PO37 6RG
Tel: 0845 365 2318 **International:** +44 (0)1983 862806 **Fax:** 01983 862806
Web: www.johansens.com/rylstonemanor **E-mail:** rylstone.manor@btinternet.com

Our inspector loved: The continuing relaxed and friendly atmosphere at this unique little hotel.

Price Guide: (including dinner)
single from £75
double from £150

Carole and Michael Hailston are the proud owners of this delightful manor house hidden away in 4½ acres of peaceful mature gardens on the edge of Shanklin. You can catch a glimpse of the sea from some of the charming bedrooms and the stylish day rooms are just the thing for a good book and afternoon tea. Of course in good weather you will probably wish to be outside for much of the day and from the garden you will be able to enjoy stunning views of Shanklin Bay and a 2-minute walk leads to the promenade and beach. The restaurants menu changes daily and is complemented by a well thought out wine list which includes some interesting local vintages.

Location: A3055, 0.5 mile; Shanklin, 0.5 mile; Cowes (Southampton) Ferry Terminal, 14.8 miles; Fishbourne (Portsmouth) Ferry Terminal, 16 miles

Attractions: Osborne House; Godshill Old Village; Arreton Manor; Carisbrooke Castle

THE HAMBROUGH

HAMBROUGH ROAD, VENTNOR, ISLE OF WIGHT PO38 1SQ
Tel: 0845 365 2517 **International:** +44 (0)1983 856333 **Fax:** 01983 857260
Web: www.johansens.com/thehambrough **E-mail:** info@thehambrough.com

Our inspector loved: This chic retreat with great food and wonderful views.

Price Guide:
single from £110
double £160–£220

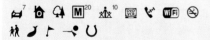

Awards/Recognition: 2 AA Rosettes 2006-2007

Location: A3055, 0.25 mile; Shanklin, 3.8 miles; Cowes (Southampton) Ferry Terminal, 15.8 miles; Fishbourne (Portsmouth) Ferry Terminal, 15miles

Attractions: Osborne House; Carisbrooke Castle; Bonchurch Pottery; Botanic Gardens; Godshill Organics

This stylish delightful hotel, high above the harbour, at the southern end of Ventnor Bay, has stunning views of the coastline, and scenic views of St Boniface Down. Two of the seven newly presented bedrooms have balconies upon which you can relax and sip a cooling drink or evening aperitif whilst watching the world drift by. The decor is minimalist throughout, the bedrooms feature flat screen TV's and DVD players - even an espresso machine. The bathrooms are a joy with underfloor heating and de luxe baths and showers. Take a coffee break, light lunch, afternoon tea, or an after dinner nightcap in the bar. Executive Chef Craig Atchinson creates the most imaginative and inspired gourmet cuisine from the finest and freshest ingredients available from the market daily.

WALLETT'S COURT HOTEL & SPA

WEST CLIFFE, ST MARGARET'S-AT-CLIFFE, DOVER, KENT CT15 6EW
Tel: 0845 365 2784 **International:** +44 (0)1304 852424 **Fax:** 01304 853430
Web: www.johansens.com/wallettscourt **E-mail:** mail@wallettscourt.com

Our inspector loved: *This historical country house and locaton with its modern approach.*

Price Guide:
single £109–£139
double £129–£169

Awards/Recognition: 2 AA Rosettes 2006-2007

Location: A2, 1 mile; M2 jct7, 30 miles; Dover, 3 miles; Gatwick Airport, 73 miles

Attractions: Dover Castle; White Cliffs of Dover; Canterbury Cathedral; Leeds Castle

This Grade II listed house was found in ruins in the late 70's by the Oakley family, who thankfully picked it up and put it back on its feet. In the main house the Jacobean staircase leads to one of the three traditional 4-poster bedrooms and across the courtyard there are 14 contemporary rooms housed in converted Kentish hay barns. On top of excellent hospitality there is a spa complete with hydrotherapy pool and treatment cabins set in the woods. The restaurant is deservedly popular locally and local ingredients are important - try the St Margaret's Bay lobster or Romney Marsh lamb. You can practice clay pigeon shooting with a professional or have a round of golf atop the White Cliffs or simply relax here for a day or two before heading over to France.

ROMNEY BAY HOUSE HOTEL

COAST ROAD, LITTLESTONE, NEW ROMNEY, KENT TN28 8QY
Tel: 0845 365 2305 **International:** +44 (0)1797 364747 **Fax:** 01797 367156
Web: www.johansens.com/romneybayhouse

Our inspector loved: *This complete haven on the very edge of Kent.*

Price Guide:
single from £60
double £90–£160

Awards/Recognition: Condé Nast Johansens Most Excellent Coastal Hotel 2006

Location: A259, 2 miles; M20 jct 11, 11 miles; New Romney, 2 miles; Gatwick Airport, 77 miles

Attractions: Dover Castle; Canterbury Cathedral; Ancient Rye; Fly to Le Touquet for lunch

Winner of the Condé Nast Johansens Most Excellent Coastal Hotel in 2006, this spectacular house mixes the historic Kent coastline with a dash of 1920's Hollywood glamour. Built for the infamous American actress and journalist Hedda Hopper, there is access to the beach, croquet lawn and golf course, while a 5-minute drive to Lydd Airport means you can fly to Le Touquet and back in no time. The chef-patron and his wife both with London hotel/restaurant backgrounds, create delicious dishes for sea-air enhanced appetites and also provide wonderful cream teas on the terrace. Upstairs, comfortable bedrooms are furnished with antiques. You can relax in the drawing room or survey the irresistible panoramic views through the telescope in the first-floor library.

THE ROYAL HARBOUR HOTEL

NELSON CRESCENT, RAMSGATE, KENT CT11 9JF
Tel: 0845 365 4853 **International:** +44 (0)1843 591514 **Fax:** 01843 570443
Web: www.johansens.com/royalharbour **E-mail:** info@royalharbourhotel.co.uk

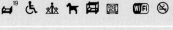

Our inspector loved: The abundance of books, and things to amuse and entertain.

Price Guide:
single from £75
double from £95

Location: A255, 2.5 miles; M2 (A2), 16.5 miles; Kent International Airport, 3.5 miles

Attractions: Fishing and Yachting Harbour; Ferry service to Ostende; Dickens Heritage; Richborough Roman Fort

A Regency townhouse overlooking Ramsgate harbour is where owner James Thomas, previously GM of a fine London boutique hotel, has put his mark. With an eye for detail, he has give the Royal Harbour a unique style - traditional yet eclectic; with fine art, quirky memorabilia and books in abundance. A record player with stacks of old vinyls awaits your attention in the snug. Lovely gestures of hospitality include a cheese board and hot drinks put out for guests returning late. Rooms vary in size, most enjoying marina views. Some feature beautiful teak four-poster beds, including the Bridal Suite, which boasts a working fireplace. In the basement - a screening room - where guest can watch films when the local film production team are not in residence. While guests dine at one of the local restaurants a hearty breakfast greets you each morning.

LITTLE SILVER COUNTRY HOTEL

ASHFORD ROAD, ST MICHAELS, TENTERDEN, KENT TN30 6SP
Tel: 0845 365 2032 **International:** +44 (0)1233 850321 **Fax:** 01233 850647
Web: www.johansens.com/littlesilver **E-mail:** enquiries@little-silver.co.uk

Our inspector loved: *The stylish new restaurant complemented by the new presentation in the lounge.*

Price Guide:
single from £60
double/twin from £95
suites from £150

Location: On the A28; M20 jct 9, 12 miles; Tenterden, 0.5 miles; Gatwick Airport, 52 miles

Attractions: Sissinghurst and Great Dixter Gardens; Ancient Rye; Leeds and Bodiam Castles; Canterbury Cathedral

An unexpected find in the Weald of Kent, you'll discover that this wood framed Tudor-style hotel welcomes you with friendly hospitality and service and makes an excellent choice for weekends and longer breaks, weddings and celebrations. Especially attractive is the Kentish oast-house inspired octagonal hall with stained-glass windows, which can accommodate up to 150 guests. The beamed lounge's blazing log fires bring warmth and pleasure to a grey winter's day. Individually furnished bedrooms and suites deliver complete comfort, some with four-poster beds, Jacuzzi baths, and views across the gardens. 2 rooms are particularly suitable for wheelchair users. Good food is never far away, with breakfast, morning coffee, lunch, afternoon tea and dinner served in the Oaks restaurant.

FERRARI'S RESTAURANT & HOTEL

THORNLEY, LONGRIDGE, PRESTON, LANCASHIRE PR3 2TB
Tel: 0845 365 3293 **International:** +44 (0)1772 783148 **Fax:** 01772 786174
Web: www.johansens.com/ferraris **E-mail:** info@ferrariscountryhouse.co.uk

Our inspector loved: *The Italian hospitality and friendliness at this family run hotel.*

Price Guide:
single £45–£90
double/twin £60–£110

Location: B5269, 1.5 miles; M6 jct 31a, 6 miles; Longridge, 1.5 miles; Preston, 8 miles

Attractions: Ribble Valley; Clitheroe; Preston; Blackpool

This impressive house was built by the Earl of Derby in 1830 as a shooting lodge, and today it's a family owned affair, with Susan Ferrari and daughter Luisa overseeing the kitchen and restaurant. Dishes are a combination of traditional English and Italian cooking, including Loin of Lamb of Rosemary and Insalata di Gamberi. The Ferraris pride themselves on a personalised wedding service, working together with each couple to provide the perfect day. Comfortable bedrooms are individually styled, some have Jacuzzis and half-tester Tudor beds, and many feature antique furniture and garden views. You're spoilt for choice with places to visit as the historic market town of Clitheroe and its famous Norman castle are on the doorstep, as well as the natural beauty of rural Lancashire.

THE INN AT WHITEWELL

FOREST OF BOWLAND, CLITHEROE, LANCASHIRE BB7 3AT
Tel: 0845 365 2546 **International:** +44 (0)1200 448222 **Fax:** 01200 448298
Web: www.johansens.com/innatwhitewell **E-mail:** reception@innatwhitewell.com

Our inspector loved: The new bar and terrace with spectacular views over the River Hodder.

Price Guide:
single £70–£95
double £96–£140
suite £118–£160

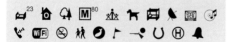

Awards/Recognition: Condé Nast Johansens Most Excellent Traditional Inn 2006; 1 AA Rosette 2007

Location: B6243, 8.25 miles; M6 jct 31a, 15 miles; Longridge, 9 miles; Clitheroe, 7 miles

Attractions: Trough of Boland; Brownsholme Hall; Clitheroe Castle; River Hodder

An art gallery and wine merchant share the premises of this friendly, welcoming early 14th century inn, once inhabited by the Keeper of the "Forêt" – the Royal hunting ground. Set within 3 acres, the inn enjoys splendid views across the dramatically undulating Trough of Bowland. All bedrooms, including the luxury rooms in the coach house, feature antiques and quality fabrics. All have hi-tech entertainment systems for video or dvd. The excellent à la carte menu, created by head chef Jamie Cadman, features predominately English country recipes such as seasonal roast game, homemade puddings and farmhouse cheeses. Good bar meals and garden lunches are also offered. 8 miles of water is available to residents where brown trout, sea trout, salmon and grayling can be caught.

HORSE & TRUMPET

OLD GREEN, MEDBOURNE, NEAR MARKET HARBOROUGH, LEICESTERSHIRE LE16 8DX
Tel: 0845 365 1879 **International:** +44 (0)1858 565000 **Fax:** 01858 565551
Web: www.johansens.com/horseandtrumpet **E-mail:** info@horseandtrumpet.com

Our inspector loved: The variety and quality of the tasting menu and its selection of wines.

Price Guide:
single from £75
double from £75

Awards/Recognition: 2 AA Rosettes 2006-2007

Location: On the B644, 10 miles; A14, 10 miles; M6 Jct 1, 20 miles; Market Harborough, 8 miles

Attractions: Rockingham Castle; Coton Manor Wildlife Garden; Burghley House; Althorp House

Facing the village bowling green, the 18th century Horse & Trumpet has been lovingly restored and converted into a restaurant with rooms by Gill Pemberton and her team. The Grade II listed main building is built from local stone, and in winter you can enjoy pre dinner drinks by the Inglenook fireplace before dining in one of the 3 attractive dining rooms. There are 4 superb bedrooms in the outbuildings, recycling many original features and materials including an old saloon bar window incorporated into the main door. On sunny days, you can appreciate alfresco dining in the secluded courtyard. Chef Gary Magnani and his team create imaginative, modern British award winning cuisine. A multi-course tasting menu is available alongside the à la carte, complemented by individually matched wines. Private dining for parties of 8 - 32 can be accommodated.

SYSONBY KNOLL HOTEL

ASFORDBY ROAD, MELTON MOWBRAY, LEICESTERSHIRE LE13 0HP
Tel: 0845 365 2385 **International:** +44 (0)1664 563563 **Fax:** 01664 410364
Web: www.johansens.com/sysonby **E-mail:** reception@sysonby.com

Our inspector loved: *The striking colour schemes and local hunting prints in the bar.*

Price Guide:
single £68
double/twin from £82
four poster from £115

Location: On the A6006; M1 jct 21a, 30-min drive; Melton Mowbray, 1 mile; East Midlands Airport, 20-min drive

Attractions: Rutland Water; Belvoir Castle; Nottingham; Oakham

Surrounded by 1.5 acres of Edwardian landscaped gardens overlooking the river Eye, Sysonby Knoll has been owned and run by the same family since 1965. The original building houses the reception and lounge areas, decorated in period style, forming part of a courtyard, with the bar, restaurant and conservatory overlooking the gardens and fields beyond. The well appointed bedrooms include 9 singles, the rest are either twin or double-bedded. The 2 stunning four-poster garden view bedrooms are perfect for a honeymoon. A wide choice of menus is available in the restaurant, featuring excellent, freshly prepared dishes and fine wines from a comprehensive list. The hotel has a total of 5 acres of grounds with coarse fishing on the River Eye. Guests with pets are always welcome.

BAILHOUSE HOTEL

34 BAILGATE, LINCOLN, LINCOLNSHIRE LN1 3AP
Tel: 0845 365 3024 **International:** +44 (0)1522 541000 **Fax:** 01522 521829
Web: www.johansens.com/bailhouse **E-mail:** info@bailhouse.co.uk

Our inspector loved: The charm and comfort of an established hotel with all the modern touches.

Price Guide: (room only)
single £64.50-£125
double £79-£175

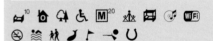

Location: Between Castle and Cathedral; A15, 1 miles; M180, 22 miles

Attractions: Lincoln Cathedral; Medieval Bishops Palace (EH); Woodhall Spa Golf Course; Trent Bridge

Dating from 1354 as a Baronial Hall and situated between a Norman Castle and the second largest Cathedral in Britain, Bailhouse is surrounded by over 1000 years of history at the heart of vibrant Lincoln. Contemporary comfort combines with charm and character, well-worn flagstones, beamed ceilings and an eclectic mix of antique and fine furnishings complement the architecture. Spacious bedrooms enjoy views over the gardens, castle or Bailgate and are decorated with fine fabrics and four-poster or brass beds. Many feature 42" plasma televisions and larger bathrooms. The attractive breakfast room doubles as a relaxed reading area. The many excellent restaurants on Bailgate are all within 2 minutes' walk. The secluded gardens feature a stone chapel and a number of self-catering cottages and secure private parking.

WASHINGBOROUGH HALL

CHURCH HILL, WASHINGBOROUGH, LINCOLN LN4 1BE
Tel: 0845 365 2792 **International:** +44 (0)1522 790340 **Fax:** 01522 792936
Web: www.johansens.com/washingboroughhall **E-mail:** enquiries@washingboroughhall.com

Our inspector loved: *The quiet and peaceful setting so close to the centre of Lincoln.*

Price Guide:
single from £70
double/twin from £95

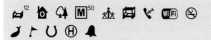

Location: A15, 4 miles; M180, 24 miles; Lincoln, 4 miles

Attractions: Lincoln Cathedral; The Aviation Heritage Centre; Horncastle; Market Rasen Racecourse

Originally built around 1700 for George Fairfax, the esteemed local Rector and his family, Washingborough Hall has always played an important part in the lives of the area and today it remains a popular place for county weddings and anniversary parties. It's a good looking Georgian manor with comfortable bedrooms and plenty of space in the drawing room to curl up with a good book. It's cool and relaxing in summer, and the large York stone open fireplace will warm you after a cheek-chilling walk in winter. Talented Lincolnshire chef, Dan Wallis creates culinary interest from local ingredients, served in the dining room overlooking the gardens. Places of interest nearby include Lincoln's 11th-century cathedral and castle, and Horncastle, renowned for its antique shops

THE CROWN HOTEL

ALL SAINTS PLACE, STAMFORD, LINCOLNSHIRE PE9 2AG
Tel: 0845 365 2451 **International:** +44 (0)1780 763136 **Fax:** 01780 756111
Web: www.johansens.com/crownstamford **E-mail:** reservations@thecrownhotelstamford.co.uk

Our inspector loved: *The way in which the mix of traditional and modern work so well.*

Price Guide:
single from £85
double from £100

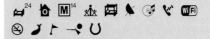

Awards/Recognition: 3 AA Rosettes 2006-2007

Location: A1, 1 mile; Peterborough, 13.5 miles

Attractions: Burghley House; Belvoir Castle; Rutland Water; Rockingham Raceway

Owned and managed by a lively, enthusiastic brother and sister team, The Crown Hotel lies in the heart of this attractive stone built town, a popular setting for many acclaimed English period dramas. They have cleverly kept key traditional elements - stone walls, beams and original floors and blended them with fresh contemporary colours, wallpaper and fabrics. Early evening the bar is a popular meeting place for locals and in summer you can relax in the side courtyard. The restaurant makes the best use of Lincolnshire's farming heritage - succulent meat and tasty seasonal vegetables are accompanied by excellent wines and real ales. A meeting room is also available off the courtyard with plenty of parking at the back. A great base when exploring this beautiful part of England.

The King's Arms Hotel

2 LION GATE , HAMPTON COURT ROAD, HAMPTON COURT, KT8 9DD
Tel: 0845 365 4857 **International:** +44 (0)208 977 1729 **Fax:** 0208 943 9838
Web: www.johansens.com/kingsarms **E-mail:** info@hamptoncourthotel.com

Our inspector loved: *This pub has everything - fantastic rooms, great food and a proper bar. It's a real find!*

Price Guide:
single from £95
double from £120
suite from £150

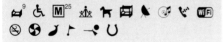

Location: Hampton Court Station, 5-min walk; London Waterloo Station, 30-min train/metro; A3, 7 miles

Attractions: Hampton Court; Bushy Park; Windsor Castle and Great Park; Sandown Park Racecourse

Reopened Christmas 2006 after a major refurbishment this pub is a real find. Close to the impressively large Lion Gates entrance to Hampton Court Palace and dating back to 1658. The owners have maintained the elements of it's heritage - deep oak tables and flagged floors in the bar, smart yet unpretentious restaurant and upstairs 9 beautifully designed rooms, with wi-fi throughout and fine Egyptian Cotton bedlinen, The bar sells wonderful real ales and the restaurant is rapidly gaining renown for its philosophy that it is possible to serve good-quality food at affordable prices. With an inspired English/Mediterranean flavour the chef has a constantly changing menu of inspired dishes to excite even the most jaded palette! The King's Arms really has grasped the way to look after the 21st century guest!

BINGHAM

61-63 PETERSHAM ROAD, RICHMOND-UPON-THAMES, SURREY TW10 6UT
Tel: 0845 365 3761 **International:** +44 (0)208 940 0902 **Fax:** 0208 948 8737
Web: www.johansens.com/bingham **E-mail:** info@thebingham.co.uk

Our inspector loved: The new meeting facilities downstairs - it would be the most stunning setting for a small and sophisticated wedding!

Price Guide:
double from £180

Location: Richmond-Upon-Thames, 5-min walk; A316, 2 miles; London Waterloo, 15-min train/metro; Heathrow Airport, 30-min drive

Attractions: Richmond Park; Twickenham Rugby; Hampton Court Palace; Richmond Town Centre and Riverside

Contemporary style in a beautiful Georgian townhouse that nestles on the tranquil banks of the Thames. Chic bedrooms combine modern elegance with classic touches. Soft greys and beige are accented with black and walnut . Envelope yourself in the duck and goose feather duvet and enjoy the rooms' digital gadgets, including high-tech music server. Two rooms feature an antique four-poster bed; some boast whirlpool baths and walk-in showers. If you can be tempted away from your room then head to the dining room to savour the award-winning Modern British cuisine. Here taking full advantage of its glorious riverside setting there are glimpses of art-deco off-set with shimmering chandeliers. On warm days the wide terrace leading down to an immaculately landscaped garden is the place to wile away time.

TREE TOPS COUNTRY HOUSE RESTAURANT & HOTEL

SOUTHPORT OLD ROAD, FORMBY, NR SOUTHPORT, MERSEYSIDE L37 0AB
Tel: 0845 365 2759 **International:** +44 (0)1704 572430 **Fax:** 01704 573011
Web: www.johansens.com/treetopscountryhouse **E-mail:** sales@treetopsformby.fsnet.co.uk

Our inspector loved: *The light and airy restaurant with the modern international dining experience.*

Price Guide:
single £63–£78
double £105–£130

Location: A565, 300yds; M57 jct 7, 16 miles; Southport, 5 miles; Liverpool, 18 miles

Attractions: Formby & Ainsdale Beaches; Southport; Liverpool Albert Dock; Numerous Championship Golf Cources

Set in 5 acres of lawns and woodland, Tree Tops is the former Dower House of Formby Hall and still retains the elegance of another age. The house has been fully restored by Lesley Winsland over the past 24 years. Spacious accommodation is available in well-appointed en-suite lodges. An outdoor heated swimming pool has direct access to the richly decorated Cocktail Lounge. Dark leather seating and subtle lighting all contribute to the overall ambience, complemented by welcoming and efficient staff. The restaurant and conservatory have been refurbished, cleverly incorporating some 21st-century ideas. Menus offer a wonderful blend of traditional and modern, English and international cuisine. Table d'hôte, à la carte and lunchtime snacks are available, using only the freshest of local produce.

FELBRIGG LODGE

AYLMERTON, NORTH NORFOLK NR11 8RA
Tel: 0845 365 2853 **International:** +44 (0)1263 837588 **Fax:** 01263 838012
Web: www.johansens.com/felbrigglodge **E-mail:** info@felbrigglodge.co.uk

Our inspector loved: The secluded and intimate luxury - a place to unwind.

Price Guide:
suite £125-£180

Location: A140, 2 miles; M11, 80 miles; Holt, 7 miles; Norwich, 21 miles

Attractions: North Norfolk Coast; Blickling Hall; Norfolk Broads; Felbrigg Hall

You can't help but be impressed by DeeDee and Philip Lomax's enthusiasm and dedication to ensuring you have a memorable stay. In a tranquil woodland setting six delightful suites offer you a real sense of peacefulness, privacy and charm. For those really wishing to hibernate there is the very spacious Oak Pavilion with its wonderful vaulted ceiling and open fire. The Ivy Restaurant is intimate and friendly, rather like the Dining Car on the Orient Express! Philip's in charge and his daily menu is influenced by the seasons. Dinner is at 7.30 and guests must confirm ahead. Dee Dee is an excellent concierge whose local knowledge can arrange amongst other things helicepter flights, horse riding, life coaching and singing. The pool adds to your options for not venturing far.

THE KINGS HEAD HOTEL

GREAT BIRCHAM, KING'S LYNN, NORFOLK PE31 6RJ
Tel: 0845 365 2567 **International:** +44 (0)1485 578 265 **Fax:** 01485 578 635
Web: www.johansens.com/kingsheadbircham **E-mail:** welcome@the-kings-head-bircham.co.uk

Our inspector loved: The bold contemporary bedrooms and total attention to detail.

Price Guide:
single £69.50–£125
double/twin £125–£200

Awards/Recognition: 3 AA Rosettes 2007-2008

Location: On the B1153; A148, 4 miles; King's Lynn, 14 miles; Norwich airport, 37 miles

Attractions: Sandringham; Burnham Market; Holkham Hall; Houghton Hall

Tall red brick chimneys and decorative gables are just two attractive features of this white-faced, Grade II Listed Victorian hotel in the heart of North Norfolk. Others include a comfortable atmosphere, stylish modern décor and spacious bedrooms. Bathrooms are particularly luxurious, and you might find that the gorgeous homemade Norfolk toiletries make it into your bag and home with you. Just as tempting are the innovative and unfussy restaurant menus which are inspired by local and seasonal ingredients. On warm days you can eat outside in the pretty courtyard. A contemporary bar offers light meals and snacks alongside local and guest ales. In-house health and beauty treatments can be arranged. Stately homes galore surround you if that's your thing, and nature lovers can head to bird sanctuaries and miles of unspoilt sandy beaches.

TITCHWELL MANOR HOTEL

TITCHWELL, KING'S LYNN, NORFOLK PE31 8BB

Tel: 0845 365 2861 **International:** +44 (0)1485 210221 **Fax:** 01485 210104
Web: www.johansens.com/titchwellmanor **E-mail:** margaret@titchwellmanor.com

Our inspector loved: *The beautiful new suites and the warm and personal welcome.*

Price Guide:
double £70-£170

Awards/Recognition: 2 AA Rosettes 2007-2008

Location: On the A149; Brancaster, 1 mile; King's Lynn, 23 miles; Norwich Airport, 40 miles

Attractions: Burnham Market; Titchwell RSPB Reserve; Holkham Hall

Once a Victorian gentlemen's club, Titchwell Manor is now one of those wonderful and rare hotels that manages to capture the period feeling of an older residence with the stylish and contemporary luxury that we all love. Always warm and welcoming, the hotel now has 25 bedrooms and the latest 13 are stunning - built around a central courtyard herb garden, where the wonderful aromas inspire the names of the rooms themselves. The conservatory dining room uses an impressive list of local fare - be it mussels and lobsters from Brancaster Staithe, Cromer crabs or Holkham venison - and a log fire burns in the lounge during the winter months. The surrounding scenery is simply stunning and a walk on Norfolk's beautiful golden beaches is an absolute must at any time of the year.

BEECHWOOD HOTEL

CROMER ROAD, NORTH WALSHAM, NORFOLK NR28 0HD
Tel: 0845 365 3032 **International:** +44 (0)1692 403231 **Fax:** 01692 407284
Web: www.johansens.com/beechwood **E-mail:** enquiries@beechwood–hotel.co.uk

Our inspector loved: *The eye for detail and passion for service.*

Price Guide:
single from £72
double from £90

Awards/Recognition: 2 AA Rosettes 2007-2008

Location: off A149; B1150, 0.5 miles; A1042, 13.5 miles; Norwich, 16.6 miles

Attractions: Felbrigg Hall (NT); Norfolk Broads; Blickling Hall; East Ruston Old Vicarage Gardens

Don Birch and Lindsay Spalding know a thing or two about immaculate detail and care for their guests. Their 1800's ivy-clad house has always had an enviable society guest list which in the past was headed by Agatha Christie and the Sheikh of Iraq. You don't have to be so illustrious to enjoy bedrooms with large windows, traditional and antique furnishings, and in some, luxurious Victorian-style bathrooms with freestanding "Mae West" style slipper baths. Inspirational evening menus from Head Chef Steven are influenced by his desire to sources all the ingredients, where possible, from within ten miles of the hotel. When in season, expect to see Sheringham lobster, Cromer crab, Thornham oysters and even Norfolk cheese. In summer enjoy cocktails in the garden after a day exploring the delightful North Norfolk coastline.

THE STOWER GRANGE

SCHOOL ROAD, DRAYTON, NORWICH, NORFOLK NR8 6EF
Tel: 0845 365 2701 **International:** +44 (0)1603 860210 **Fax:** 01603 860464
Web: www.johansens.com/stowergrange **E-mail:** enquiries@stowergrange.co.uk

Our inspector loved: The comfortable and homely atmosphere together with the warm and genuine welcome.

Price Guide:
single £75
double £95
suite £150

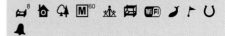

Once a rectory and a lovely home Stower Grange now offers guests a peaceful retreat. The fine lawns with mature trees invite you to sit beneath them and do nothing but relax. Owners Richard and Jane Fannon encourage a friendly, informal atmosphere, and in winter stoke up open fires to add to the welcome. There are 8 individually decorated rooms, one with an oak four-poster if you're feeling particularly romantic. The restaurant, known locally as a "special place" for dinner ensures good eating, with imaginative cooking by chef, David Kilmister. A good alternative to a Norwich city hotel, from here you can venture out and about to historic houses including Sandringham, the Norfolk Coast and horseracing at Fakenham.

Location: A1067, 0.23 miles; A140, 2.5 miles; Norwich Airport, 2.7 miles; Norwich 4 miles

Attractions: Norfolk Broads; Norwich Castle Museum & Norwich Art Gallery; Norwich Cathedral; Blickling Hall (NT)

THE OLD RECTORY

103 YARMOUTH ROAD, NORWICH, NORFOLK NR7 OHF
Tel: 0845 365 2614 **International:** +44 (0)1603 700772 **Fax:** 01603 300772
Web: www.johansens.com/oldrectorynorwich **E-mail:** enquiries@oldrectorynorwich.com

Our inspector loved: The character, individualism and attention to detail in every room.

Price Guide:
single £85-£110
double £115-£145

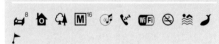

Awards/Recognition: 2 AA Rosettes 2007-2008

Location: A47, 2 miles; Norwich, 2 miles; Norwich Airport, 4 miles

Attractions: Whitlingham Country Park; Norwich Cathedral; Sandringham

The promise of a warm welcome and personal service will draw you to this Wisteria clad Grade II listed Georgian house. Set in an acre of mature gardens on the outskirts of Norwich overlooking the Yare Valley the spacious bedrooms and elegant Drawing Room offer a great place to relax. Chris and Sally Entwistle understand hospitality and are the proud winners of a Green Tourism Business Scheme Award for 2007. The tempting dinner menu is changed daily, and if you must talk business the Wellingtonia Room and Conservatory, overlooking the pool terrace and gardens, provide a unique venue for meetings, private lunches or dinners. If you really need to escape, the Dowagers Cottage in the grounds is a comfortable self-catering option.

Broad House

THE AVENUE, WROXHAM, NORFOLK NR12 8TS
Tel: 0845 365 4856 **International:** +44 (0)1603 783567 **Fax:** 01603 782033
Web: www.johansens.com/broadhouse **E-mail:** philip@broadhousehotel.co.uk

Our inspector loved: The walk through the trees and meadow down to the boat house, alongside Wroxham Broad.

Price Guide:
double from £130
suite £190

An idyllic old English home in a tranquil rural location, 7 miles from Norfolk and along side the Norfolk Broads, which are well worth a little exploration. The coast just 12 miles away and fishing, golf and country walks all conveniently nearby. This is a charming retreat, originally a 18th century Queen Anne Estate House which in its new role as a boutique hotel has been stylishly decorated with great care and attention to detail. The 14 rooms all have there own personality and enjoy views of the extensive grounds and gardens surrounding the grade II listed building. The owners' admirable aim is to source all of their products from Norfolk, from soaps to puddings. The effect: a very unique and genuine Norfolk experience.

Location: Just off the B1140; A1151, 0.7 miles; Norwich, 8 miles

Attractions: The Norfolk Broads; Blickling Hall; North Norfolk Coast; Norwich Castle

THE NEPTUNE INN & RESTAURANT

85 OLD HUNSTANTON ROAD, OLD HUNSTANTON, NORFOLK PE36 6HZ
Tel: 0845 365 2604 **International:** +44 (0)1485 532122 **Fax:** 01485 535314
Web: www.johansens.com/theneptune **E-mail:** reservations@theneptune.co.uk

Our inspector loved: *The warm welcome and the fresh and smart feel of everything.*

Price Guide:
single from £45
double from £70

Awards/Recognition: 1 AA Rosette 2007-2008

Location: On the A149; King's Lynn, 19 miles; Norwich Airport, 36 miles

Attractions: Sandringham; Holkham Hall; Houghton Hall; Many famous golf courses

Experience New England here on the North Norfolk coastline. There's something so calming and peaceful about The Neptune that we can only praise it's owners for their vision and dedication. A 19th-century coaching inn that now presents minimalist bedrooms with clean lines and white, handmade New England furniture. Public rooms soothe jangled nerves with their mellow tones, fresh flowers and inviting Lloyd Loom sofas and chairs, while a talented chef whips up a storm in the restaurant using the finest local ingredients. Explore one of the most protected coastal areas in England, the stately homes of Holkham and Houghton and the Queen's own retreat at Sandringham.

WAREN HOUSE HOTEL

WAREN MILL, BAMBURGH, NORTHUMBERLAND NE70 7EE
Tel: 0845 365 2785 **International:** +44 (0)1668 214581 **Fax:** 01668 214484
Web: www.johansens.com/warenhouse **E-mail:** enquiries@warenhousehotel.co.uk

Our inspector loved: The delicious dinner using locally sourced produce.

Price Guide:
single £85–£143
double £113–£175
suite £157–£223

"To visit the North East and not to stay here, would be foolish indeed", so says one of many complimentary entries in the hotel's visitors' book. This delightful, traditional country house will meet all your expectations. Set in 6 acres of gardens and woodland on the edge of Budle Bay Bird Sanctuary overlooking Holy Island and close to majestic Bamburgh Castle. Antique furnishings and immaculate decor create a warm ambience. Choose from a daily changing menu and complementary fine wines in the candle-lit dining room surrounded by family portraits. Owners Anita and Peter don't cater for under 14s, so peace and tranquility are assured even in the summer months. Dogs are welcome by prior arrangement. There is a boardroom for executive meetings and special breaks are available.

Location: B1342, 200yds; A1, 2 miles; Bamburgh, 3 miles; Alnwick, 15 miles

Attractions: Bamburgh Castle; Holy Island & Farne Islands; Alnwick Gardens; Budle Bay Wildlife Sanctuary

The Otterburn Tower

OTTERBURN, NORTHUMBERLAND NE19 1NS

Tel: 0845 365 3748 **International:** +44 (0)1830 520620 **Fax:** 01830 521504
Web: www.johansens.com/otterburntower **E-mail:** info@otterburntower.com

Our inspector loved: The delicious dinner of home - farmed lamb and home - grown vegetables.

Price Guide:
single £65
double £130–£230
suite £230

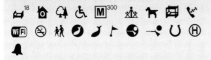

Location: A 696, 100yds; A68, 2 miles; A 1 M, 26 miles; Newcastle Airport, 25 miles

Attractions: Alnwick Castle & Gardens; Hadrians Wall; Kielder Water & Forest Park

Standing regally at the heart of a 32 acre estate in the Redesdale valley this magestic building dates back to the 11th century ; founded by a cousin of William the Conqueror. Painstakingly restored, the building retains stunning original features, from oak panelling, leaded panes and stained glass. The 18 stylish and unique rooms include The Library Room, featuring a beautiful four poster bed, oak panelling and well-stocked bookshelves. Admire the extensive terraced lawns and flower-abundant gardens from the Morning Room. Dining at the Otterburn Tower is a delight, with all ingredients for the imaginative dishes supplied by either Longwitton Farm, covering over 3000 acres to the south-east of the hotel and run by the hotel owner's son, John Goodfellow Junior, or other locally accredited sources. The hotel owns a stretch of the river Rede, and the chefs take full advantage of the fresh trout and salmon in season.

THE ORCHARD HOUSE

HIGH STREET, ROTHBURY, NORTHUMBERLAND NE65 7TL
Tel: 0845 365 3726 **International:** +44 (0)1669 620 684 **Fax:** 01669 620 684
Web: www.johansens.com/orchardhouse **E-mail:** info@orchardhouserothbury.com

Our inspector loved: *The luxurious comfort of the bedrooms.*

Price Guide:
single £88-£148
double £88-£170

Location: B6341, 20yds; A697, 6 miles; A1, 7 miles; Alnwick, 11 miles

Attractions: Cragside Hall; Alnwick Castle & Gardens; Cheviot Hills; Northumberland National Park

A striking grey stone, grade II listed Georgian House situated on the High Street in the pretty town of Rothbury. The stylish, contemporary bedrooms are fragranced with fresh flowers and feature beds dressed with sumptuous duck down duvets and crisp white Egyptian linen. Canapés, chocolates and champagne breakfasts can all be arranged for extra indulgence. The drawing room, furnished with antiques and filled with fresh flowers, is elegant, warm and inviting; wile away your evening here and enjoy the bar service. The Orchard House does not cater for dinner, however the owners will gladly recommend local restaurants. Be sure to savour the lavish breakfast, with its emphasis on local organic produce, both hearty traditional and contemporary dishes are offered, and the extensive sideboard will also keep you busy!

GREENWOOD LODGE

5 THIRD AVENUE, SHERWOOD RISE, NOTTINGHAM, NG7 6JH
Tel: 0845 365 2891 **International:** +44 (0)115 962 1206 **Fax:** 0115 962 1206
Web: www.johansens.com/greenwoodlodge **E-mail:** pdouglas71@aol.com

Our inspector loved: This quiet haven so near to the centre of Nottingham.

Price Guide:
single £45–£60
double £75–£95

Location: City Centre, 1 mile; A610, 2 miles; M1 jct 26, 6 miles; East Midlands Airport, 30-min drive

Attractions: Nottingham Castle; Lace Market; Theatre; National Arena Ice Rink

Greenwood Lodge enjoys a quiet, secluded location in the heart of a conservation area, yet is conveniently just 1 mile from Nottingham city centre. Built in 1834, the lodge is set in a mature courtyard garden, filled with lovingly tended shrubs and trees. Immaculately maintained throughout, the lodge features antique furniture and paintings and retains a sense of traditional refinement as well as home-from-home charm. The attractive rooms are individually decorated in fresh colour schemes and feature antique furniture and paintings. Three feature striking four poster beds. A notable breakfast menu is served in the airy conservatory and whilst lunch or dinner are not provided guests are given plenty of recommendations for eating out close by. Of course you may just be happy to curl up in the beautiful lounge with a drink and a good book.

COCKLIFFE COUNTRY HOUSE HOTEL

BURNTSTUMP COUNTRY PARK, BURNTSTUMP HILL, NOTTINGHAMSHIRE NG5 8PQ
Tel: 0845 365 3237 **International:** +44 (0)115 968 0179 **Fax:** 0115 968 0623
Web: www.johansens.com/cockliffe **E-mail:** enquiries@cockliffehouse.co.uk

Our inspector loved: *The striking new Brasserie.*

Price Guide:
single from £75
double £95–£150

Location: Off the A614, 2 miles; M1 jct 26, 9 miles; Nottingham, 7 miles; East Midlands, 23 miles

Attractions: Nottingham Castle; Sherwood Forest; Southwell Minster; Newstead Abbey

Situated in the heart of Robin Hood country, Cockliffe is an unusually designed 17th-century house standing in 3 acres of gardens adjacent to Burntstump Country Park. Dane and Jane Clarke rescued the house from disrepair 13 years ago and are proud of their renovations, many of which reflect the original features. Décor and furnishings are elegant and tasteful and most rooms afford splendid views over the garden. The 10 bedrooms are individually designed and comfortably appointed. Most have Jacuzzi's, period furniture and beautiful curtain fabrics chosen by Jane Clarke. The brasserie and fine dining restaurant offer excellent and imaginative menus using local produce and game when in season. The adjoining cocktail bar is perfect for pre-meal drinks. A conference room with high-tech facilities is available.

LANGAR HALL

LANGAR, NOTTINGHAMSHIRE NG13 9HG
Tel: 0845 365 1983 **International:** +44 (0)1949 860559 **Fax:** 01949 861045
Web: www.johansens.com/langarhall **E-mail:** imogen@langarhall.com

Our inspector loved: The old world charm, the tranquillity, and the imaginative food.

Price Guide:
single £75–£115
double/twin £90–£210
suite £210

Location: A52, 4 miles; A46, 5 miles; Nottingham, 19 miles; East Midlands Airport, 26 miles

Attractions: Belvoir Castle; Trent Bridge cricket; Nottingham Castle; Stilton cheese making

Combining the charm of a traditional private home and good country living Langar Hall stands quietly secluded, overlooking parkland where sheep graze among ancient trees. The family home of Imogen Skirving, its site is historic, and the house itself dates back to 1837. Today, bedrooms are delightful with lovely views of the gardens and moat, the restaurant - very popular locally - serves English dishes of local meat, poultry, game, fish, and garden vegetables in season. Beyond the croquet lawn you can get lost in a romantic network of medieval fishponds teeming with carp, and further afield, the hotel is perfect for cricket at Trent Bridge, trips to Belvoir Castle and visits to the academics at Nottingham University. Dogs can also enjoy the Hall's comforts by prior arrangement.

BURFORD LODGE HOTEL & RESTAURANT

OXFORD ROAD, BURFORD, OXFORDSHIRE OX18 4PH
Tel: 0845 365 3215 **International:** +44 (0)1993 823354
Web: www.johansens.com/burfordlodge **E-mail:** info@burfordlodge.com

Our inspector loved: The wonderful enthusiasm of the owners and their staff in offering the best for their guests.

Price Guide:
single £98
double/twin £118
suite £140

Location: A40, 50 yds; M40, M5, M4, 25 miles; Burford, 0.50 miles; Birmingham, 52 miles

Attractions: Oxford; Cheltenham; Cotswolds; Blenheim Palace

Reminiscent of its beginnings as an elegant country residence, this Victorian hotel has undergone a remarkable refurbishment. Owners Graham and Paula Cox have taken great care to blend traditional style with modern amenities, mixing power showers with Victorian style sit-in baths. The popular restaurant serves a seasonal menu with plenty of fresh fish delivered daily from the coast. The chocolate fountain is certain to be a hit with the youngsters, and for the adults the menu offers the chance to cook their own food at your table on volcanic stones. Burford is a delightful village with many antique and craft shops, and is an ideal base if you wish to travel to Oxford or Cheltenham, explore the Cotswolds or play a round of golf at the Burford Golf Course.

THE LAMB INN

SHEEP STREET, BURFORD, OXFORDSHIRE OX18 4LR
Tel: 0845 365 2576 **International:** +44 (0)1993 823155 **Fax:** +44 (0)1993 822228
Web: www.johansens.com/lambinnburford **E-mail:** info@lambinn-burford.co.uk

Our inspector loved: This lovely old inn with a mix of traditional cosiness and fabulous contempory touches such as the stunning new allium room.

Price Guide: (room only)
single £145-£165
double £165-£195
suite £195-£255

Awards/Recognition: 2 AA Rosettes 2006-2007

Location: A40, 1 mile; M40, 20 miles; Burford, 30yds; Birmingham Airport, 50 miles

Attractions: Cotswold Tours; Cheltenham Racecourse; Cotswold Wildlife Park; Sherbourne Estate(NT)

Walk into The Lamb Inn and instantly recapture something of the 14th-century - flagged floors, antiques, and the flicker of log fires on gleaming copper, brass and silver. Cleverly amongst the traditional elements is a complimentary tone of the contemporary, in particular in the stunning new Allium suite which adds an indulgent feel. The attractive bar invites you into its sumptuous sofas and overstuffed chairs. Bar meals and the more formal, award winning restaurant specialise in fresh fish, and in summer you can eat outside in the pretty walled garden. Located near the heart of Burford you might like to browse through antiques shops or laze by the waters of the River Windrush. You're within easy reach of Oxford, Cheltenham, Stow-on-the-Wold and many other quintessential Cotswold villages.

FALLOWFIELDS

KINGSTON BAGPUIZE WITH SOUTHMOOR, OXON OX13 5BH
Tel: 0845 365 3288 **International:** +44 (0)1865 820416 **Fax:** 01865 821275
Web: www.johansens.com/fallowfields **E-mail:** stay@fallowfields.com

Our inspector loved: This charming and welcoming country house hotel with its homely comforts and sunny restaurant.

Price Guide:
single from £120
double £150–£170

Awards/Recognition: 2 AA Rosettes 2007-2008

Location: A420, 1 mile; A415, 1 mile; M40 jct 8, 20 miles; Oxford, 10 miles

Attractions: Oxford; Vale of the White Horse; Riverside Walks; The Cotswolds

Brimming with character, Fallowfields, home to Begum Aga Khan, dates back more than 300 years. Today, this is an extremely comfortable, welcoming and spacious country house hotel set in 2 acres of pretty gardens and surrounded by 10 acres of grassland. Each of the guest rooms is large and traditionally decorated, some with four-poster or coroneted beds. The drawing room and bar are elegant and relaxing, and even cosier in winter months with crackling log fires. Dine in the light and airy restaurant or alfresco patio and enjoy contemporary dishes prepared by Head Chef Oliver Richings. The library is the perfect place for private dining. The peaceful ambience of the hotel also provides an ideal environment for high-level strategy and senior management retreats.

THE JERSEY ARMS

MIDDLETON STONEY, BICESTER, OXFORDSHIRE OX25 4AD
Tel: 0845 365 2563 **International:** +44 (0)1869 343234 **Fax:** 01869 343565
Web: www.johansens.com/jerseyarms **E-mail:** jerseyarms@bestwestern.co.uk

Our inspector loved: *The cosy bar and restaurant.*

Price Guide:
single from £85
double from £99
suite from £130

Location: A34, 3 miles; M40, 3 miles; Bicester, 4 miles; Birmingham, 45 miles

Attractions: Silverstone; Blenheim Palace; Bicester Village (shopping); Oxford

This inn has certainly moved on from its early days back in 1241 when it was listed as providing "necessaries as food and drink." Today comfortable bedrooms and an inviting atmosphere will ensure you'll have all that's necessary, and more. Donald and Helen Livingston are only the third family to own it in 700 years and appreciate the importance of keeping many of the historical features amongst the more modern furnishings. An upper and lower dining room offer informal and tasty menus. On winter evenings you can snuggle up next to the open log fire in the bar, or in the warmer months there's a secluded courtyard garden to enjoy. This is an idyllic Oxfordshire village, Woodstock, Blenheim Palace and the famous "Bicester Village" shopping outlet are nearby.

THE NUT TREE INN

MURCOTT, KIDLINGTON, OXFORDSHIRE OX5 2RE
Tel: 0845 365 3789 **International:** +44 (0)1865 331253
Web: www.johansens.com/nuttreeinn **E-mail:** imog79@hotmail.com

Our inspector loved: *The enticing mix of country pub and sophisticated restaurant.*

Price Guide:
starters £6.95–£9
main £11–£22
desert £5.50–£7.50
set menu mon-fri (lunch) and mon-thurs (evening)
2 course £12; 3 course £15, sunday menu from £12

Awards/Recognition: 2 AA Rosettes 2007-2008

Location: A34, 6 miles; M40 jct 9, 6 miles; Oxford, 10 miles

Attractions: Oxford; Bicester Shopping Village; Boarstal Duck Decoy; Nature Reserve

The Nut Tree Inn effortlessly and unaffectedly combines a country pub setting with the informal sophisticated of a great restaurant. Savour real ale from the cask before sampling the fabulous modern British cuisine. Previously, owner Mike was the youngest holder of a Michelin Star and you can therefore expect some wonderfully creative dishes with seasonal flavours used to their best. The great thing is you don't have to pay the earth, menus start from £12. The traditional thatched pub boasts large grounds, which include a game of Aunt Sally. During the summer, dine at the inviting al fresco dining area in the company of the Gloucester Old Spot Tamworth pigs stabled nearby. The Inn does not offer accommodation, however the staff will readily recommend nearby bed & breakfast accommodation.

WESTON MANOR

WESTON-ON-THE-GREEN, OXFORDSHIRE OX25 3QL
Tel: 0845 365 2798 **International:** +44 (0)1869 350621 **Fax:** 01869 350901
Web: www.johansens.com/westonmanor **E-mail:** reception@westonmanor.co.uk

Our inspector loved: The mix of traditional and contemporary.

Price Guide:
single from £99
double from £121
suite from £195

Awards/Recognition: 2 AA Rosettes 2007-2008

Location: A34, 0.5 mile; M40 jct 9, 2 miles; Oxford, 10 miles; Heathrow Airport, 52 miles

Attractions: Bicester shopping village; Blenheim Palace; Gateway to Cotswolds; Oxford

You'll pass through imposing wrought-iron gates and tall grey stone pillars before reaching the impressive entrance to this manor house, once ancestral home of the Earls of Abingdon and Berkshire and owned by Henry VIII. Many bedrooms, including 4 in a cottage and 16 in the coach-house, have antique furniture, while all have garden views. The magnificent vaulted, oak-panelled Baronial Hall with its Rosette-awarded menus, overlooking the beautiful grounds, create a feeling of aristocratic grandeur. If you are planning on getting together with friends or colleagues there is plenty of flexibility with seven private meeting rooms. If you're feeling brave why not visit for an exciting murder mystery weekend, hosted at the hotel throughout the year.

THE KINGS HEAD INN & RESTAURANT

THE GREEN, BLEDINGTON, NR KINGHAM, OXFORDSHIRE OX7 6XQ
Tel: 0845 365 2568 **International:** +44 (0)1608 658365 **Fax:** 01608 658902
Web: www.johansens.com/kingshead **E-mail:** kingshead@orr-ewing.com

Our inspector loved: This character filled inn in a lovely village setting.

Price Guide:
double £55–£60
double £70–£125

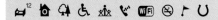

Location: A429, 4 miles; M40, 30 miles; Chipping Norton, 6 miles; Birmingham, 40 miles

Attractions: Cotswolds; Oxford; Stratford-upon-Avon; Blenheim Palace

Fulfilling all your expectations of a traditional English inn, the King's Head sits beside a village green where in summer you can see Morris dancers in action or just relax by the babbling brook. Archie and Nicola Orr-Ewing have done an exceptional job over the last few years of turning this 16th Centrury cider house into a destination in its own right. Inside there are exposed stone walls, original beams, inglenook fireplace and an old settle. Charming bedrooms are in the main building above the bar or set around the courtyard. In the friendly bar there's a wide selection of real ales, robust meals at lunchtime and in the evenings. Keeping things local, farmer and uncle to Archie supplies the fine Aberdeen Angus beef and vegetables are grown on the nearby famous Evesham Vale.

THE SPREAD EAGLE HOTEL

CORNMARKET, THAME, OXFORDSHIRE OX9 2BW
Tel: 0845 365 2694 **International:** +44 (0)1844 213661 **Fax:** 01844 261380
Web: www.johansens.com/spreadeaglethame **E-mail:** spreadeagleeventl@btconnect.com

Our inspector loved: The quaintness of this old coaching Inn.

Price Guide:
single from £99.95
double from £114.95
suite from £209.95

Awards/Recognition: 1 AA Rosette 2005-2006

Location: On the A418; M40 Jct 8 southbound Jct6 northbound, 6 miles, 16.5 miles; Heathrow, 36 miles

Attractions: Waddesdon Manor; Oxford; Blenheim Palace; Vale of Aylesbury

Thames' mile-long main street is worth a wander before you finally settle at this hotel that's stood tall and proud in town since the 16th-century. Over the years it's played host to Charles II, French prisoners from the Napoleonic wars, famous politicians and writers such as Evelyn Waugh. Former proprietor John Fothergill introduced haute cuisine to the provinces and the brasserie, named in his honour, serves tasty English and French cuisine made with fresh local produce including Oxfordshire beef. There is a cosy and unpretentious feel to this old coaching inn and is in a great location to head out to the beautiful countryside and its tiny villages, or historic Blenheim Palace and Waddesdon Manor.

THE FEATHERS

MARKET STREET, WOODSTOCK, OXFORDSHIRE OX20 1SX
Tel: 0845 365 2491 **International:** +44 (0)1993 812291 **Fax:** 01993 813158
Web: www.johansens.com/feathers **E-mail:** enquiries@feathers.co.uk

Our inspector loved: The location in the centre of Woodstock and the really cosy feel of this atmospheric hotel.

Price Guide:
single £99–£139
double/twin from £165
suite from £225

Awards/Recognition: 2 AA Rosettes 2006-2007

Location: A44, 0.5 mile; M40, 9 miles; Oxford, 9 miles,; Heathrow, 45 miles

Attractions: Blenheim Palace; Cotswolds; Oxford; Stowe Gardens

Independently owned and managed, this 17th century town house hotel can adapt to suit your mood and the season, with log fires and traditional English furnishings drawing you into its warmth in winter and the recently redesigned courtyard garden providing the perfect spot for lunch or afternoon tea in the summer. At the heart of historical Woodstock, one of England's most attractive Cotswold country towns dating back to the 12th century, the hotel is also renowned for its award winning cuisine. The menu changes regularly, inspired by local, seasonal produce. In the bedrooms you will find hospitality trays and pillow menus. Indulge yourself in beauty treatments and a revitalising massage at Preen The Feather's beauty suite. The Drawing Room is the perfect place for meetings. Food & Travel magazine Gastro Pub of The Year 2006/07

DUKE OF MARLBOROUGH COUNTRY INN

WOODLEYS, WOODSTOCK, OXFORD OX20 1HT
Tel: 0845 365 3273 **International:** +44 (0)1993 811460 **Fax:** 01993 810165
Web: www.johansens.com/dukeofmarlborough **E-mail:** sales@dukeofmarlborough.co.uk

Our inspector loved: *The friendly bar, spacious rooms and good central location.*

Price Guide:
single £70
double/twin £85–£110

Location: A44, 20yds; M40, 6 miles; Woodstock, 1 mile; Heathrow Airport, 60 miles

Attractions: Blenheim Palace; Woodstock; Stratford Upon Avon; Cotswold Tours

This friendly, traditional English inn, situated on the A44 is just a few minutes from the pretty town of Woodstock. You will find the accommodation in a separate building, designed to reflect its rural setting and its' 13 bedrooms are spacious and comfortable. With a focus on good service and hospitality, the Duke of Marlborough serves thoughtfully prepared seasonal dishes in the pub style restaurant and the menus make good use of locally sourced produce. The menu also offers chefs specials – wholesome steaks with a choice of delicious sauces whilst other dishes include fish, vegetarian options and a childrens menu. The welcoming bar offers an extensive wine list and a selection of real ales. The beer garden and patio provides a safe and secure area for youngsters when the weather is fine.

BARNSDALE LODGE

THE AVENUE, RUTLAND WATER, NEAR OAKHAM, RUTLAND LE15 8AH
Tel: 0845 365 3028 **International:** +44 (0)1572 724678 **Fax:** 01572 724961
Web: www.johansens.com/barnsdalelodge **E-mail:** enquiries@barnsdalelodge.co.uk

Our inspector loved: The bright airy corridors and the plethora of pictures.

Price Guide:
single from £65
double/twin from £80
superior from £105

Awards/Recognition: 1 AA Rosette 2006-2007

Location: A606, 0.9 miles; A1, 7.5 miles; Oakham, 3 miles; East Midlands Airport, 42 miles

Attractions: Oakham; Vale of Belvoir; Rutland Water; Burghley House

Overlooking Rutland Water, surrounded by green hills and standing at the head of a tree-lined avenue, this former 17th-century farmhouse, built of local stone is an idyllic retreat for those wishing to escape. Fully restored and converted, you will find every comfort available. The furnishings and décor are superb and the well appointed bedrooms offer relaxation; 2 have been specifically designed for disabled guests, some are interconnecting and many offer panoramic views south over Rutland Water. Richard Carruthers, the talented head chef of Bluebird fame, offers an inspirational new bistro-style menu using organic and local produce, free-range eggs from the Gainsborough Estate and damson jam from the orchards, complemented by a cellar of fine wines. A multitude of water sports can also be arranged.

THE LAKE ISLE HOTEL & RESTAURANT

16 HIGH STREET EAST, UPPINGHAM, RUTLAND LE15 9PZ
Tel: 0845 365 2573 **International:** +44 (0)1572 822951 **Fax:** 01572 824400
Web: www.johansens.com/lakeislehotel **E-mail:** info@lakeisle.co.uk

Our inspector loved: The animated wine-orientated restaurant.

Price Guide:
standard £75
superior £100

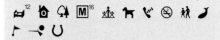

Location: Just off A6003; A43, 13 miles

Attractions: Rutland Water; Uppingham School; Burghley House; Oakham

There has been plenty of praise poured on owners Richard and Janine Burton whose charming, warm and hospitable natures have ensured a large, regular following. You'll appreciate over 350 years of character at The Lake Isle Hotel & Restaurant. Entered from a quiet courtyard, downstairs a log fire for cold nights and upstairs a relaxing lounge overlooking the pretty High Street of this charming town famous for Uppingham School. Food and wine are taken very seriously here and under the disciplined eye of chef Stuart Mead the restaurant offers imaginative seasonal menus, and a wine list ranging from regional labels to old clarets. Monthly wine dinners are great fun and to save you from driving you can simply roll upstairs to a comfortable night's sleep.

PEN-Y-DYFFRYN COUNTRY HOTEL

RHYDYCROESAU, NEAR OSWESTRY, SHROPSHIRE SY10 7JD
Tel: 0845 365 2106 **International:** +44 (0)1691 653700 **Fax:** 01978 211004
Web: www.johansens.com/penydyffryn **E-mail:** stay@peny.co.uk

Our inspector loved: *its wonderful views, delicious dining too. Just unwind and enjoy.*

Price Guide:
single £84
double £110–£170

Awards/Recognition: 2 AA Rosettes 2007-2008

Location: A 5, 4 miles; A483, 4 miles; Chester, 28 miles; Shrewsbury, 20 miles

Attractions: Erddig (NT); Powis Castle (NT); Chirk Castle (NT); Lake Vyrnwy

Enjoying breathtaking Welsh mountain views from high on the last hill in Shropshire, this captivating former Condé Nast Johansens Best Value for Money award-winning hotel, offers you the chance to totally relax and unwind. Built in 1845 as a Georgian rectory for a Celtic scholar, the Grade II listed property now happily rests in the hands of owners Miles and Audrey Hunter, who provide a well-established discreet service and cosy atmosphere. All bedrooms, some of which have Jacuzzis or spa baths, overlook the attractive terraced gardens, while 4 rooms in the coach-house have private patios. Chef David Morris - awarded 2 AA Rosettes - creates menus from local, often organic, produce. Peruse the exciting wine list with many organic wines alongside non-alcoholic organic drinks. Chester and Shrewsbury are nearby and the local area offers hill walking, riding, golf, and trout fishing.

SOULTON HALL

NEAR WEM, SHROPSHIRE SY4 5RS
Tel: 0845 365 2356 **International:** +44 (0)1939 232786 **Fax:** 01939 234097
Web: www.johansens.com/soultonhall **E-mail:** enquiries@soultonhall.co.uk

Our inspector loved: This historic hall, true to its origins and Ideal for small gatherings.

Price Guide:
single from £62.50
double from £95

Location: On the B5065; A49, 2 miles; A5, 11 miles; M56, 25 miles

Attractions: Ironbridge; Hawkstone Country Park; West Midlands Shooting Ground (advance booking required); Shrewsbury

Dating from the 15th and 17th centuries, this imposing Tudor manor with magnificent pillared courtyard stands in 550 acres of parkland. Owners, the Ashton family are descendants of the first protestant Lord Mayor of London who bought Soulton Hall in 1556, and have restored the property whilst retaining many of its unique features in the 6 spacious bedrooms; 4 in the main building and 2 in the nearby Carriage House. The converted Soulton Court was built in 1783 as stables and its stone-flagged floor, and beams make it an ideal venue for private dining, weddings and conferences. Ann Ashton exercises her skills in traditional English cooking, specialities might include, hand-raised game pie and butter baked salmon served with saffron oil. Game from the estate in season and fruit from the garden.

COMPTON HOUSE

TOWNSEND, AXBRIDGE, SOMERSET BS26 2AJ
Tel: 0845 365 3243 **International:** +44 (0)1934 733944 **Fax:** 01934 733945
Web: www.johansens.com/comptonhouse **E-mail:** info@comptonhse.com

Our inspector loved: *Location and tasteful presentation throughout.*

Price Guide:
single from £75
double/twin £95–£130

Location: On the A371; M5 jct 21, 10 miles; Bristol, 18.3 miles

Attractions: Cheddar Gorge; Wells Cathedral; Bath; Glastonbury

This impressive 17th-century, Grade II listed manor house is situated in historic Axbridge, at the foot of the Mendip Hills, commanding spectacular views over the Somerset Levels to Glastonbury Tor. Surrounded by an expansive and secluded lawned garden, Compton House dates back to Elizabethan times and oak panelling, elegant mouldings and wonderful fireplaces feature throughout. Enthusiastic owners, Patricia and Robert Tallack, whose interest is routing local walks, have continually pursued excellence, earning the hotel a reputation for comfort, hospitality and service. The generous bedrooms have many original features, and Patricia uses Fairtrade and West Country produce for the superb dishes served in the attractive dining room, following apèritifs, if desired, on the sun-catching terrace. Exclusive use for house parties, meetings and weddings can be arranged.

WOODLANDS COUNTRY HOUSE HOTEL

HILL LANE, BRENT KNOLL, NR BRISTOL, SOMERSET TA9 4DF
Tel: 0845 365 3242 **International:** +44 (0)1278 760232 **Fax:** 01278 769090
Web: www.johansens.com/woodlandshotel **E-mail:** info@woodlands-hotel.co.uk

Our inspector loved: *The sincere welcome and feeling of wanting to stay.*

Price Guide:
single £69-£99
double £99-£135
suite £155

Location: A38, 3 miles; M5 jct 22, 5 miles; Bristol, 24 miles

Attractions: Glastonbury Tor; Cheddar Gorge; Wookey Hole; Somerset Levels; Bath

A very warm welcome greets you at this relaxed but so professionally run small hotel. Peter and Glenda Botes with years of hospitality experience behind them recently purchased Woodlands and are clearly putting their mark upon it. They have created a tranquil home-from-home ambience in the picturesque setting of the Somerset countrysite. The individual and classically decorated guestrooms all enjoy magnificent rural views. After a day using the hotel's bicycles or visiting nearby attractions such as Cheddar and Bath, head to the cosy bar for an aperitif. Gourmands will enjoy the engaging, creative cuisine of the restaurant's seasonally changing menu, with all dishes prepared using the finest west countries produce. In summer the outdoor pool is a welcome retreat.

BELLPLOT HOUSE HOTEL & THOMAS'S RESTAURANT

HIGH STREET, CHARD, SOMERSET TA20 1QB
Tel: 0845 365 3033 **International:** +44 (0)1460 62600 **Fax:** 01460 62600
Web: www.johansens.com/bellplothouse **E-mail:** info@bellplothouse.co.uk

Our inspector loved: *This delightful small town house oozing warmth, comfort, relaxation and superb cuisine.*

Price Guide:
single from £109
double from £122
all exclusive use from £1300

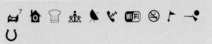

Escape to this delightful Georgian bolthole, full of lovely period features and décor that reflects its 1729 beginnings. The 7 bedrooms are named after the female deed holders who once owned Bellplot and feature crisp white linens, TVs and facilities for Internet users and business guests. Owners Betty and Dennis Jones pride themselves on their warm welcome, and Head Chef Thomas Jones excels in the culinary department. After a drink in the bar, relax in the restaurant, 1 of only 4 in Somerset to be awarded 'Taste of the West'. Sumptuous dishes include Lyme Bay crab cake followed by whole baby spring poussin, but make sure you save room for desserts such as baked lemon tart with orange coulis and luxurious bread and butter pudding.

Awards/Recognition: 1 AA Rosette 2006-2007

Location: On the A30; A358, 1 miles; M5 jct 25, 12 miles; Honiton, 14 miles

Attractions: Forde Abbey; Barrington Court (NT); Lyme Regis; Exeter

THREE ACRES COUNTRY HOUSE

THREE ACRES, BRUSHFORD, DULVERTON, SOMERSET TA22 9AR
Tel: 0845 365 2751 **International:** +44 (0)1398 323730
Web: www.johansens.com/threeacres **E-mail:** enquiries@threeacrescountryhouse.co.uk

Our inspector loved: *The warm welcome from the moment you step out of the car and the generous hospitality.*

Price Guide:
single £55–£70
double/twin £80–£110
exclusive use £600 maximum 12

Location: B3222, 0.5 miles; A396, 1.3 miles; M5 jct 27, 17.6 miles; Dulverton, 2 miles

Attractions: Exmoor National Park; Wimbleball Lake; Knightshayes Court(NT); 4X4 Off-road Safari

You may have to look carefully but on the edge of Exmoor hidden by trees is the peaceful Three Acres. The house has been decorated with relaxation in mind, spacious rooms, generous sofas, log fires and a bar that leads onto a sun terrace. Bedrooms are individually styled and have plenty of personal character. There is no morning rush for breakfast, which includes delicious daily specials using fresh local produce. Lunch and dinner are not catered for however owners Edward and Julie are more than happy to recommend excellent restaurants, cafés and pubs close at hand, although for exclusive use guests dinner can be provided by prior arrangement. The unspoilt Dulverton's art galleries and antique shops are also nearby. Country sports and activities can be arranged including fishing, shooting, hunting and sailing.

FARTHINGS COUNTRY HOUSE HOTEL & RESTAURANT

HATCH BEAUCHAMP, NEAR TAUNTON, SOMERSET TA3 6SG

Tel: 0845 365 3290 **International:** +44 (0)1823 480664 **Fax:** 01823 481118

Web: www.johansens.com/farthings **E-mail:** info@farthingshotel.co.uk

Our inspector loved: *Attention to detail and the free range chickens who provide fresh eggs for breakfast.*

Price Guide:
single £110
double/twin £130
suite £175

Awards/Recognition: 1 AA Rosette 2007-2008

Location: A358, 1.5 miles; M5 jct 25, 4 miles; A303, 4.6 miles; Taunton, 7.6 miles

Attractions: Exmoor; Montacute House; Cheddar Gorge; Forde Abbey

Overlooking the village green of peaceful Hatch Beauchamp in the heart of Somerset, it's hard to believe that the hotel is only 5 miles from Taunton and the M5. Relaxing and informal, you can enjoy drinks and canapés in the garden on a warm summer's evening, and log fires in the cosy lounge or bar in winter. The AA 3 Star, Farthings is privately owned with tasteful bedrooms, and the family and staff are on hand with locally sourced food, cooked and presented in the AA Rosette-awarded restaurant. There are many attractions in the area such as Barrington Court, Montacute House, Hestercombe Gardens and West Somerset Railway. Wells Cathedral, Cheddar Gorge, Longleat Safari Park and the cities of Exeter and Bristol are all easily accessible.

BERYL

WELLS, SOMERSET BA5 3JP
Tel: 0845 365 3034 International: +44 (0)1749 678738 Fax: 01749 670508
Web: www.johansens.com/beryl E-mail: stay@beryl-wells.co.uk

Our inspector loved: *Everything from the moment of arrival.*

Price Guide:
single £65–£85
double £85–£130

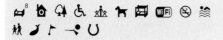

Location: B3139, 0.36 miles; A371, 2.16 miles; Bath, 21 miles

Attractions: Wells Cathedral; Cheddar Caves & Gorge; Longleat House; Roman Baths

This 19th-century, 5 Star, Gothic mansion is a real treasure, set in 13 acres of parkland and gardens, which have been skillfully restored. Beryl is tastefully furnished with antiques and offers you hospitality of the highest order. Holly Nowell and her daughter Mary-Ellen are charming hostesses, and take pride in the great attention to detail evident throughout the house. Guests are invited to use the honesty bar in the Green Room or enjoy drinks and wines on the lawn in summer. Holly and Mary-Ellen are happy to organise group bookings and make reservations for overnight guests at the many first-class restaurants and pubs situated nearby. The bedrooms have interesting views and offer every comfort. Take a dip in Beryl's outdoor pool from May to September.

GLENCOT HOUSE

GLENCOT LANE, WOOKEY HOLE, NEAR WELLS, SOMERSET BA5 1BH
Tel: 0845 365 1769 **International:** +44 (0)1749 677160 **Fax:** 01749 670210
Web: www.johansens.com/glencothouse **E-mail:** relax@glencothouse.co.uk

Our inspector loved: Location - presentation and the idea of taking it over for a private house party.

Price Guide:
double £165–£260
exclusive use £4,000

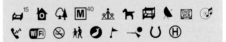

This late Victorian mansion, built in grand Jacobean style is situated at the foot of the Mendip Hills. Glencot House is set in 18 acres of secluded gardens and parkland with a gently meandering trout-filled river. A Grade II listed building, the house has been sensitively restored to create a fine country house hotel. The tranquil atmosphere is matched by friendly service. Beautiful interiors include carved ceilings and dressers, walnut panelling, huge fireplaces and crystal chandeliers. Each of the comfortable and individually decorated bedrooms feature period antiques, some have four-poster beds and enjoy views over the garden or surrounding countryside. Evening relaxation can be enjoyed in the cosy drawing room or library before sampling a delicious set menu in the elegant candlelit dining room.

Location: A371, 0.60 miles; Wells, 2.4 miles; Bristol, 22.3 miles; Bath, 23.4 miles

Attractions: Glastonbury; Cheddar Gorge; Somerset Levels; Wookey Hole Caves

KARSLAKE COUNTRY HOUSE

HALSE LANE, WINSFORD, EXMOOR NATIONAL PARK, SOMERSET TA24 7JE
Tel: 0845 365 1935 **International:** +44 (0)1643 851242 **Fax:** 01643 851242
Web: www.johansens.com/karslake **E-mail:** enquiries@karslakehouse.co.uk

Our inspector loved: *Location and warm welcome in this little gem.*

Price Guide:
single £55-£70
double £75-£110
exclusive use half board £1000

Awards/Recognition: 1 AA Rosette 2006-2007

Location: A396, 1.66 miles; A361, 19 miles; M5 jct 27, 25 miles

Attractions: Salmon and Trout Fishing; Exmoor Pony Centre; Dunster Castle; Tarr Steps

This 15th-century Malthouse was subsequently named after Sir John Burgess Karslake, a prominent lawyer and MP during the 1860s. Nestling in the wooded hills of Exmoor, Karslake is ideally located for exploring Devon's coasts. Owners Nick and Juliette Mountford have devoted themselves to this oasis, where views of the Exe Valley and the hotel's garden can be seen from 3 of the 5 bedrooms. The four-poster room offers total luxury. The accredited restaurant uses seasonal, local produce, and homemade bread, jams and marmalades at breakfast. The wine list is comprehensive and the bar is well-stocked. Packed lunches can be provided if you wish to explore the countryside. Relaxation treatments such as aromatherapy, lymphatic drainage massage and cranio-sacral therapy are provided by Karslake's health therapist.

THE BILDESTON CROWN

104 HIGH STREET, BILDESTON, IPSWICH IP7 7EB
Tel: 0845 365 2860 **International:** +44 (0)1449 740 510 **Fax:** 01449 741 843
Web: www.johansens.com/bildestoncrown **E-mail:** info@thebildestoncrown.co.uk

Our inspector loved: The range of eye-catching modern and traditional pictures througout the hotel.

Price Guide:
single £70-£90
double £120-£180
suite £220

Awards/Recognition: 3 AA Rosettes 2007-2008

Location: On the B1115; A12, 11 miles; A14, 16 miles; Bury St Edmunds, 18 miles

Attractions: Lavenham; Long Melford; Gainsboroughs House; Constable Country

Dating back to the 15th century, this charming, totally refurbished, timber framed former village coaching inn effortlessly blends the old with the new without losing any of the character since its first wall was laid in 1495. Bedrooms are all individually styled and downstairs the restaurant and lounge are decorated in the striking combination of red walls and original wooden beams. The restaurant's menu includes original dishes that feature beef and lamb reared on the inn's very own farm and game transported from their Scottish estate. Open fires make for a cosy rural retreat in the colder months and in summer a charming courtyard is the focus for entertaining. Classical pictures abound throughout, reminders that this is Constable Country.

CLARICE HOUSE

HORRINGER COURT, HORRINGER ROAD, BURY ST EDMUNDS SUFFOLK IP29 5PH
Tel: 0845 365 3235 **International:** +44 (0)1284 705550 **Fax:** 01284 716120
Web: www.johansens.com/clarice **E-mail:** bury@claricehouse.co.uk

Our inspector loved: *The wide range of treatments and the swimming pool.*

Price Guide:
single £55–£75
double/twin £85–£100

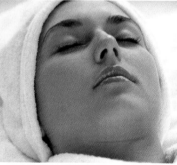

Awards/Recognition: 1 AA Rosette 2006-2007

Location: On the A143; A14, 2.3 miles

Attractions: Cambridge; Ely; Newmarket Racecourse

Clarice House is a residential spa within a beautifully refurbished neo-Jacobean mansion set in 20 acres of Suffolk countryside and ancient woodland. The excellent restaurant is open to residents and non-residents and for those choosing to stay for bed and breakfast, the bedrooms are comfortable and well-appointed. A variety of Spa Break packages include dinner and full use of the spa facilities, The hi-tech gym includes personal programme management and a team of dedicated instructors who offer daily classes. A 20-metre indoor swimming pool leads into a spa bath, steam room and sauna. The suite of beauty salons offers a wide range of indulgent treatments from the more traditional to holistic treatments such as reflexology, reiki and Indian head massage.

THE SWAN INN

PETWORTH ROAD, CHIDDINGFOLD, SURREY GU8 4TY
Tel: 0845 365 3749 **International:** +44 (0)1428 682073 **Fax:** 01428 683259
Web: www.johansens.com/swansurrey **E-mail:** enquiries@theswaninn.biz

Our inspector loved: This pub just has it for me. Great food and great decor - stylish and unpretentious! Well worth a drive out of London for!

Price Guide:
single from £70
double/twin from £70
suite from £85

    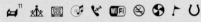

Stylish, modern and unpretentious are the best words to describe this wonderful inn that lies in this delightfully English little enclave of Surrey. With 11 carefully designed rooms in contemporary muted colours and luxurious bathrooms in relaxing marble and stone this really is a break from the traditional chintz pub! The restaurant serves some beautifully prepared dishes worthy of a top London address, and yet Chiddingfold itself has an intimate and pretty little village green that evokes memories of bygone summers watching cricket and sipping tea or Pimms. It's only an hour's drive from London and the ideal spot for a quick midweek break or weekend getaway!

Location: On the A283; Guildord, 13.5 mile; London Waterloo, 40-min train

Attractions: Petworth House; Ramster Gardens; Lurgashall Winery

The Hope Anchor Hotel

WATCHBELL STREET, RYE, EAST SUSSEX TN31 7HA
Tel: 0845 365 2519 **International:** +44 (0)1797 222216 **Fax:** 01797 223796
Web: www.johansens.com/hopeanchor **E-mail:** info@thehopeanchor.co.uk

Our inspector loved: The always impeccable housekeeping at this pleasing hotel at the heart of Old Rye.

Price Guide:
single from £65
double from £75
suite from £95

Location: A259, 0.5 mile; M20 jct 10, 21 miles; Hastings, 12 miles; Gatwick Airport, 62 miles

Attractions: Battle Abbey; Sissinghurst Gardens; Smallhythe Place; Rye Harbour Nature Reserve

Many a child's imagination was captured by Malcolm Saville's books, and you'll find yours inspired by this mid-18th century inn that was featured in them. Its beautiful old timbers, nooks and crannies and secret passages possess immense character and charm, as does its enviable position with stunning views across Romney Marsh, Camber Castle and the rivers Brede and Tillingham. Bedrooms offer double and family accommodation, the bar and restaurant are friendly, and menus make good use of fresh, seasonally available local ingredients. Rye itself was described as, "about as perfect as a small town can get," by the Daily Telegraph and landmarks such as Mermaid Street, Church Square, Lamb House and the 13th-century Ypres Tower are all within a few minutes' stroll.

BURPHAM COUNTRY HOUSE

THE STREET, BURPHAM, NEAR ARUNDEL, WEST SUSSEX BN18 9RJ
Tel: 0845 365 2851 **International:** +44 (0)1903 882160 **Fax:** 01903 884627
Web: www.johansens.com/burphamcountryhouse **E-mail:** info@burphamcountryhouse.com

Our inspector loved: The stunning downland village setting.

Price Guide:
single from £50
double £90–£100
four poster/luxury room £130-£140

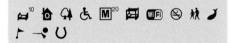

With its flint and thatched cottages scattered on grassy hillocks in the water-meadows of the River Arun, and stunning views over the chalky uplands of the South Downs, it is little wonder that Burpham is considered one of Sussex's prettiest villages. It has a quality of timelessness about it and is the perfect setting for this 18th-century former hunting lodge. An excellent place to explore the South Downs Way and the delights of Arundel. You couldn't expect a friendlier welcome than that from owners Steve and Jackie Penticost, who have refurbished their guest rooms in the most stylish and comfortable of ways, tended a superb country garden in which to relax in contemplation, and built a good reputation for food.

Location: A27, 2.5 miles; M27 jct 12, 20 miles; Arundel, 3 miles; Gatwick Airport, 25 miles

Attractions: Goodwood House and Estate; South Downs; Arundel and Petworth Antiques; Weald and Downland Museum

THE MILL HOUSE HOTEL

MILL LANE, ASHINGTON, WEST SUSSEX RH20 3BX

Tel: 0845 365 2598 **International:** +44 (0)1903 892426 **Fax:** 01903 893846
Web: www.johansens.com/millhousehotelashington **E-mail:** info@millhousehotelsussex.co.uk

Our inspector loved: *Its unexpected hideaway location.*

Price Guide:
single from £59
double from £92
suite from £125

Location: A24, 0.5 mile; M23 jct 11, 20 miles; Worthing, 12 miles; Gatwick, 28 miles

Attractions: South Downs; Thakeham House; Regency Brighton; Arundel Castle

This enchanting Grade II listed country house exudes warmth and character, tucked away in the pretty West Sussex countryside. Interesting antiques can be found in the public areas and beautiful paintings adorn the walls, forming a lasting testament to their 17th-century origins. After renovation and careful refurbishment, the house combines an authentic charm of a bygone era with the convenience of modern facilities, complemented by traditional, attentive service. Individual styled bedrooms are comfortable and the attractive gardens are ideal for relaxing. Food lovers will enjoy the excellent cuisine, expertly prepared from the finest local ingredients served with a good selection of wines, liqueurs and cognacs. The meeting room will accommodate up to 48 people and is perfect for small conferences and private dining.

BEECHFIELD HOUSE

BEANACRE, WILTSHIRE SN12 7PU
Tel: 0845 365 3031 **International:** +44 (0)1225 703700 **Fax:** 01225 790118
Web: www.johansens.com/beechfieldhouse **E-mail:** reception@beechfieldhouse.co.uk

Our inspector loved: *The friendly welcome at this very pretty Victorian House set in beautiful grounds.*

Price Guide:
single from £90
double from £125
family from £145
four poster from £150

Location: On the A350; M4 jct 17, 15-min drive; Lacock, 2 miles; Bath, 11 miles

Attractions: Bath; Cotswolds; Longleat; Lacock

Venture down the drive of this privately owned country house hotel and you will be turning your back on the outside world and entering a tranquil retreat where old style courtesy and first class service complement more modern facilities. Whether you are coming to visit the surrounding attractions or to just switch off, you will find something to help you unwind. The heated pool is gorgeous in the summer, whilst in the winter the open fires are as warm as the welcome. A relaxing candle-lit dinner can be enjoyed from an ever changing menu offering a wide variety of dishes, many created from locally sourced and home grown produce. Walk around the beautiful grounds or take advantage of the in-house beauty treatment centre using the Decleor product range. All bedrooms are comfortable and well appointed with kingsize beds and large multichannel LCD TVs. Crisp Eqyptian cotton sheets, fluffy towels and Molton Brown goodies add to the sense of indulgence.

WIDBROOK GRANGE

WIDBROOK, BRADFORD-ON-AVON, NEAR BATH, WILTSHIRE BA15 1UH
Tel: 0845 365 2805 **International:** +44 (0)1225 864750/863173
Web: www.johansens.com/widbrookgrange **E-mail:** stay@widbrookgrange.co.uk

Our inspector loved: *The friendly welcome and feeling of being at home.*

Price Guide:
single £95–£120
double £120–£130
four poster £140
family rooms from £160.50

Awards/Recognition: 1 AA Rosette 2006-2007

Location: Off the A363; Bradford-on-Avon, 1.3 miles; M4 jct 18, 19 miles; Bath, 6.8 miles

Attractions: Bath; Longleat; Laycock Abbey Stonehenge

Widbrook Grange, home of owners Jane and Peter Wragg is an elegant 250 year old Georgian three star country house hotel peacefully located in 11 acres of grounds and rolling countryside on the outskirts of medieval Bradford-on-Avon, only 20 minutes from the historic city of Bath. There are wonderful country walks from the hotel and spacious grounds in which children can play in safety. Service is attentive yet unobtrusive and it has an informal intimate relaxing atmosphere with peaceful gardens, cosy lounges and log fires on cold winter nights. Its award winning restaurant serves fine modern European cuisine complemented by an interesting selection of New and Old World wines. The spacious and tastefully decorated bedrooms in the main house, courtyard and garden include romantic four posters, family rooms and rooms with facilities for disabled guests. There is a heated indoor swimming pool, a gym and meeting rooms.

THE OLD MANOR HOTEL

TROWLE, NEAR BRADFORD-ON-AVON, WILTSHIRE BA14 9BL
Tel: 0845 365 2613 **International:** +44 (0)1225 777393 **Fax:** 01225 765443
Web: www.johansens.com/oldmanorbath **E-mail:** romanticbeds@oldmanorhotel.com

Our inspector loved: The interesting antiques, pictures and quirky features throughout.

Price Guide:
single £70–£90
superior/twin £90–£95
four poster £110
luxury £130

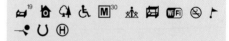

Location: On the A363; Bradford-on-Avon, 1.9 miles; Bath, 9.8 miles

Attractions: Roman Baths; Bowood House; Longleat; Stonehenge

The Old Manor is typical of this kind of Grade II* listed property in that it is a jumble of old farm buildings now converted to hotel use. This is definitely where a great deal of its charm comes from. Tim Burnham, the slightly eccentric and equally jumbled owner has filled the place with interesting curios and antiques creating a unique atmosphere. Charming bedrooms include antique half tester and four poster beds. The restaurant, formerly the milking parlour, is dominated by a huge ashlar fireplace unearthed during refurbishments. Upcoming renovations include a luxurious suite comprising the 1st floor of the manor plus landscaping and a pond outside reception. Don't forget to pop in the pub-style bar for a pint of the local brew. A great place to take over exclusively for a wedding or a gathering of friends.

THE CASTLE INN

CASTLE COMBE, WILTSHIRE SN14 7HN

Tel: 0845 365 2894 **International:** +44 (0)1249 783030 **Fax:** 01249 782315
Web: www.johansens.com/castleinn **E-mail:** enquiries@castle-inn.info

Our inspector loved: A fabulous traditional inn, so welcoming and in one of England's prettiest villages.

Price Guide:
single £69.50-£150
double £110-£175

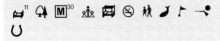

Location: M4 jct 17, 5 miles; A420, 1 mile; Chippenham Railway Station, 6 miles

Attractions: Bath; Lacock; Bradford on Avon

A charming country hotel nestling in a wooded Cotswold valley and conveniently located for historic Bath. Castle Combe often referred to as the "Prettiest Village in England" is intriguingly also home to a renowned classic race circuit. Here little has changed architecturally since the 15th century and every property is now a listed monument. The famous Castle Inn stands in the market place, and has been lovingly restored to preserve and enhance its matchless charm. The guest rooms are tastefully decorated with antique furniture and rich fabrics, in a manner in keeping with a building that retains many of its original features. The ambient restaurant, relaxed garden room and cosy bar offer a range of tempting menus to suit every taste, from five course indulgence to light bar snacks.

STANTON MANOR HOTEL & GALLERY RESTAURANT

STANTON SAINT QUINTIN, NEAR CHIPPENHAM, WILTSHIRE SN14 6DQ
Tel: 0845 365 2364 **International:** +44 (0)1666 837552 **Fax:** 01666 837022
Web: www.johansens.com/stantonmanor **E-mail:** reception@stantonmanor.co.uk

Our inspector loved: *The beautifully kept extensive gardens.*

Price Guide:
single £110–£115
double £140–£190
double superior deluxe £220

Location: A429, 1 mile; M4 jct 17, 1 mile; Chippenham, 5 miles; Bath, 17 miles

Attractions: Thermae Bath Spa; Stourhead Garden and House; Longleat; Tewkesbury Abbey

Listed in the Domesday-book and whilst more recently rebuilt in 1840, the original Dovecot still exists. There is a very clever and comfortable mix of the traditional and contemporary. Magnificent Tudor fireplaces and stone flooring blend with strong bold modern fabrics. Bedrooms are spacious, 4 have four-poster beds, some a private patio and some ideal for families. Owners Robert and Linda Davis take great care with the detail and they have an obvious love of the East which shows in the art lining the walls of the elegant Gallery restaurant. You can buy the art and all proceeds go to support a children's orphanage in Vietnam. Head Chef Paul Hudson and his team are creative in their interpretation of British cuisine using seasonal local ingredients. A super location not far from the M4, at the gateway to the Costwolds.

THE LAMB AT HINDON

HIGH STREET, HINDON, WILTSHIRE SP3 6DP

Tel: 0845 365 2574 **International:** +44 (0)1747 820 573 **Fax:** 01747 820 605
Web: www.johansens.com/lambathindon **E-mail:** info@lambathindon.co.uk

Our inspector loved: The cosy feel of a real traditional inn.

Price Guide:
single £70
double/twin £99–£135

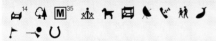

Location: Just off B3089; A303, 1.2 miles; Salisbury, 19 miles

Attractions: Longleat; Stonehenge; Cranborne Chase; Old Wardour Castle

A 12th century public house that by the 1870's was considered a 'favourable' stop for coaches travelling between London and the West Country. Its characterful interiors with rich colours, flagstone floors, tartan fabrics and wooden beams are in keeping with its sense of history. Some of the charming and spacious bedrooms have four-posters, and there are ample corners throughout for you to relax in, including the Whisky & Cigar Bar and the cosy Snug. A Scottish flavour influences food, with ingredients sourced whenever possible from local or Scottish suppliers. Rare wines from the award-winning Boisdale selection make an appearance, and in addition to real ales the malt whisky menu is reputedly the largest in Wiltshire.

THE BELL AT RAMSBURY

RAMSBURY, MARLBOROUGH, WILTSHIRE SN8 2PE
Tel: 0845 365 3769 **International:** +44 (0)1672 520230 **Fax:** 01672 520832
Web: www.johansens.com/bellatramsbury **E-mail:** jeremy@thebellramsbury.com

Our inspector loved: *The Chapter Room for private dining with its bold and interesting art work.*

Price Guide:
starter from £6.95
main from £10.95
dessert from £5.25

Location: B4192, 3.5 miles; A419, 6 miles; M4 Jct 15, 10 miles; Marlborough, 6.5 miles

An inviting traditional inn located in the heart of a pretty Wiltshire village. Currently without accommodation but a great choice for taking a detour to experience exceptional food and warm hospitality. The enticing menu features a variety of traditional British cuisine. Wherever possible, produce is locally sourced from within Wiltshire and Berkshire. Mouth-watering dishes include local 28 day ribeye steak with béarnaise sauce and sausages made with Ramsbury Gold Beer. Seafood lovers are spoilt for choice, with lobster, scallops and local Kennet crayfish all offered. Peruse the extensive list of fine wines for the perfect accompaniment to your meal, and look out for regional "wines of the month". The monthly wine events are always good fun and for more intimate gatherings or meeting there's the striking Chapter Room adorned with bold artwork.

THE PEACOCK INN

WORCESTER ROAD, BORASTON, TENBURY WELLS, WORCESTERSHIRE WR15 8LL
Tel: 0845 365 2634 **International:** +44 (0)1584 810506 **Fax:** 01584 811236
Web: www.johansens.com/peacockboraston **E-mail:** thepeacockinn001@aol.com

Our inspector loved: *The dining area in the old stables.*

Price Guide:
single £55
double £75

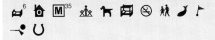

Location: On the A456; M5 jct 6, 28 miles; Worcester, 23 miles; Birmingham International Airport, 50 miles

Attractions: Market Town of Tenbury Wells; Worcester; Ludlow; Hereford

You'll receive a warm welcome at The Peacock Inn, the owner knows a thing or too about hospitality, creating a warm welcoming atmosphere with an eye for detail and discreet service. The five bedrooms clearly all have their own identity; 2 featuring local, hand-crafted oak four-posters and the deluxe room housing an original 125-year-old roll-top bath. In true traditional British Inn style fine ales, lagers and wines can be sampled and enjoyed in the wood-panelled bar. Food is not for the faint-hearted, as dishes include mille feuilles of black pudding and apple, goats cheese and truffle oil crostinis, noisettes of lamb and Aberdeen Angus steaks. Exclusive fishing is available on the Teme just 100 yards away.

ROYAL FORESTER COUNTRY INN

CALLOW HILL, NEAR BEWDLEY, WORCESTERSHIRE DY14 9XW
Tel: 0845 365 2865 **International:** +44 (0)1299 266 286
Web: www.johansens.com/royalforester **E-mail:** contact@royalforesterinn.co.uk

Our inspector loved: *The gorgeous colour schemes in the bedrooms.*

Price Guide:
single from £55
double from £79

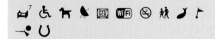

Location: On the A456; M5 jct 6, 18 miles; Bewdley, 2 miles; Birmingham International Airport, 55-min drive

Attractions: Bewdley; Severn Valley Steam Railway; Witley Court; Shelsley Walsh Hill Climb

This beautifully refurbished and modernized old inn has origins dating back to 1411. The charming restaurant is a "meandering-shape" with old floors and walls which showcase murals of Wyre Forest scenes and characters from over a 100 years ago. Great emphasis is put on creating seasonal menus and building a complementary wine list, needless to say it is a popular spot for resident and non-residents alike, the surprisingly moderate rates are an added bonus. The 7 bedrooms, named after fruits, have been styled with rich fabrics and bold colours and as you would expect come with all the 21st century gadgets a modern guest would require. Opposite the ancient and alluring Wyre Forest is ideal for riding or walking and the hotel can arrange stabling and livery.

THE OLD RECTORY

IPSLEY LANE, IPSLEY, NEAR REDDITCH, WORCESTERSHIRE B98 0AP
Tel: 0845 365 2615 **International:** +44 (0)1527 523000 **Fax:** 01527 517003
Web: www.johansens.com/oldrecipsley **E-mail:** ipsleyoldrectory@aol.com

Our inspector loved: The conservatory and especially its warm colours.

Price Guide:
single from £99
double/twin from £124

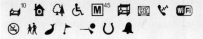

Location: A435, 2 miles; M42 jct 3, 7 miles; Redditch, 3 miles; Birmingham International, 13 miles

Attractions: Stratford-upon-Avon; Warwick Castle; The Cotswolds; Birmingham Bullring

The great-grandson of Sir Christopher Wren 'modernised' The Old Rectory in 1812 whilst living in the house for 40 years. The property has endured over 500 years of history and the Domesday Book lists a building on this site which borders the Roman built Icknield Street. Today you can experience warm and relaxed hospitality. The bedrooms are all quite different; one is reputedly haunted, others have exposed beams and one has a barrel ceiling. Take dinner in the conservatory where menus offer dishes prepared on the premises, using the freshest seasonal produce. Coffee and liqueurs may be enjoyed in the snug or lounge, whilst the beautiful gardens with their rhododendrons, Portuguese laurel, old oak, cedar, silver birch and weeping ash trees, beckon to be explored.

COLWALL PARK

COLWALL, NEAR MALVERN, WORCESTERSHIRE WR13 6QG
Tel: 0845 365 3238 **International:** +44 (0)1684 540000 **Fax:** 01684 540847
Web: www.johansens.com/colwallpark **E-mail:** hotel@colwall.com

Our inspector loved: The warm and friendly welcome and the relaxing atmosphere.

Price Guide:
single £80-£90
double/twin £120-£150
suite £150-£170

Awards/Recognition: 2 AA Rosettes 2007-2008

Location: On the B4218; M50/M50, 10 miles; Malvern, 3 miles; Birmingham, 38 miles

Attractions: Worcester; Hereford; Gloucester; Eastnor Castle

Dust off your walking boots for a stay at this country house hotel on the sunny western side of the Malvern Hills, with footpaths from the hotel leading directly to the hills and their spectacular scenery. Efficient, knowledgeable and very friendly staff, winners of the prestigious AA Courtesy and Care Award, will show you to your room where, as well as high standard furnishings and features, you'll find tea, coffee and home-made biscuits. The award-winning Seasons restaurant is a contemporary furnished oak-panelled room serving gourmet dishes, while the popular Lantern Bar, a meeting place for locals and residents, crackles with a log fire during winter and offers real ales, good house wines and an exciting menu of freshly made meals and snacks.

THE WHITE LION HOTEL

HIGH STREET, UPTON-UPON-SEVERN, NEAR MALVERN, WORCESTERSHIRE WR8 0HJ
Tel: 0845 365 2738 **International:** +44 (0)1684 592551 **Fax:** 01684 593333
Web: www.johansens.com/whitelionupton **E-mail:** info@whitelionhotel.biz

Our inspector loved: *Henry Fielding's "Wild Goose" bedroom with beams and strikingly coloured bathroom tiles.*

Price Guide:
single from £70–£90
double from £99
four-poster from £125

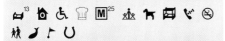

Awards/Recognition: 1 AA Rosette 2006-2007

Location: On the A4104; A38, 1.5 miles; M5 jct 7, 8 miles; Worcester, 11 miles

Attractions: Worcester; Malvern Hills; Ledbury; Tewkesbury Abbey

In his 1749 novel, "The History of Tom Jones", Henry Fielding described the hotel as "the fairest Inn on the street" and "a house of exceedingly good repute", so owners Jon and Chris Lear have taken him at his word, upholding a tradition of hospitality, good food & drink. Bedrooms from various periods date back to 1510 - again, with literary aspirations, the Rose Room and Wild Goose Room are named in a Fielding book. The award-winning Pepperpot Brasserie serves fine dishes with flair and plenty of seasonal influence. As a member of CAMRA – supporters for Real Ale the bar is appropriately stocked for aficionados and each summer hold their own mini-beer festival. Other great days out locally include The Three Counties Show Ground and The Upton jazz festival.

THE AUSTWICK TRADDOCK

AUSTWICK, VIA LANCASTER, NORTH YORKSHIRE LA2 8BY
Tel: 0845 365 2396 **International:** +44 (0)15242 51224 **Fax:** 015242 51796
Web: www.johansens.com/austwick **E-mail:** info@austwicktraddock.co.uk

Our inspector loved: *The delicious dinner at this family-run country hotel.*

Price Guide:
single £80–£120
double/twin £140–£190

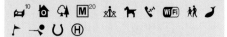

Awards/Recognition: 1 AA Rosette 2007-2008

Location: A65, 1 mile; M6 jct 36, 30 miles; Settle, 4 miles; Kirkby Lonsdale, 12 miles

Attractions: Ingleborough Cave; The 3 peaks of Whernside, Pen-y-ghent, Ingleborough; Settle; Yorkshire Dales

Set in 2 acres of peaceful, landscaped gardens in the heart of the Yorkshire Dales National Park is this fine Georgian country house hotel and restaurant, oozing character, charm and the friendliest of hospitality. Here you are surrounded by some of the most sensational limestone scenery in Europe, including several magnificent caves with dazzling stalagmites and stalagatites, which have yielded finds from pre-history. You can relax after walking and sightseeing tours in the comfortable bar and lounge, warmed in winter by open log fires. Bedrooms are individually designed and beautifully furnished with English antiques. The restaurant won Organic Restaurant of the Year 2006 and Chef, Tom Eunson, produces excellent Modern British cuisine, complemented by an extensive wine list. Special breaks are available on request.

STOW HOUSE

AYSGARTH, LEYBURN, NORTH YORKSHIRE DL8 3SR
Tel: 0845 365 2379 **International:** +44 (0)1969 663635
Web: www.johansens.com/stowhouse **E-mail:** info@stowhouse.co.uk

Our inspector loved: *The panoramic views over Wensleydale from the four-poster bed.*

Price Guide:
single £44–£55
double/twin £72–£96

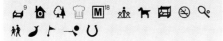

Location: A684, 50yds; Leyburn, 8 miles; Hawes, 9 miles; Harrogate, 42 miles

Attractions: Aysgarth Falls; Bolton Castle; Fountains Abbey; Yorkshire Dales National Park

This charming former Victorian Vicarage stands in 2 acres of mature grounds just a 10-minute walk from Aysgarth Falls in the heart of beautiful Wensleydale. Built in 1876 for Fenwick William Stow, Rural Dean of Wensleydale and over the years lovingly restored, it has 9 comfortable bedrooms, all with a lovely outlook including 2 larger luxury bedrooms, one with a four-poster. The lounge opens onto lawn and gardens with a stunning view towards Bishopdale. In the dining room you can enjoy dishes created by chef, Michael Sullivan, using the freshest of local produce. Ideal for house parties and shooting parties, you can have exclusive use of the hotel. There are wonderful walks direct from the door and the area abounds in historic castles, abbeys and stately homes.

THE DEVONSHIRE FELL

BURNSALL, SKIPTON, NORTH YORKSHIRE BD23 6BT
Tel: 0845 365 2462 **International:** +44 (0)1756 718111 **Fax:** 01756 710564
Web: www.johansens.com/devonshirefell **E-mail:** res@devonshirehotels.co.uk

Our inspector loved: *The bright, vivid colours of the décor, and the magnificent views.*

Price Guide:
single £110
double/twin £145–£198
suite £213–£220

Location: On the B6160; A59, 6 miles; Skipton, 7 miles; Harrogate, 22 miles

Attractions: Bolton Abbey Estate; Yorkshire Dales; Malham Cove; Skipton Castle

The Devonshire Fell is in a rare location where the views are simply stunning. Step inside to meet bold bright colours created by The Duchess of Devonshire. Large comfortable sofas, a wood burning stove and original contemporary art combine to create an inviting atmosphere. This is very much "city chic in the countryside" with impeccable standards throughout. Menus are sourced locally, wherever possible, and from the kitchen gardens at its sister hotel in Bolton Abbey. The 10 bedrooms and 2 family suites incorporate fresh and vivid colours, CD/DVD players and flat-screen TVs and of course breathtaking views. Aromatherapy treatments are offered at the on-site Beauty Studio and you have complimentary use of the spa and leisure facilities at The Devonshire Health Spa at nearby Bolton Abbey. The Dalzell Room is perfect for private events.

THE RED LION

BY THE BRIDGE AT BURNSALL, NEAR SKIPTON, NORTH YORKSHIRE BD23 6BU
Tel: 0845 365 2671 **International:** +44 (0)1756 720204 **Fax:** 01756 720292
Web: www.johansens.com/redlionburnsall **E-mail:** redlion@daelnet.co.uk

Our inspector loved: *Having lunch on the River Bank Terrace overlooking the River Wharf.*

Price Guide:
single £60–£115
double £127.50–£155

Awards/Recognition: 2 AA Rosette 2007-2008

Location: On the B6160; A59, 6 miles; Skipton, 10 miles; Leeds/Bradford Airport, 18 miles

Attractions: Harewood House; Harrogate; York; Upper Wharfdale

Formally a Ferryman's Inn, this 16th century property is now run by the Grayshon family, and the bedrooms, all traditional – beamed ceilings, antiques and Victorian brass beds, reflect their aim to retain this hotel's character and charm. Most have wonderful views across the glorious countryside that encompasses the village green, river and Burnsall Fell. The bar is a popular meeting place for locals and has an impressive selection of cask conditioned real ale. Fine wines and food are served in the restaurant where dishes reflect local produce and the creativity that well deserves its AA Rosette. Local dishes include rabbit braised in ale served with herb dumplings, or partridge with apricot seasoning and game chips. There is private fishing on the River Wharfe and pheasant shooting over 3000 acres on the nearby Grimwith Estate.

HOB GREEN HOTEL, RESTAURANT & GARDENS

MARKINGTON, HARROGATE, NORTH YORKSHIRE HG3 3PJ
Tel: 0845 365 1867 **International:** +44 (0)1423 770031 **Fax:** 01423 771589
Web: www.johansens.com/hobgreen **E-mail:** info@hobgreen.com

Our inspector loved: *Strolling around the large, lovingly tended Victorian walled herb, vegetable and cutting flower garden.*

Price Guide:
single £95–£118
double/twin £110–£155
suite £135–£175

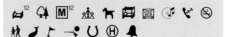

Location: A61, 2.5 miles; A1 M jct 17, 7 miles; Harrogate, 4.5 miles

Attractions: Historic City of Ripon, 6 miles; Ripon Racecourse, 6.5 miles; Harrogate, 6.5 miles; Fountains Abbey and Studley Royal Water Gardens (NT), 8.5 miles

A charming "country house" set in 870 acres of farm and woodland, Hob Green gazes upon some of Yorkshire's most dramatic scenery. Bedrooms are tasteful, and the drawing room and hall, warmed by log fires in cool weather, are comfortably furnished. Sit, relax and "antique spot" the gorgeous furniture, porcelain and pictures. The restaurant's reputation is excellent, and much of its fresh produce grows in the hotel's own garden. Interesting menus are complemented by a good choice of wines, which are sensibly priced. Every whim is catered for here, so all you need to do is enjoy it! For a dose of culture and history, Fountains Abbey and Studley Royal Water Gardens are nearby, or you can ride at the Yorkshire Riding Centre.

Ox Pasture Hall Country Hotel

LADY EDITH'S DRIVE, RAINCLIFFE WOODS, SCARBOROUGH, NORTH YORKSHIRE YO12 5TD
Tel: 0845 365 3461 **International:** +44 (0)1723 365295 **Fax:** 01723 355156
Web: www.johansens.com/oxpasturehall **E-mail:** oxpasturehall@btconnect.com

Our inspector loved: *The lovely location of this peaceful country hotel.*

Price Guide:
single from £110
double £150-£180
suite £210

Location: A171, 1.5 miles; A170, 4 miles; Scarbrough, 3 miles; York, 38 miles

Attractions: Scarborough; Duncombe Hall; North Yorkshire Moors Railway; Whitby Abbey

Stunningly located in 17 acres of its own landscaped gardens and grounds and nestled amongst the meadows and woodlands of the magnificent North Yorkshire Moors National Park. This hotel offers quiet luxury and yet is only 3 miles from the centre of the seaside resort of Scarborough. Spacious bedrooms in the main hall overlook the manicured gardens, which are uniquely framed by the backdrop of Raincliffe Woods and others, including three 4-posters are set around a lovely wisteria clad garden courtyard. You can choose to dine in the Courtyard Restaurant or Brasserie, both of which are perfect to relax, unwind and enjoy an excellent meal at the end of the day. On warmer nights you can also dine and take drinks on the terrace.

DUNSLEY HALL

DUNSLEY, WHITBY, NORTH YORKSHIRE YO21 3TL
Tel: 0845 365 3276 **International:** +44 (0)1947 893437 **Fax:** 01947 893505
Web: www.johansens.com/dunsleyhall **E-mail:** reception@dunsleyhall.com

Our inspector loved: *The peacock strutting around the gardens of this coastal hotel.*

Price Guide:
single from £95
double/twin from £149
four poster from £180
deluxe from £198

Awards/Recognition: 1 AA Rosette 2007-2008

Location: A171, 2 miles; Whitby, 3 miles; Scarborough, 21 miles

Attractions: Whitby Abbey; Robin Hoods Bay; North Yorkshire Moors Steam Railway; Birthplace of Captain Cook

Dunsley Hall hotel stands in 4 acres of magnificent landscaped gardens in the North Yorkshire Moors National Park and has remained virtually unaltered since it was built at the turn of the 20th century. Some of the individually decorated bedrooms, 2 with four-poster beds, enjoy a fantastic view of the sea, just a few minutes walk away, and feature fine fabrics and furniture. All bedrooms are non-smoking. Mellow oak panelling, a handsome Inglenook carved fireplace and stained glass windows enhance the drawing room's relaxing and restful atmosphere. From the Oak Room, Terrace Suite or Pyman Bar, you can enjoy award-winning regional dishes and seafood specialities made from only the freshest of ingredients. There is also a self catering holiday cottage available by prior request.

MARMADUKES HOTEL

ST PETERS GROVE, BOOTHAM, YORK, NORTH YORKSHIRE YO30 6AQ
Tel: 0845 365 4852 **International:** +44 (0)1904 640099
Web: www.johansens.com/marmadukes **E-mail:** mail@marmadukeshotels.co.uk

Our inspector loved: *The handcrafted beds and antique furniture.*

Price Guide:
single £95
double £155
suite £350

Awards/Recognition: 1 AA Rosette 2007-2008

Location: Town Centre, 0.3 miles; A19, 0.3 miles

Attractions: York Minster; Castle Howard; Jorvik Centre; North York Moors

Ideally located in the heart of historic York, in its own peaceful grounds and just a short stroll from York Minster and the ancient city walls. Originally a Victorian gentleman's residence, this unique, AA 4 Star boutique hotel combines classical style with modern elegance. The 19 rooms are individually decorated with carefully selected antiques and offset by stunning Italian fabrics. Bed frames have been handcrafted and handmade mattresses are covered in the crispest Egyptian cotton. For a truly romantic break, reserve the Loft Suite, luxurious and contemporary this suite features a private lounge with champagne table, dressing room and the stunning bathroom boasts a barrel sauna with CD music system and a double ended bath for two. Continue to indulge with a candle-lit dinner at their Victorian Chop House, Monty's Grill, serving the best of traditional British cuisine.

HEY GREEN COUNTRY HOUSE HOTEL

WATERS ROAD, MARSDEN, WEST YORKSHIRE HD7 6NG
Tel: 0845 365 1846 **International:** +44 (0)1484 848000 **Fax:** 01484 847605
Web: www.johansens.com/heygreen **E-mail:** info@heygreen.com

Our inspector loved: *This peaceful retreat in "The Last of the Summer Wine" country.*

Price Guide:
single £89-£149
double £119-£179

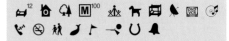

Awards/Recognition: 2 AA Rosettes 2007-2008

Location: A62, 0.33 miles; Marsden, 1 mile; Oldham, 8 miles; Huddersfield, 10 miles

Attractions: Standedge Canal Tunnel; Start of Pennine Way; Last ot the Summer Wine Country; Bronte Country

With an imposing pillared entrance, this traditional solidly built West Yorkshire hotel stands overlooking the spectacular Colne Valley, midway between Huddersfield and Oldham. You don't have to wander far from its landscaped grounds to find rolling green pastures, dry stone walls, and little grey farms tucked into the hills. A warm ambience welcomes you back to the house, where attention to your needs is a staff priority. Each bedroom has character and little personal touches, with most offering panoramic views. The restaurant is housed in the oldest part of the hotel, built in about 1710, and has a superb flagstone floor and open fire burning in winter. The excellent à la carte menu offers traditional British cuisine. After dinner you can relax in the comfortable conservatory.

Image from Fáilte Ireland

Ireland

For further information on Ireland, please contact:

The Irish Tourist Board
(Bord Fáilte Éireann)
Baggot Street Bridge
Dublin 2
Tel: +353 (0)1 602 4000 or +44 (0)1850 230 330
Internet: www.ireland.ie

Tourism Ireland
Tourism Centre
Suffolk Street
Dublin 2
Tel: +353 (0)1 605 7700
Internet: www.discoverireland.com

Northern Ireland Tourist Information
Belfast Welcome Centre
47 Donegall Place
Belfast, BT1 5AD
Tel: +44 (0)28 9024 6609
Internet: www.gotobelfast.com

or see **pages 197-200** for details of local historic houses, castles and gardens to visit during your stay.

For additional places to stay in Ireland, turn to **pages 194-196** where a listing of our Recommended Hotels & Spas Guide can be found.

ARD NA SIDHE

KILLARNEY, KILLORGLIN, CO KERRY, IRELAND
Tel: 00 353 66 976 9105 **Fax:** 00 353 66 976 9282
Web: www.johansens.com/ardnasidhe **E-mail:** sales@kih.liebherr.com

Our inspector loved: The feeling of tranquility and privacy. A place to reflect and replenish your energy.

Price Guide:

(open 17th May – 15th October 2008)
single €150-€270
double €170-€300

Location: Killorglin, 4 miles; Killarney N22, 18 miles; Kerry Airport, 20 miles

Attractions: Dingle Bay; Gap of Dunloe; Ring of Kerry

Standing majestically above the iridescent waters of Caragh Lake is a Victorian mansion whose name romantically translates to "the hill of the fairies". It's the sheer tranquillity of the place that seems to get under your skin from the moment you step out of the car. There is an old world enchantment about the hotel with its classical style, antique furnishings and paintings. After a relaxed dinner adjourn to the terrace and night sky, or alternatively a large cosy sofa and a crackling peat fire. Botany enthusiasts will enjoy the award-winning gardens, which are haven for ferns, hybrid rhododendrons, fuchias and Lavateras. Paths and cuttings wind their way through the grounds and on the lakeside you can take the rowing boat out to explore or to try a spot of fishing.

BALLYSEEDE CASTLE

TRALEE, CO KERRY, IRELAND
Tel: 00353 66 712 5799 **Fax:** 00353 66 712 5287
Web: www.johansens.com/ballyseedecastle **E-mail:** info@ballyseedecastle.com

Our inspector loved: *The character of this handsome small castle and the friendly atmosphere.*

Price Guide: (euro)
single from €119
double €170-€239

Location: off the N21; Tralee, 3 miles; Kerry Airport, 8 miles; Killarney, 20 miles

Attractions: Ring of Kerry; Dingle Peninsular; Lakes of Killarney; Tralee and Ballybunion Championship golf courses

Drive through an imposing granite gateway to reach this small and impressive ivy-enveloped castle. Once the chief garrison of the Fitzgeralds, Earls of Desmond, the castle retains its historic grandeur though you'll find the warm welcome more relaxed now. The flagstone hallway has a dramatic feel with Doric columns, a fine bifurcating oak staircase and marble fireplace. The restaurant prides itself on menus inspired by local produce and the drawing rooms are flooded with day light from elegant tall windows that make them ideal for enjoying an Irish afternoon tea. A recent conversion of the old stables has given the castle 10 new contemporary bedrooms whilst those upstairs are more traditional. The owner Marnie Corscadden is a third generation hotelier and along with Arthur her wonderfully docile Irish wolfhound will ensure a memorable stay.

TEMPLE COUNTRY RETREAT & SPA

HORSELEAP, MOATE, CO. WESTMEATH
Tel: 00 353 57 933 5118 **Fax:** 00 353 57 933 5008
Web: www.johansens.com/templespa **E-mail:** relax@templespa.ie

Our inspector loved: *The tranquil and relaxing atmosphere at this country retreat.*

Price Guide: (euro)
single from €175
double from €250
suite from €350

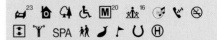

A contemporary destination spa within an hour's drive of Dublin, Temple stands on the siter of an ancient monastery and subtly echoes the architectural forms of its predecessor. The philosophy is simple: "eat healthily, drink wisely and sleep well". The Garden Room restaurant serves innovative and flavoursome dishes using largely locally sourced, organic produce; and the seasonally varying menu is perfectly complemented by a bottle of organic wine. The 23 elegant rooms, flooded with natural light, are decorated in soothing natural tones and enjoy panoramic views of the surrounding Irish countryside; the 2 suites each boast a private jacuzzi and balcony. Enjoy an indulgent spa treatment, or daily activities such as early morning walks through the parkland; or simply savour "doing nothing" at this tranquil retreat.

Location: N6, 3 miles; Dublin, 60-min drive

Attractions: Numerous Golf Courses; Cycling Routes; Moate Museum; Athlone

Scotland

For further information on Scotland, please contact:

Visit Scotland
Ocean Point 1,
94 Ocean Drive, Leith
Edinburgh EH6 6JH
Tel: +44 (0)131 472 2222 or +44 (0)1463 716 996
Internet: www.visitscotland.com

Greater Glasgow & Clyde Valley Tourist Board
Tel: +44 (0)141 204 4400
Internet: www.seeglasgow.com

Edinburgh & Lothians Tourist Board
Tel: +44 (0)845 2255 121
Internet: www.edinburgh.org

The Scottish Borders Tourist Board
Tel: 0870 608 0404
Internet: www.scot-borders.co.uk

or see **pages 197-200** for details of local historic houses, castles and gardens to visit during your stay.

For additional places to stay in Scotland, turn to **pages 194-196** where a listing of our Recommended Hotels & Spas Guide can be found.

NORWOOD HALL

GARTHDEE ROAD, CULTS, ABERDEEN, AB15 9FX
Tel: 0845 365 3462 **International:** +44 (0)1224 868951 **Fax:** 01224 869868
Web: www.johansens.com/norwoodhall **E-mail:** info@norwood-hall.co.uk

Our inspector loved: The period decor especially the tapestry on the walls in the restaurant.

Price Guide:
single £105–£205
double £125–£225

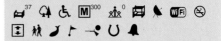

Awards/Recognition: 1 AA Rosette 2007-2008

Location: A90, 1 mile; Aberdeen City Centr,e, 3 miles; Aberdeen Airport, 7 miles

Attractions: Castle Trail; Whiskey Trail; Museums & Art Galleries; Championship Golf Courses

Norwood Hall stands in an area of outstanding natural beauty, at the gateway to Royal Deeside, 3 miles from the centre of historic and increasingly cosmopolitan Aberdeen. This 19th century mansion house has been lovingly restored and has a relaxed and comfy atmosphere. Its Victorian heritage has been well preserved with grand rooms some wood panelled and some with 'A' listed wallpaper. There are gorgeous fabrics, one gold embossed and stained glass windows and intricate cornices. Bedrooms include deluxe junior suites, four poster rooms and the particularly beautiful original house rooms. Wile away your evenings in the beautiful dining room, lined with tapestry work and where award-winning chefs combine the finest local ingredients to delight the tastebuds then retire to the Library for a great selection of Scotch.

HIGHLAND COTTAGE

BREADALBANE STREET, TOBERMORY, ISLE OF MULL PA75 6PD
Tel: 0845 365 1849 **International:** +44 (0)1688 302030
Web: www.johansens.com/highlandcottage **E-mail:** davidandjo@highlandcottage.co.uk

Our inspector loved: *Special highland hospitality and exceptional food.*

Price Guide:
single from £120
double from £150
sea-facing/four poster from £185

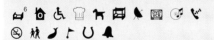

Awards/Recognition: 2 AA Rosettes 2007–2008

Location: Town Centre, 5-min walk; A848, 0.3 miles; A85, 32 miles

Attractions: Day-trip to Iona; Visit Staffa and the Treshnish Isles; Climb Ben More

Tobermory harbour must be one of the most distinctive in Britain. It's characteristic and colourful houses and shops provide a picturesque introduction to the Isle of Mull. This intimate, AA 3 Red Star, small hotel captures its essence high above the bustling harbour yet only a 5-minute walk from the town's main streets and Fisherman's Pier. Sunny public rooms offer you the perfect spot to read the paper, and bedrooms, decorated in island style, are cheerful and homely. This is Jo and David Currie's home and their cosy, intimate restaurant unsurprisingly uses top quality local ingredients; seafood comes direct from the Tobermory boats, caught by locals and the meat is of West Highland stock.

CULZEAN CASTLE – THE EISENHOWER APARTMENT

MAYBOLE, AYRSHIRE KA19 8LE
Tel: 0845 365 3257 **International:** +44 (0)1655 884455 **Fax:** 01655 884503
Web: www.johansens.com/culzeancastle **E-mail:** culzean@nts.org.uk

Our inspector loved: *The height of luxury with magnificent views.*

Price Guide:
(including breakfast and afternoon tea)
single from £140
double from £225

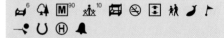

Take care when looking down! A 6 bedroom presidential apartment retained for General Eisenhower in his lifetime when the Castle was handed over to the National Trust for Scotland in 1945. Enter through the extremely impressive armoury at the front door, and as you arrive on the top floor you'll know that you are entering a rather splendid home. "This is a place I can relax" said Eisenhower, and that sentiment is exemplified by the friendly staff looking after you. Whether you are travelling on your own, as a couple, or maybe wishing to book all the rooms for that special party, the Castle will make you feel most welcome. Excellent links courses in the area and you have access to the Castle and its 560-acre country park with its woodlands, deer park and Victorian Vinery during opening hours.

Location: Just off the A719; A77, 4 miles; Ayr, 12 miles; Prestwick Airport, 16 miles

Attractions: Ayr - Home of Robert Burns; Brodick Castle on the Isle of Arran; Championship Golf Courses

BALCARY BAY HOTEL

AUCHENCAIRN, NR CASTLE DOUGLAS, DUMFRIES & GALLOWAY DG7 1QZ
Tel: 0845 365 3026 **International:** +44 (0)1556 640217/640311 **Fax:** 01556 640272
Web: www.johansens.com/balcarybay **E-mail:** reservations@balcary-bay-hotel.co.uk

Our inspector loved: *The idyllic setting, peaceful surroundings and the immaculate presentation.*

Price Guide:
single £69
double/twin £124–£160

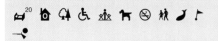

Awards/Recognition: 2 AA Rosettes 2006-2007

Location: Off the A711, 0.9 miles; Auchencairn, 2 miles; Castle Douglas, 9 miles

Attractions: Various Golf Courses; Galloway Wildlife Conservation Park; Threave Castle; Threave Estate and Gardens

At the end of a narrow lane, and enjoying a surprisingly warm, Gulf Stream climate, this traditional, secluded hideaway on the Solway Firth is still close to the bustling market town of Dumfries. You will have the reassuring intimacy of a family-run hotel, whilst enjoying all the ingredients for a peaceful, romantic visit. As you sit in the lounge overlooking the bay, only the call of sea birds and gently lapping waves compete for your attention. You should make the most of local delicacies such as lobster, prawns and salmon, and the great coastal walks that this corner of Scotland has to offer. Nearby are several excellent golf courses, salmon rivers and trout lochs, sailing, shooting, riding and bird-watching.

CORSEWALL LIGHTHOUSE HOTEL

CORSEWALL POINT, NEAR KIRKCOLM, STRANRAER, DG9 OQG
Tel: 0845 365 2859 **International:** +44 (0)1776 853220 **Fax:** 01776 854231
Web: www.johansens.com/lighthousehotel **E-mail:** info@lighthousehotel.co.uk

Our inspector loved: *The comfort of a small, unique hotel with a functioning lighthouse.*

Price Guide: (including breakfast and dinner)
double £140-£250
suite £210-£280

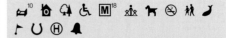

Awards/Recognition: 1 AA Rosette 2007-2008

Location: A718, 4 miles; Stranraer Ferry, 11 miles; Prestwick Airport, 60 miles

Attractions: Mull of Galloway Lighthouse; Culzean Castle; Logan Botanic Gardens

Perched high on a clifftop, just yards from a glazier-like face, Corsewall Lighthouse is either being dashed by high rising storm spray or smoothed by calmer summer waters at its rocky foot. This sparkling white lighthouse is a gorgeous little retreat that exudes the warmth, charm and romance of its early 19th-century origins with the comforts and style of a very unique hotel. It's a delightfully restored "A" listed national treasure that you will adore. Views are dazzling by day and star-scattered by night, taking in meadowland and a spectacular seascape brightened by several other working Scottish and Irish lighthouses whose knife-like beams warn of inshore dangers. Flexible accommodation includes two 2-bedroom suites, and the restaurant menu is inspired by seasonal offerings from both the sea and land.

TRIGONY HOUSE HOTEL

CLOSEBURN, THORNHILL, DUMFRIES AND GALLOWAY DG3 5EJ
Tel: 0845 365 1869 **International:** +44 (0)1848 331211
Web: www.johansens.com/trigony **E-mail:** info@trigonyhotel.co.uk

Our inspector loved: *Relaxed Edwardian country house hotel set in acres of gardens and woodland.*

Price Guide:
double £140-£150

Location: Just off the A76; Dumfries, 12.7 miles; Glasgow Airport, 55 miles

Attractions: Drumlanrig Castle; Ellisland Farm; Glenkiln Sculptor Park; Solway Coast Rockcliffe

The former shooting lodge for Closeburn Castle stands in over four acres of gardens and mature woodland in the heart of picturesque Dumfriesshire. Current owners Adam and Jan have created a charming country house hotel, offering guests the relaxed ambience and comfort of a family home. The bedrooms are all individually styled and most enjoy garden views and look across to the Lowther hills to the east or the Kier hills to the west. The Garden Suite boasts its own conservatory from which to admire the hotel's stunning setting. Well deserving of their Gold Plate and "Superb Breakfast" commendation by Hotel Review Scotland their culinary inspiration doesn't stop there. Classic rustic Scottish and English dishes along with European peasant fare is served in the elegant, sun-bathed restaurant, overlooking the lovingly maintained gardens, or in the cosy bar beside a welcoming open fire. Closed 25th and 26th December.

THE PEAT INN

PEAT INN, BY CUPAR, FIFE KY15 5LH
Tel: 0845 365 2637 **International:** +44 (0)1334 840206 **Fax:** 01334 840530
Web: www.johansens.com/thepeatinn **E-mail:** stay@thepeatinn.co.uk

Our inspector loved: The impressive refurbishment that has transformed the restaurant and bedrooms.

Price Guide:
single £125
double/twin £165

Certainly a challenge for Geoffrey and Katherine Smeddle in taking over what was, for over 30 years, one of Scotland's finest restaurants, but they have already put their own stamp on this 1700s coaching inn, creating a relaxed atmosphere where you cannot help but enjoy delicious food from the kitchen. Dishes are based on the best of what is seasonally available, meat from the Highlands, locally grown vegetables and freshly caught fish. A Bordeaux-based friend of the family acts as consultant for the excellent wine list and cellar. Just behind the restaurant, The Residence provides 8 bedroom suites with Italian marble bathrooms and views over the surrounding farmland. The Peat Inn remains one of Scotland's shining lights!

Location: B941, 1.5 miles; A915, 6 miles; M90, 27 miles; Edinburgh, 44 miles

Attractions: St Andrews; Secret Bunker; Falkland Palace; Scottish Fisheries Museum, Anstruther

THE STEADINGS AT THE GROUSE & TROUT

FLICHITY, FARR, SOUTH LOCH NESS, INVERNESS IV2 6XD
Tel: 0845 365 2698 **International:** +44 (0)1808 521314 **Fax:** 01808 521741
Web: www.johansens.com/steadings **E-mail:** stay@steadingshotel.co.uk

Our inspector loved: The wide open spaces and hares boxing just in front of the house!

Price Guide:
single £68
double £95

Location: The B851 ; A9 to Fort Augustus Road, 7 miles; Inverness, 12 miles; Inverness Airport, 20 miles

Attractions: Culloden Battlefield; Loch Ness; Inverness City Centre

The wonderful panoramic scenery and wildlife to be seen from the conservatory of this rustic, unpretentious inn is second to none. Built in 1860, the property was originally outbuildings, thankfully salvaged from the Flichity Inn, destroyed in 1964. Jump on the whisky trail and explore the castles, lochs and glens of the hidden Highlands, while looking out for herds of deer, wild goats, grouse, and heron landing on the Flichity Loch - if you're really lucky you might even spot osprey whisking away a salmon, or a stoat playing with the resident hare family on the hotel's lawn. Enjoy a local beer in The Grouse & Trout Lounge Bar and delicious Scottish and international food alongside an excellent wine list and, of course, fine Scottish malt whiskies.

GRESHORNISH HOUSE HOTEL

EDINBANE, BY PORTREE, ISLE OF SKYE IV51 9PN
Tel: 0845 365 1798 **International:** +44 (0)1470 582266 **Fax:** 01470 582345
Web: www.johansens.com/greshornishhouse **E-mail:** info@greshornishhouse.com

Our inspector loved: Very welcoming-charming drawing room with wood-panelling and large open fire.

Price Guide:
single £60–£165
double £120–£165
family £162.50–£225

Experience the open-door policy of this typical family run Skye manor house, very much in keeping with the island's hospitable traditions. Secluded in a beautiful lochside setting, the oldest part of the building dates back to the mid-18th century. The bedrooms are distinctive and comfortable - one allegedly haunted. However, there is nothing spooky in the candle-lit dining room, where an abundance of local seafood, game, Skye lamb, Scotch beef and cheeses are on offer. After dinner enjoy snooker and chess, or take a quiet moment by the drawing room fire to really appreciate a good malt whisky. The hotel is the perfect base for exploring the north end of Skye, or simply a place to relax and unwind whilst being looked after by a delightful team of people. Non-Smoking throughout the hotel.

Location: A850, 2.5 miles; Dunvegan, 6.5 miles; Portree, 17 miles

Attractions: Dunvegan Castle; Talisker Distillery; Edinbane Pottery; Skyeskyns Tannery

TORAVAIG HOUSE

KNOCK BAY, SLEAT, ISLE OF SKYE IV44 8RE
Tel: 0845 365 2756 **International:** +44 (0)1471 833231 **Fax:** 01471 833231
Web: www.johansens.com/toravaig **E-mail:** info@skyehotel.co.uk

Our inspector loved: *Crisp fresh atmosphere in a most scenic area.*

Price Guide: (including dinner)
double £110–£120

Location: On A851; Broadford, 12 miles; Skye Bridge, 16.5 miles; Portree, 37 miles

Attractions: Talisker Distillery and Visitor Centre; Sea Trips; Dunvegan Castle; Portree

Owners Anne Gracie and Kenneth Gunn have turned Toravaig House into a luxurious, affordable hotel, somewhere you'll happily spend time and deservedly recognised by its many awards. Overlooking the Sound of Sleat, its comfortable bedrooms, all named after Hebridean Islands, have little Scottish touches, and the elegant Iona restaurant, serves first class food from fresh local produce. Of course the great outdoors has masses to offer here, with fantastic low-level walking and climbing in the Cuillin Mountains. Even better, Ken's affinity with the sea is illustrated by daily skippered charters on the hotel's yacht, "Solus," take you around the south of Skye and the mainland. Skye's Sleat Peninsula, a hotbed of highland culture as well as being renowned for its musical events, holds a splendid Feis in mid-July.

RUDDYGLOW PARK

LOCH ASSYNT, BY LAIRG, SUTHERLAND IV27 4HB
Tel: 0845 365 2315 **International:** +44 (0)1571 822216 **Fax:** 01571 822216
Web: www.johansens.com/ruddyglowpark **E-mail:** info@ruddyglowpark.com

Our inspector loved: *Very relaxed homely atmosphere in stunning mountainous location.*

Price Guide:
double £115–£195
suite from £150

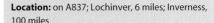

Location: on A837; Lochinver, 6 miles; Inverness, 100 miles

Attractions: Stalking; Geopark; Eas-Coul-Aulin via Kylesku; Cape Wrath

Owned and run by Patricia Filmer-Sankey, a parish of Assynt native, this small, quiet country house's unusual name is inspired by the 1920s National Hunt racehorse, "Ruddyglow," ridden by Patricia's father, the late Captain Filmer-Sankey. Winner of over 27 races. In the dining room you can enjoy extensive organic Continental buffets and traditional full Scottish breakfasts. Dinners created from organic, local produce can be prepared by prior arrangement. The house has a superb elevated position with spectacular views from the terraces over acres of much loved and well tended woodland gardens, majestic mountains and Scottish lochs. The comfortable traditional bedrooms feature Egyptian cotton bed linen, pure Hungarian goose down duvets and velvety bathrobes, Jacuzzi baths and bathroom accessories to ensure an indulgent experience.

FORSS HOUSE HOTEL

FORSS, NEAR THURSO, CAITHNESS KW14 7XY
Tel: 0845 365 1749 **International:** +44 (0)1847 861201 **Fax:** 01847 861301
Web: www.johansens.com/forsshousehotel **E-mail:** anne@forsshousehotel.co.uk

Our inspector loved: *Delicious dinner- all local produce.*

Price Guide:
single £75–£90
double/twin £110–£145
suite £210

Awards/Recognition: 1 AA Rosettes 2007-2008

Location: On the A836; A9, 4.6 miles; Thurso, 5 miles; Wick Airport, 27 miles

Attractions: John O'Groats; Castle of Mey; Old Pulteney Distillery; Orkney

If you love open spaces and the grand landscapes of the Scottish Highlands you will adore this 200 year old house, carefully restored by the owners, who also refurbished Ackergill Tower. The bedrooms in the main house have been carefully decorated with luxurious soft furnishings and feature elegant, tiled bathrooms. Take breakfast in the light and airy conservatory, whilst the more classic dining-room is the perfect setting for intimate dinners. Each dish is prepared with a simplicity that retains the true flavours of the finest local ingredients, seasonal meat and fish sourced from surrounding estates, rivers and the coastline of Forss. Matched by an extensive and inspiring wine collection. The house nestles in a tree-lined glen with its own swirling river for fishing.

KNOCKOMIE HOTEL

GRANTOWN ROAD, FORRES, MORAYSHIRE IV36 2SG
Tel: 0845 365 1963 **International:** +44 (0)1309 673146 **Fax:** 01309 673290
Web: www.johansens.com/knockomiehotel **E-mail:** stay@knockomie.co.uk

Our inspector loved: Panelled whisky bar with it's huge collection.

Price Guide:
single £115
double/twin £170
four poster £210

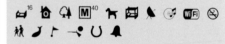

Awards/Recognition: Condé Nast Johansens / Taittinger Wine List Award 2006

Location: On A940; 1.6 miles south of Forres; Forres Railway Station, 1.5 miles; Inverness Airport, 20 miles

Attractions: Cawdor Castle; Brodie Castle; Malt Whisky Trail; Loch Ness

Defined by the Arts and Crafts movement, this elegant house was transformed in 1914 into what it is today. Paying guests are recorded as early as the 1840s, although its metamorphosis into a stylish hotel is somewhat more recent! Owners, Gavin and Penny Ellis have created a personal, intimate atmosphere, with just 16 bedrooms, and you can kick back and relax from the moment you arrive. This is Malt Whisky country, so do visit one of the local distilleries, and with Loch Ness to the west and Speyside to the east, you're surrounded by beautiful places. At the end of a full day's exploring or playing golf on one of a number of championship and challenging courses look forward to a drink in the delightful and well-stocked bar followed by carefully prepared menus balancing traditional Scottish ingredients with lighter dishes.

CRINGLETIE HOUSE

EDINBURGH ROAD, PEEBLES EH45 8PL
Tel: 0845 365 3251 **International:** +44 (0)1721 725750 **Fax:** 01721 725751
Web: www.johansens.com/cringletiehouse **E-mail:** enquiries@cringletie.com

Our inspector loved: The gardens, carpets of flowers, changing with the season - stunning!

Price Guide:
single from £165
double/twin £220–£290
suite £374

Awards/Recognition: 2 AA Rosettes 2006-2007

Location: On the A703; A8, 19.5 miles; Peebles, 3 miles; Edinburgh Airport, 28 miles

Attractions: Traquair House; Abbotsford House, Floors Castle, Abbeys

A distinguished baronial mansion set within 28 acres, the AA 4 Red Star Cringletie House is the epitome of fine country living. The individually decorated bedrooms have breathtaking views over the surrounding Peebleshire countryside. The panelled dining room has an impressive carved oak and marble fireplace, many original artworks and an eye catching hand painted ceiling depicting a heavenly classical scene. Highly acclaimed cuisine is created with flair and imagination designed around the fruits and vegetables available in Scotland's only 17th-century walled kitchen garden. Specialities include fresh game and fish. You can play outdoor chess or boule in the woodland garden, attempt the 9-hole putting green or play lawn croquet. Other activities can be arranged. Cringletie is a good base from which to explore the rich heritage of the Borders.

CASTLE VENLAW

EDINBURGH ROAD, PEEBLES EH45 8QG
Tel: 0845 365 3226 **International:** +44 (0)1721 720384 **Fax:** 01721 724066
Web: www.johansens.com/venlaw **E-mail:** stay@venlaw.co.uk

Our inspector loved: *A really traditional hotel with a relaxed and friendly attitude - particularly liked the romantic suites!*

Price Guide:
double/twin £120–£180
four poster £175–£250
romantic suite £195–£295

Awards/Recognition: 2 AA Rosettes 2007-2008

Location: Just off the A703; Edinburgh, 40-min drive; Glasgow, 90-min drive

Attractions: Traquair House; Neidpath Castle; Dawyck and Kailzie Gardens; Edinburgh Castle

Built as a private residence in 1782 the Castle is a short distance from Edinburgh yet within the peaceful Borders countryside overlooking the royal and ancient town of Peebles. This acclaimed 4-star hotel maintains country house traditions and a relaxed informality, from the Library with its oak panelling and log fire, to the 12 bedrooms and suites - all named after Scotland's finest malt whiskies. Enjoy the recently added four-poster romantic suites as well as the spacious restaurant offering menus where delicious local produce such as Borders salmon, lamb and game are given an international flavour. Explore the countryside where historic ruins can be appreciated. Short breaks are available all year and the Castle is available for exclusive use for parties and weddings.

Image from britainonview.com

Wales

For further information on Wales, please contact:

Wales Tourist Board
Brunel House, 2 Fitzalan Road, Cardiff CF24 0UY
Tel: +44 (0)29 2049 9909
Web: www.visitwales.com

North Wales Tourism
77 Conway Road, Colwyn Bay, Conway LL29 7LN
Tel: +44 (0)1492 531731
Web: www.nwt.co.uk

Mid Wales Tourism
The Station, Machynlleth, Powys SY20 8TG
Tel: (Freephone) 0800 273747
Web: www.visitmidwales.co.uk

South West Wales Tourism Partnership
The Coach House, Aberglasney, Carmarthenshire SA32
8QH
Tel: +44 (0)1558 669091
Web: www.swwtp.co.uk

or see **pages 197-200** for details of local historic
houses, castles and gardens to visit during your stay.

For additional places to stay in Wales,
turn to **pages 194-196** where a listing of our
Recommended Hotels & Spas Guide can be found.

JABAJAK VINEYARD (RESTAURANT WITH ROOMS)

BANC Y LLAIN, LLANBOIDY ROAD, WHITLAND, CARMARTHENSHIRE SA34 0ED
Tel: 0845 365 2839 **International:** +44 (0)1994 448786
Web: www.johansens.com/Jabajak **E-mail:** amanda@jabajak.co.uk

Our inspector loved: The concept of Jabajak, and delicious dining.

Price Guide:
double (single occupancy) £57.50-£92.50
double from £80
honeymoon/farmhouse suite from £110

This charming former farm, with a carriage house, stable, grain store and milking parlour, is now a delightful relaxing retreat in the rather unique setting of a newly planted Welsh vineyard. It's about great food and hospitality, 3 restaurants, a lounge bar and 5 bedrooms. Owners Julian and Amanda have been inspirational in creating this haven and have taken endless care with the menus to reflect the best of local ingredients. Non-residents are welcome in the large Grain Store restaurant (great for party takeovers), the bistro and the more intimate 'Nook gallery' in the eaves of the building, however guests also have the advantage of their own lounge with fire, games and big sofa in which to relax after a day exploring the beautiful surrounding countryside. Bedrooms feature carved furniture and views over the six acres of landscaped grounds.

Location: A40, 3 miles; M4, 28 miles; Severn Bridge, 104 miles; Gateway to Ireland Pembroke Dock, 30 miles

Attractions: Preseli Mountains and Pembrokeshire National Park; Cardiganshire Coast; Laugharne, home of Dylan Thomas; Botanical Garden of Wales

TAN-Y-FOEL COUNTRY HOUSE

CAPEL GARMON, NR BETWS-Y-COED, CONWY LL26 0RE
Tel: 0845 365 2387 **International:** +44 (0)1690 710507 **Fax:** 01690 710681
Web: www.johansens.com/tanyfoel **E-mail:** enquiries@tyfhotel.co.uk

Our inspector loved: *The whole concept, relaxing room, amazing views and very special dining. A gem.*

Price Guide: (including dinner)
double (single occupancy) from £152
double from £224

Awards/Recognition: 3 AA Rosettes 2007-2008; Condé Nast Johansens Most Excellent Country House 2006

Location: A470, 2 miles; A55, 16 miles; A5, 4 miles; Betws-y-Coed, 3.1 miles

Attractions: Snowdonia; Narrow Gauge and Mountain Railways; Conwy Castle; Anglesey

Contemporary and bijou, this Welsh stone house blends country elegance with striking bedrooms within a spectacular location, offering fabulous views of the lush Conwy Valley and rugged Snowdonia. Bedrooms are individually styled and you cannot help but admire the attention to detail. Taking advantage of the fertile surroundings, owner Janet, a member of "The Master Chefs of Great Britain", sources the best local produce - fresh fish, Welsh black beef and organically grown vegetables for her creative menus and daughter Kelly complements both parents with her own skills. We liked the house so much we awarded it Condé Nast Johansens - Most Excellent Country House 2006 award, and the Welsh Tourist Board concurred, with the accolade of 5 stars for its Country House Guest Accommodation. A no smoking policy prevails.

SYCHNANT PASS HOUSE

SYCHNANT PASS ROAD, CONWY LL32 8BJ
Tel: 0845 365 2384 **International:** +44 (0)1492 596868
Web: www.johansens.com/sychnant **E-mail:** bre@sychnant-pass-house-co.uk

Our inspector loved: *The 2 new suites with hot tubs on their private balconies.*

Price Guide:
single £75-£160
double/twin £95-£170
suite £140-£180

Awards/Recognition: 1 AA Rosette 2006-2007

Location: A55, 2 miles; Conwy, 2 miles; Valley Airport, 33 miles; Holyhead Port for Ireland, 38 miles

Attractions: Snowdonia; Conwy Castle; Superb Golf Courses; Bodnant Garden

Idyllically situated in the foothills of Snowdonia National Park, Sychnant Pass House has won many accolades as an outstanding small country house that perfectly blends elegance with charm. Surrounded by 3 acres of wild garden, unfenced roads, wandering sheep and roaming wild ponies. Owners Bre and Graham Carrington Sykes are fastidious about standards and are renowned for their welcoming, warm personalities. You can choose from a variety of rooms; each delightfully decorated and fitted to the highest criteria. 2 ground floor bedrooms feature French windows leading onto a terrace and 4 suites have sitting rooms. Some rooms have galleries and terraces and all enjoy mountain and countryside views towards the medieval walled town of Conwy. You can also enjoy excellent and imaginative cuisine in the candle-lit restaurant.

PORTH TOCYN COUNTRY HOUSE HOTEL

ABERSOCH, PWLLHELI, GWYNEDD LL53 7BU
Tel: 0845 365 2136 **International:** +44 (0)1758 713303 **Fax:** 01758 713538
Web: www.johansens.com/porthtocyn **E-mail:** bookings@porthtocyn.fsnet.co.uk

Our inspector loved: This little bit of vintage heaven, with 21st century features - blissful.

Price Guide: (including continental breakfast)
single from £70
double/twin from £93

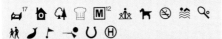

Awards/Recognition: 2 AA Rosettes 2006-2007

Location: A499, 3 miles; A479, 9 miles; Chester, 100 miles; Shrewsbury, 104 miles

Attractions: Plas Glyn-Y-Weddw Gallery; Bardsey Island; Plas Yn Rhiw; Heritage Coast Line

A rare treat, this country house seaside hotel appeals whether you want to kick a football around or doze in the garden with one eye on views across Cardigan Bay. The Fletcher-Brewer family have owned this white building, once a row of miners' cottages, for 3 generations and welcome guests of all ages. Continuity is the essence of Porth Tocyn and it is to be treasured. Most bedrooms have sea views, some are for families, and 3 on the ground floor are ideal for those with mobility problems. Grown-ups can enjoy cocktails before memorable dinners, and lunch is informal, on the terrace or by the pool. Glorious beaches, water sports, golf, tennis and riding provide fun for the young and young at heart.

Bae Abermaw

PANORAMA HILL, BARMOUTH, GWYNEDD LL42 1DQ
Tel: 0845 365 3023 **International:** +44 (0)1341 280550 **Fax:** 01341 280346
Web: www.johansens.com/baeabermaw **E-mail:** enquiries@baeabermaw.com

Our inspector loved: *Fantastic views. Delicious fish from the bay.*

Price Guide:
single £86–£110
double/twin £126–£165

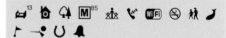

Awards/Recognition: 1 AA Rosette 2006-2007

Location: A496, 0.25 miles; A470, 8 miles; Birmingham Airport, 108 miles; Manchester Airport, 110 miles

Attractions: Mawddach Esta; Snowdonia; Royal St Davids Golf Course; Portmeirion

First time visitors to this hillside hotel overlooking the lovely Mawddach Estuary and backed by Snowdonia National Park are in for a surprise as it's owners David and Suzi Reeve, and Andrew Roberts-Evans have created an impressive retreat. The hotel offers the best of everything and sets itself above the label of "seaside hotel". Cool neutral colours - white, cream, flax, beige - stripped floorboards and streamlined sofas suggest a minimalist feel, whilst deep blue is the prominent colour in the excellent restaurant. The cuisine has some modern and exciting interpretations of classic British dishes with a French influence. Local produce is much in use, particularly Welsh black beef, marsh lamb and sole, plus a choice of vegetarian options. Bedrooms are stylishly decorated and feature deep baths and luxurious toiletries.

LLWYNDU FARMHOUSE

LLANABER, NR BARMOUTH, GWYNEDD LL42 1RR
Tel: 0845 365 3721 **International:** +44 (0)1341 280144 **Fax:** 01341 281236
Web: www.johansens.com/llwyndu **E-mail:** intouch@llwyndu-farmhouse.co.uk

Our inspector loved: *Its informality, and simplicity, the epitomy of a historic 16th century building.*

Price Guide: (including dinner)
double from £144

Location: A 496, 0.25 miles; A 470, 12 miles; A487, 14 miles

Attractions: Snowdonia National Park; Portmeirion; LLeyn Peninsula; Barmouth Panorama Walk

If you are look for something historic and unspoilt this should be on your list. Overlooking a secluded bay this grade II listed farmhouse has been lovingly restored by owners Peter and Paula Thompson. Full of character and charm, many quirky original features have been kept including the inglenook fireplaces, stone staircase and even a sink fitted into a door. Two of the three bedrooms have four posters and whilst all have up to date comforts they exude the personality of a welcoming 16th century home. In the evenings you can dine by candle light in the cosy and warm restaurant, perfect for an intimate evening or gathering of friends. Dishes are imaginatively prepared by Peter who uses fresh Welsh ingredients with flair. You shouldn't leave without trying a national favourite - Welsh rarebit with laver bread.

The Bell At Skenfrith

SKENFRITH, MONMOUTHSHIRE NP7 8UH
Tel: 0845 365 2403 **International:** +44 (0)1600 750235 **Fax:** 01600 750525
Web: www.johansens.com/bellskenfrith **E-mail:** enquiries@skenfrith.co.uk

Our inspector loved: *The lovely bedrooms and idyllic location on the edge of the River Monnow.*

Price Guide:
single £75–£120 (not available at weekends)
double/twin £105–£160
four-poster from £185

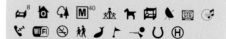

A beautifully renovated 17th-century coaching inn surrounded by unspoilt Monmouthshire countryside and overlooking historic castle ruins. It's a dream come true if you're looking for a quiet retreat to escape to, with its roaring log fires, flagstone floors, stunning oak beams and deep sofas. Bedrooms are homely with pure wool Welsh blankets, finest linen and views of the Welsh hills or River Monnow. In the evenings you'll be happy to sip a glass of wine or real ale before tucking into an organically produced dinner created by the award winning kitchen. Wanting to grow many of their own ingredients this year they have successfully developed a Kitchen Garden which now helps flavour the imaginative menus.

Awards/Recognition: 2 AA Rosettes 2007-2008; Condé Nast Johansens Most Excellent Traditional Inn 2007

Location: Off the B4521; A466, 3.4 miles; A49, 7.2 miles; Monmouth, 8 miles

Attractions: Llanthony Priory, Abergavenny; Tintern Abbey; Monmouth; Ross-on-Wye

PENALLY ABBEY

PENALLY, TENBY, PEMBROKESHIRE SA70 7PY
Tel: 0845 365 2103 **International:** +44 (0)1834 843033 **Fax:** 01834 844714
Web: www.johansens.com/penallyabbey **E-mail:** penally.abbey@btinternet.com

Our inspector loved: *The relaxed atmosphere, enchanting location and variety of accommodation.*

Price Guide:
single £130
double/twin £146–£188
suite £230

Location: A4139, 0.5 mile; M4, 38 miles; Swansea, 48 miles; Bristol, 124 miles

Attractions: Caldey Island; Pembroke Castle; Tenby; National Botanical Gardens Aberglasney

This impressive hotel's wisteria-clad stone walls, built on the site of an ancient abbey, glistens with decorative windows through which you can enjoy panoramic views across the gardens to Carmarthen Bay and Caldey Island. All 3 limestone buildings blend the best of the old with the new. Reminiscent of a country seat, the original Abbey House has a superbly proportioned lounge with Adams fireplace, family photos and comfy leather Chesterfields. Next door the intimate Coach House's 4 rooms each have a private entrance, while uncluttered St Deiniol's Lodge features rich wooden furniture, leather sofas and marble bathrooms - the ultimate in urban chic. Relax in the restaurant beneath high coved ceilings and crystal chandeliers, and brave Welsh waters with water skiing, surfing and sailing nearby.

WOLFSCASTLE COUNTRY HOTEL & RESTAURANT

WOLF'S CASTLE, HAVERFORDWEST, PEMBROKESHIRE SA62 5LZ
Tel: 0845 365 2817 **International:** +44 (0)1437 741225 **Fax:** 01437 741383
Web: www.johansens.com/wolfscastle **E-mail:** enquiries@wolfscastle.com

Our inspector loved: *The fish pie!*

Price Guide:
single £65-£90
double/twin £95-£130

Awards/Recognition: 1 AA Rosette 2007-2008

Location: Just off the A40; Fishguard, 7 miles; Haverfordwest, 7 miles; Cardiff, 100 miles

Attractions: Pembrokeshire Coast National Park; St Davids Cathedral and Bishops Palace; Skomer and Ramsey Island

Situated in the glorious Pembrokeshire countryside, this former vicarage has a welcoming atmosphere. Andrew Stirling the owner/manager of 28 years, is supported by a close network of staff, several of whom have been at Wolfscastle for many years. The charming non-smoking bedrooms, including 4 luxurious Executive Suites, combine elegant period décor with contemporary facilities. Try the excellent restaurant where you can taste delicious menus based on fresh local produce. After a day walking the coastal paths, enjoy the log fire in the bar. Both dining areas offer an à la carte and bar menu. The main function room is ideal for conferences and social events and opens onto a magnificent patio/garden area. For smaller parties choose the Barclay Suite, named after the retired pianist.

GLANGRWYNEY COURT

GLANGRWYNEY, NR CRICKHOWELL, POWYS NP8 1ES
Tel: 0845 365 1764 **International:** +44 (0)1873 811288 **Fax:** 01873 810317
Web: www.johansens.com/glangrwyneycourt **E-mail:** info@glancourt.co.uk

Our inspector loved: *The gardens, perfect for lazing around or playing games. Cosy in winter too.*

Price Guide:
single £60-£85
double/twin £75-£120
suite £95-£180

Location: A40, 0.25 mile; A465, 2 miles; Cardiff, 40 miles; Bristol, 55 miles

Attractions: Hay on Wye; Brecon Beacons; Tredegar House and Park; Sdwd yr Eira Falls

Owner Christina Jackson has created a charming and tranquil hideaway, which is certainly more than just a Bed and Breakfast. The mansion has a relaxed, lived-in feel. It is a place where you can unwind amidst antiques, family bric-a-brac, and the log fire in the main sitting room. The charming, well-equipped Gardner's Cottage has its own facilities. All the bedrooms are beautifully furnished and offer views over the listed gardens, which are lovely to explore along with the surrounding countryside. Tennis, croquet and boules can be enjoyed on site; riding, fishing, shooting, wonderful walks and excellent restaurants are on the doorstep. Glangrwyney Court is perfect if you're looking for an informal setting for a small wedding or business event.

EGERTON GREY

PORTHKERRY, NR CARDIFF, VALE OF GLAMORGAN CF62 3BZ

Tel: 0845 365 3281 **International:** +44 (0)1446 711666 **Fax:** 01446 711690
Web: www.johansens.com/egertongrey **E-mail:** info@egertongrey.co.uk

Our inspector loved: *A beautiful house with some wonderful original features close to Cardiff Airport.*

Price Guide:
single £90–£120
double/twin £130–£150

Location: A4226, 2 miles; M4 jct 33, 11 miles; Cardiff, 12 miles

Attractions: Cardiff Castle; The Welsh Folk Museum; Castle Coch

This early 19th century, distinguished former rectory was opened as a small luxury hotel in 1988. Tucked away in 7 acres of gardens in a secluded, wooded valley in the Vale of Glamorgan, you can enjoy glorious views towards Porthkerry Park and the sea. The house's historic character has been carefully preserved with interiors that complement its architectural heritage. The Edwardian drawing room has intricate plaster mouldings, chandeliers, and an open fireplace, whilst the library overlooks the garden. Several of the 9 immaculately presented bedrooms have Victorian baths. The main restaurant, once a billiard room, creates an air of intimacy with its original Cuban mahogany panelling and candle-lit tables. Owners Richard Morgan-Price and Huw Thomas take great pride in presenting high-quality cuisine and fine wines.

Hotels & Spas, Great Britain & Ireland

All the properties listed below can be found in our Recommended Hotels & Spas, Great Britain & Ireland 2008 Guide. More information on our portfolio of guides can be found on page 247.

Channel Islands

The Atlantic Hotel and Ocean Restaurant	Jersey	**0845 365 2395**
The Club Hotel & Spa, Bohemia Restaurant	Jersey	0845 365 2419
Longueville Manor	Jersey	0845 365 2038

England

The Bath Priory Hotel and Restaurant	Bath & NE Somerset	0845 365 2397
The Bath Spa Hotel	Bath & NE Somerset	0845 365 2398
Dukes Hotel	Bath & NE Somerset	0845 365 3274
Homewood Park	Bath & NE Somerset	0845 365 1875
Hunstrete House	Bath & NE Somerset	0845 365 1906
The Park	Bath & NE Somerset	0845 365 2619
The Royal Crescent Hotel	Bath & NE Somerset	0845 365 2679
Luton Hoo Hotel, Golf & Spa	Bedfordshire	0845 365 3458
Moore Place Hotel	Bedfordshire	0845 365 2075
The Bear Hotel	Berkshire	0845 365 2401
Cliveden	Berkshire	0845 365 3236
The Crab at Chieveley	Berkshire	0845 365 2437
Donnington Valley Hotel and Spa	Berkshire	0845 365 3267
Fredrick's – Hotel Restaurant Spa	Berkshire	0845 365 1758
The French Horn	Berkshire	0845 365 2496
The Great House	Berkshire	0845 365 2513
Oakley Court Hotel	Berkshire	0845 365 2092
The Vineyard At Stockcross	Berkshire	0845 365 2716
New Hall	Birmingham	0845 365 2083
Danesfield House Hotel and Spa	Buckinghamshire	0845 365 3261
Hartwell House Hotel, Restaurant & Spa	Buckinghamshire	0845 365 1824
The Kings Hotel	Buckinghamshire	0845 365 2841
Stoke Park Club	Buckinghamshire	0845 365 2374
Stoke Place	Buckinghamshire	0845 365 2843
Cambridge Garden House	Cambridgeshire	0845 365 2879
Hotel Felix	Cambridgeshire	0845 365 1897
Green Bough Hotel	Cheshire	0845 365 1796
Mere Court Hotel	Cheshire	0845 365 2058
Nunsmere Hall	Cheshire	0845 365 2089
Rowton Hall Hotel, Health Club & Spa	Cheshire	0845 365 2308
Alverton Manor	Cornwall	0845 365 3609
Budock Vean - The Hotel on the River	Cornwall	0845 365 3212
Fowey Hall Hotel & Restaurant	Cornwall	0845 365 1754
The Garrack Hotel & Restaurant	Cornwall	0845 365 2497
Hell Bay	Cornwall	0845 365 1837
Meudon Hotel	Cornwall	0845 365 2059
The Nare Hotel	Cornwall	0845 365 2603
The Polurrian Hotel	Cornwall	0845 365 2849
The Rosevine Hotel	Cornwall	0845 365 2678
St Michael's Hotel & Spa	Cornwall	0845 365 2358
Talland Bay Hotel	Cornwall	0845 365 2386
Armathwaite Hall Hotel	Cumbria	0845 365 3617
Farlam Hall Hotel	Cumbria	0845 365 3289
Gilpin Lodge	Cumbria	0845 365 1762
Holbeck Ghyll Country House Hotel	Cumbria	0845 365 1872
The Inn on the Lake	Cumbria	0845 365 2548
Lakeside Hotel on Lake Windermere	Cumbria	0845 365 1978
Linthwaite House Hotel	Cumbria	0845 365 2031
The Lodore Falls Hotel	Cumbria	0845 365 2581
Lovelady Shield Country House Hotel	Cumbria	0845 365 2042
Netherwood Hotel	Cumbria	0845 365 2082
Rampsbeck Country House Hotel	Cumbria	0845 365 2138
Rothay Manor	Cumbria	0845 365 2307
Sharrow Bay Country House Hotel	Cumbria	0845 365 2346
Tufton Arms Hotel	Cumbria	0845 365 2766
Callow Hall	Derbyshire	0845 365 3221
East Lodge Country House Hotel	Derbyshire	0845 365 3278
The Izaak Walton Hotel	Derbyshire	0845 365 2561
The Arundell Arms	Devon	0845 365 2394
Buckland-Tout-Saints	Devon	0845 365 3211
Gidleigh Park	Devon	0845 365 1759
The Horn of Plenty Country House Hotel	Devon	0845 365 2534
Hotel Riviera	Devon	0845 365 1904
Langdon Court Hotel & Restaurant	Devon	0845 365 1985
Lewtrenchard Manor	Devon	0845 365 2018
Northcote Manor Country House Hotel	Devon	0845 365 2087
Orestone Manor & The Restaurant at Orestone Manor	Devon	0845 365 2095
Soar Mill Cove Hotel	Devon	0845 365 2349
The Tides Reach Hotel	Devon	0845 365 2713
Watersmeet Hotel	Devon	0845 365 2793
Woolacombe Bay Hotel	Devon	0845 365 2819
Moonfleet Manor	Dorset	0845 365 2074
Plumber Manor	Dorset	0845 365 2134
The Priory Hotel	Dorset	0845 365 2651
Stock Hill Country House Hotel	Dorset	0845 365 2371
Summer Lodge Country House Hotel	Dorset	0845 365 2381
Headlam Hall	Durham	0845 365 1827
Burleigh Court	Gloucestershire	0845 365 3217
Calcot Manor Hotel & Spa	Gloucestershire	0845 365 3220
Charingworth Manor	Gloucestershire	0845 365 3298
Corse Lawn House Hotel	Gloucestershire	0845 365 3249
Cotswold House Hotel	Gloucestershire	0845 365 3250
Cowley Manor	Gloucestershire	0845 365 3452
The Dial House	Gloucestershire	0845 365 2463
The Grapevine Hotel	Gloucestershire	0845 365 2508
The Greenway	Gloucestershire	0845 365 2514
The Hare and Hounds Hotel	Gloucestershire	0845 365 2518
Hotel On The Park	Gloucestershire	0845 365 1903
Lords of the Manor Hotel	Gloucestershire	0845 365 2041
Lower Slaughter Manor	Gloucestershire	0845 365 2047

Hotels & Spas, Great Britain & Ireland

All the properties listed below can be found in our Recommended Hotels & Spas, Great Britain & Ireland 2008 Guide.
More information on our portfolio of guides can be found on page 247.

The Noel Arms Hotel	Gloucestershire	0845 365 2608
Stonehouse Court Hotel	Gloucestershire	0845 365 2378
The Swan Hotel At Bibury	Gloucestershire	0845 365 2709
Washbourne	Gloucestershire	0845 365 2791
Thornbury Castle	S Gloucestershire	0845 365 2749
Audleys Wood	Hampshire	0845 365 2899
Chewton Glen	Hampshire	0845 365 3233
Chilworth Manor	Hampshire	0845 365 3234
Esseborne Manor	Hampshire	0845 365 3284
Hotel TerraVina	Hampshire	0845 365 2871
The Montagu Arms Hotel	Hampshire	0845 365 2601
New Park Manor & Bath House Spa	Hampshire	0845 365 2084
Passford House Hotel	Hampshire	0845 365 2097
Tylney Hall	Hampshire	0845 365 2782
Westover Hall	Hampshire	0845 365 3425
Castle House	Herefordshire	0845 365 3225
Shendish Manor Hotel & Golf Club	Hertfordshire	0845 365 3427
St Michael's Manor	Hertfordshire	0845 365 2359
West Lodge Park Country House Hotel	Hertfordshire	0845 365 2794
Eastwell Manor	Kent	0845 365 3279
The Spa Hotel	Kent	0845 365 2693
Eaves Hall	Lancashire	0845 365 3280
The Farington Lodge Hotel	Lancashire	0845 365 3429
The Gibbon Bridge Hotel	Lancashire	0845 365 2501
Stapleford Park Country House Hotel	Leicestershire	0845 365 2367
The George Of Stamford	Lincolnshire	0845 365 3295
41	London	0845 365 3601
51 Buckingham Gate Luxury Suites and Apartments	London	0845 365 2653
Beaufort House	London	0845 365 3029
Cannizaro House	London	0845 365 3222
The Capital Hotel & Restaurant	London	0845 365 2413
The Egerton House Hotel	London	0845 365 2483
Hendon Hall Hotel	London	0845 365 1839
Jumeirah Carlton Tower	London	0845 365 1932
Jumeirah Lowndes Hotel	London	0845 365 1934
Kensington House Hotel	London	0845 365 1936
The Mandeville Hotel	London	0845 365 2589
The Mayflower Hotel	London	0845 365 2591
The Milestone Hotel & Apartments	London	0845 365 2594
The Richmond Gate Hotel and Restaurant	London	0845 365 2674
Sofitel St James	London	0845 365 2351
The Sumner	London	0845 365 2703
Twenty Nevern Square	London	0845 365 2769
Congham Hall	Norfolk	0845 365 3244
Fawsley Hall	Northamptonshire	0845 365 3291
Rushton Hall	Northamptonshire	0845 365 2316
Whittlebury Hall	Northamptonshire	0845 365 2804
Matfen Hall	Northumberland	0845 365 2057
Lace Market Hotel	Nottinghamshire	0845 365 1973
Langar Hall	Nottinghamshire	0845 365 1983
Ye Olde Bell	Nottinghamshire	0845 365 3457
Le Manoir Aux Quat' Saisons	Oxfordshire	0845 365 2014
Phyllis Court Club	Oxfordshire	0845 365 2107
The Springs Hotel & Golf Club	Oxfordshire	0845 365 2697
Hambleton Hall	Rutland	0845 365 1809
Dinham Hall	Shropshire	0845 365 3266
Avon Gorge Hotel	Somerset	0845 365 3451
The Castle at Taunton	Somerset	0845 365 2415
Charlton House & The Sharpham Park Restaurant	Somerset	0845 365 2876
Combe House Hotel	Somerset	0845 365 3240
Mount Somerset Country House Hotel	Somerset	0845 365 2076
Ston Easton Park	Somerset	0845 365 2376
Hoar Cross Hall Spa Resort	Staffordshire	0845 365 1864
Brudenell Hotel	Suffolk	0845 365 3209
Hintlesham Hall	Suffolk	0845 365 1857
The Ickworth Hotel and Apartments	Suffolk	0845 365 2539
Ravenwood Hall Country Hotel	Suffolk	0845 365 2139
Seckford Hall	Suffolk	0845 365 2319
The Swan Hotel	Suffolk	0845 365 2708
The Westleton Crown	Suffolk	0845 365 2731
Foxhills	Surrey	0845 365 1756
Grayshott Spa	Surrey	0845 365 1789
Lythe Hill Hotel & Spa	Surrey	0845 365 2052

Ashdown Park Hotel and Country Club	**East Sussex**	**0845 365 2896**
Dale Hill	East Sussex	0845 365 3259
Deans Place Hotel	East Sussex	0845 365 3264
The Grand Hotel	East Sussex	0845 365 2504
Horsted Place Country House Hotel	East Sussex	0845 365 1893
Lansdowne Place, Boutique Hotel & Spa	East Sussex	0845 365 1987
Newick Park	East Sussex	0845 365 2085
The PowderMills	East Sussex	0845 365 2648
Rye Lodge	East Sussex	0845 365 2317
Amberley Castle	West Sussex	0845 365 3612
Bailiffscourt Hotel & Spa	West Sussex	0845 365 3025
Millstream Hotel	West Sussex	0845 365 2067
Ockenden Manor	West Sussex	0845 365 2093
The Spread Eagle Hotel & Health Spa	West Sussex	0845 365 2695
The Vermont Hotel	Tyne & Wear	0845 365 2714
Ardencote Manor Hotel	Warwickshire	0845 365 3615
Billesley Manor	Warwickshire	0845 365 3036
Ettington Park	Warwickshire	0845 365 3286
Mallory Court	Warwickshire	0845 365 2053
Nailcote Hall	Warwickshire	0845 365 2078
Wroxall Abbey Estate	Warwickshire	0845 365 2835
Bishopstrow House & Spa	Wiltshire	0845 365 3038

Hotels & Spas, Great Britain & Ireland

All the properties listed below can be found in our Recommended Hotels & Spas, Great Britain & Ireland 2008 Guide. More information on our portfolio of guides can be found on page 247.

Howard's House	Wiltshire	0845 365 1905
Lucknam Park, Bath	Wiltshire	0845 365 2048
The Pear Tree At Purton	Wiltshire	0845 365 2635
Whatley Manor	Wiltshire	0845 365 2801
Woolley Grange	Wiltshire	0845 365 2831
Brockencote Hall	Worcestershire	0845 365 3204
Buckland Manor	Worcestershire	0845 365 3210
The Cottage in the Wood	Worcestershire	0845 365 2431
Dormy House	Worcestershire	0845 365 3269
The Elms	Worcestershire	0845 365 2485
The Evesham Hotel	Worcestershire	0845 365 2487
The Lygon Arms	Worcestershire	0845 365 2586
The Devonshire Arms Country House Hotel & Spa	North Yorkshire	0845 365 2461
The Grange Hotel	North Yorkshire	0845 365 2507
Grants Hotel	North Yorkshire	0845 365 1784
Grinkle Park Hotel	North Yorkshire	0845 365 3421
Hob Green Hotel, Restaurant & Gardens	North Yorkshire	0845 365 1867
Judges Country House Hotel	North Yorkshire	0845 365 1928
Middlethorpe Hall Hotel	North Yorkshire	0845 365 2061
Monk Fryston Hall Hotel	North Yorkshire	0845 365 2073
The Pheasant	North Yorkshire	0845 365 2641
Simonstone Hall	North Yorkshire	0845 365 2348
The Worsley Arms Hotel	North Yorkshire	0845 365 2746
Whitley Hall Hotel	South Yorkshire	0845 365 2803
42 The Calls	West Yorkshire	0845 365 3602

Ireland

Cabra Castle	Cavan	00 353 42 9667030
Longueville House & Presidents' Restaurant	Cork	00 353 22 47156

Harvey's Point	**Donegal**	**00 353 74 972 2208**
Brooks Hotel	Dublin	00 353 1 670 4000
Abbeyglen Castle	Galway	00 353 95 21201
Cashel House	Galway	00 353 95 31001
Renvyle House Hotel	Galway	00 353 95 43511

St. Clerans Manor House	Galway	00 353 91 846555
Ballygarry House	Kerry	00 353 66 7123322
The Brehon	Kerry	00 353 64 30700
Cahernane House Hotel	Kerry	00 353 64 31895
Hotel Dunloe Castle	Kerry	00 353 64 44111
Park Hotel Kenmare & Sámas	Kerry	00 353 64 41200
Sheen Falls Lodge	Kerry	00 353 64 41600
Killashee House Hotel & Villa Spa	Kildare	00 353 45 879277
Mount Juliet Conrad	Kilkenny	00 353 56 777 3000
Ashford Castle	Mayo	00 353 94 95 46003
Knockranny House Hotel & Spa	Mayo	00 353 98 28600
The Hunting Lodge	Monaghan	00 353 4788100
Nuremore Hotel and Country Club	Monaghan	00 353 42 9661438
Dunbrody Country House & Cookery School	Wexford	00 353 51 389 600
Kelly's Resort Hotel & Spa	Wexford	00 353 53 32114
Marlfield House	Wexford	00 353 53 94 21124

Scotland

Darroch Learg	Aberdeenshire	0845 365 3263
Ardanaiseig	Argyll & Bute	0845 365 3614
Loch Melfort Hotel & Restaurant	Argyll & Bute	0845 365 2036
Cally Palace Hotel	Dumfries & Galloway	0845 365 2873
Kirroughtree House	Dumfries & Galloway	0845 365 1962
Channings	Edinburgh	0845 365 3229
Mar Hall Hotel & Spa	Glasgow	0845 365 2054
Bunchrew House Hotel	Highland	0845 365 3214
Cuillin Hills Hotel	Highland	0845 365 3255
Drumossie Hotel	Highland	0845 365 3272
Inverlochy Castle	Highland	0845 365 1926
Rocpool Reserve	Highland	0845 365 2304
The Torridon	Highland	0845 365 2037
Dalhousie Castle and Spa	Midlothian	0845 365 3260
Ballathie House Hotel	Perth & Kinross	0845 365 3027
The Royal Hotel	Perth & Kinross	0845 365 2681
Glenapp Castle	South Ayrshire	0845 365 1768

Wales

Miskin Manor Country House Hotel	Cardiff	0845 365 2069
Falcondale Mansion Hotel	Ceredigion	0845 365 3287
Ynyshir Hall	Ceredigion	0845 365 3426
Bodysgallen Hall & Spa	Conwy	0845 365 3039
St Tudno Hotel & Restaurant	Conwy	0845 365 2361
Hotel Maes-Y-Neuadd	Gwynedd	0845 365 1902
Palé Hall	Gwynedd	0845 365 2096
Penmaenuchaf Hall	Gwynedd	0845 365 2104
Tre-Ysgawen Hall Country House Hotel	Isle of Anglesey	0845 365 2846
The Trearddur Bay Hotel	Isle of Anglesey	0845 365 3459
Llansantffraed Court Hotel	Monmouthshire	0845 365 2035
Celtic Manor Resort	Newport	0845 365 3297
Warpool Court Hotel	Pembrokeshire	0845 365 2786
The Lake Country House and Spa	Powys	0845 365 2571
Lake Vyrnwy Hotel	Powys	0845 365 1976
Llangoed Hall	Powys	0845 365 2034
Holm House	Vale of Glamorgan	0845 365 2869

Historic Houses, Castles & Gardens

We are pleased to feature over 140 places to visit during your stay at a Condé Nast Johansens Recommendation.
More information about these attractions, including opening times and entry fees, can be found on www.johansens.com

England

Bath & North East Somerset

Cothay Manor– Greenham, Wellington, Bath & North East Somerset TA21 0JR.
Tel: 01823 672 283
Great House Farm – Wells Rd, Theale, Wedmore, Bath & North East Somerset
BS28 4SJ. Tel: 01934 713133
Orchard Wyndham – Williton, Taunton, Bath & North East Somerset TA4 4HH.
Tel: 01984 632309

Bedfordshire

Woburn Abbey – Woburn, Bedfordshire MK17 9WA.
Tel: 01525 290666
Moggerhanger Park – Park Road, Moggerhanger, Bedfordshire MK44 3RW .
Tel: 01767 641007

Buckinghamshire

Doddershall Park – Quainton, Buckinghamshire HP22 4DF.
Tel: 01296 655238
Nether Winchendon House – Nr Aylesbury, Buckinghamshire HP18 0DY.
Tel: 01844 290199
Stowe Landscape Gardens – Stowe, Buckingham, Buckinghamshire MK18 5EH.
Tel: 01280 822850
Waddesdon Manor – Waddesdon, Nr Aylesbury, Buckinghamshire HP18 0JH.
Tel: 01296 653211

Cambridgeshire

The Manor – Hemingford Grey, Huntingdon, Cambridgeshire PE28 9BN.
Tel: 01480 463134

Cheshire

Cholmondeley Castle Gardens – Malpas, Cheshire SY14 8AH.
Tel: 01829 720383
Dorfold Hall – Nantwich, Cheshire CW5 8LD. Tel: 01270 625245
Rode Hall and Gardens – Scholar Green, Cheshire ST7 3QP.
Tel: 01270 882961

Co Durham

The Bowes Museum – Barnard Castle, Co Durham DL12 8NP.
Tel: 01833 690606

Cumbria

Holker Hall and Gardens – Cark-in-Cartmel, nr Grange-over-Sands,
Cumbria LA11 7PL. Tel: 015395 58328
Isel Hall – Cockermouth, Cumbria CA13 0QG.
Tel: 01900 821778
Muncaster Castle, Gardens & Owl Centre – Ravenglass, Cumbria CA18 1RQ.
Tel: 01229 717 614

Derbyshire

Haddon Hall – Bakewell, Derbyshire DE45 1LA. Tel: 01629 812855
Melbourne Hall & Gardens – Melbourne, Derbyshire DE73 1EN.
Tel: 01332 862502
Renishaw Hall Gardens – Nr Sheffield, Derbyshire S21 3WB.
Tel: 01246 432310

Devon

Anderton House – Goodleigh, Devon. Tel: 01628 825920
Bowringsleigh – Kingsbridge, Devon TQ7 3LL. Tel: 01548 852014
Downes – Crediton, Devon EX17 3PL. Tel: 01392 439046

Dorset

Mapperton Gardens – Mapperton, Beaminster, Dorset DT8 3NR.
Tel: 01308 862645
Minterne Gardens – Minterne Magna, Nr Dorchester, Dorset DT2 7AU.
Tel: 01300 341 370
Moignes Court – Owermoigne, Dorchester, Dorset DT2 8HY. Tel: 01305 853300

Durham

Auckland Castle – Bishop Auckland, Durham DL14 7NR. Tel: 01388 601627

East Yorkshire

Burton Agnes Hall & Gardens – Burton Agnes, Diffield,
East Yorkshire YO25 4NB. Tel: 01262 490 324

Essex

The Gardens of Easton Lodge – Warwick House, Easton Lodge, Great Dunmow,
Essex CM6 2BB. Tel: 01371 876979
Ingatestone – Hall Lane, Ingatestone, Essex CM4 9NR. Tel: 01277 353010

Historic Houses, Castles & Gardens

We are pleased to feature over 140 places to visit during your stay at a Condé Nast Johansens Recommendation. More information about these attractions, including opening times and entry fees, can be found on www.johansens.com

Gloucestershire

Cheltenham Art Gallery & Museum – Clarence Street, Cheltenham, Gloucestershire GL50 3JT. Tel: 01242 237431

Frampton Court – Frampton-on-Severn, Gloucester, Gloucestershire GL2 7DY. Tel: 01452 740267

Hardwicke Court – Nr Gloucester, Gloucestershire GL2 4RS. Tel: 01452 720212

Old Campden House – Chipping Campden, Gloucestershire. Tel: 01628 825920

Sezincote House & Garden – Moreton-in-Marsh, Gloucestershire GL56 9AW. Tel: 01386 700444

Sudeley Castle Gardens and Exhibitions – Winchcombe, Gloucestershire GL54 SJP. Tel: 01242 602308

Hampshire

Avington Park – Winchester, Hampshire SO21 1DB. Tel: 01962 779260

Beaulieu – Beaulieu Enterprises Ltd, John Montagu Bldg, Hampshire SO42 7ZN. Tel: 01590 612345

Broadlands – Romsey, Hampshire SO51 9ZD. Tel: 01794 505055

Buckler's Hard – Beaulieu, Brockenhurst, Hampshire. Tel: 01590 614641

Gilbert White's House & The Oates Museum – Selborne, Nr. Alton, Hampshire GU34 3JH. Tel: 01420 511275

Greywell Hill House – Greywell, Hook, Hampshire RG29 1DG.

Pylewell Park Gardens – South Baddesley, Lymington, Hampshire SO41 55J. Tel: 1725513004

Hertfordshire

Ashridge – Berkhamsted, Hertfordshire HP4 1NS. Tel: 01442 841027

Hatfield House – Hatfield, Hertfordshire AL9 5NQ. Tel: 01707 287010

Isle of Wight

Deacons Nursery (H.H) – Moor View, Godshill, Isle of Wight PO38 3HW. Tel: 01983 840 750 or 522

Kent

Cobham Hall – Cobham, Nr Gravesend, Kent DA12 3BL. Tel: 01474 823371

The Grange – Ramsgate, Kent. Tel: 01628 825925

Groombridge Place Gardens & Enchanted Forest – Groombridge, Tunbridge Wells, Kent TN3 9QG. Tel: 01892 863999

Hever Castle and Gardens – Nr Edenbridge, Kent TN8 7NG. Tel: 01732 865224

Marle Place Gardens – Marle Place Road, Brenchley, Kent TN12 7HS. Tel: 01892 722304

The New College of Cobham – Cobhambury Road, Cobham, Nr Gravesend, Kent DA12 3BG. Tel: 01474 812503

Penshurst Place and Gardens – Penshurst, Nr Tonbridge, Kent TN11 8DG. Tel: 01892 870307

Lancashire

Stonyhurst College – Stonyhurst, Clitheroe, Lancashire BB7 9PZ. Tel: 01254 826345

Townhead House – Slaidburn, via Clitheroe, Lancashire BBY 3AG. Tel: 01772 421566

London

Handel House Museum – 25 Brook Street, London W1K 4HB. Tel: 020 7495 1685

Pitzhanger Manor House – Walpole Park, Mattock Lane, Ealing, London W5 5EQ. Tel: 020 8567 1227

St Paul's Cathedral – The Chapter House, St Paul's Churchyard, London EC4M 8AD. Tel: 020 7246 8350

Sir John Soane's Museum – 13 Lincoln's Inn Fields, London WC2A 3BP. Tel: 020 7405 2107

Syon House – Syon Park, Brentford, London TW8 8JF. Tel: 0208 560 0881

Norfolk

Walsingham Abbey Grounds – Little Walsingham, Norfolk NR22 6BP. Tel: 01328 820259

Northamptonshire

Cottesbrooke Hall and Gardens – Nr Northampton, Northamptonshire NN6 8PF. Tel: 01604 505808

Haddonstone Show Gardens – The Forge House, Church Lane, Northamptonshire NN6 8DB. Tel: 01604 770711

Northumberland

Chipchase Castle & Gardens – Wark on Tyne, Hexham, Northumberland NE48 3NT. Tel: 01434 230203

Oxfordshire

Kingston Bagpuize House – Abingdon, Oxfordshire OX13 5AX. Tel: 01865 820259

Mapledurham House – Nr Reading, Oxfordshire RG4 7TR. Tel: 01189 723 350

Stonor Park – Nr Henley-on-Thames, Oxfordshire RG9 6HF. Tel: 01491 638587

Sulgrave Manor – Manor Road, Sulgrave, Banbury, Oxfordshire OX17 2SD. Tel: 01295 760205

Historic Houses, Castles & Gardens

We are pleased to feature over 140 places to visit during your stay at a Condé Nast Johansens Recommendation.
More information about these attractions, including opening times and entry fees, can be found on www.johansens.com

Wallingford Castle Gardens – Castle Street, Wallingford, Oxfordshire OX10 0AL.
Tel: 01491 835 373

Wilmington Priory – Wilmington, Nr Eastbourne, East Sussex BN26 5SW.
Tel: 01628 825920

Shropshire

Weston Park – Weston-under-Lizard, Nr Shifnal, Shropshire TF11 8LE.
Tel: 01952 852100

Somerset

Hestercombe Gardens – Cheddon Fitzpaine, Taunton, Somerset TA2 8LG.
Tel: 01823 413923
Number One Royal Crescent – Bath Preservation Trust, Bath,
Somerset BA1 2LR. Tel: (01225) 428126
Robin Hood's Hut – Halswell, Goathurst, Somerset. Tel: 01628 825925

Staffordshire

Ancient High House – Greengate Street, Stafford, Staffordshire ST16 2JA.
Tel: 01785 619 131
Izaak Walton's Cottage – Worston Lane, Shallowford, Staffordshire ST15 0PA.
Tel: 01785 760 278
Stafford Castle & Visitor Centre – Newport Road, Stafford,
Staffordshire ST16 1DJ. Tel: 01785 257 698
Whitmore Hall – Whitmore, Nr Newcastle-under-Lyme, Staffordshire ST5 5HW.
Tel: 01782 680478

Suffolk

Ancient House – Clare, Suffolk CO10 8NY. Tel: 01628 825920
Freston Tower – Near Ipswich, Suffolk. Tel: 01628 825920
Kentwell Hall – Long Melford, Sudbury, Suffolk CO10 9BA. Tel: 01787 310207
Newbourne Hall – Newbourne, Nr Woodbridge, Suffolk IP12 4NP.
Tel: 01473 736764

Surrey

Claremont House – Claremont Drive, Esher, Surrey KT10 9LY.
Tel: 01372 473623
Goddards – Abinger Common, Dorking, Surrey RH5 6TH. Tel: 01628 825920
Guildford House Gallery – 155 High Street, Guildford, Surrey GU1 3AJ.
Tel: 01483 444740
Loseley Park – Guildford, Surrey GU3 1HS. Tel: 01483 304 440

East Sussex

Anne of Cleves House – 52 Southover High Street, Lewes, East Sussex BN7 1JA.
Tel: 01273 474610
Bentley Wildfowl & Motor Museum – Halland, Nr Lewes, East Sussex BN8 5AF.
Tel: 01825 840573
Charleston – Firle, Nr Lewes, East Sussex BN8 6LL. Tel: 01323 811626
Gardens and Grounds of Herstmonceux Castle – Hailsham,
East Sussex BN27 1RN. Tel: 01323 833816
Michelham Priory – Upper Dicker, Hailsham, East Sussex BN27 3QS.
Tel: 01323 844 224

West Sussex

Denmans Garden – Denmans Lane, Fontwell, West Sussex BN18 0SU.
Tel: 01243 542808

Firle Place – Nr Lewes, West Sussex BN8 6LP. **Tel: 01273 8583**
Fishbourne Roman Palace – Salthill Road, Fishbourne, Chichester, West Sussex
PO19 3QR. Tel: 01243 785859
Goodwood House – Goodwood, Chichester, West Sussex PO18 0QP.
Tel: 01243 538449
High Beeches Gardens – Handcross, West Sussex RH17 6HQ. Tel: 01444 400589
Leonardslee Lakes and Gardens – Lower Beeding, West Sussex RH13 6PP.
Lewes Castle – Barbican House, 169 High Street, Lewes,
West Sussex BN7 1YE. Tel: 01273 486 290
Marlipins Museum – High Street, Shoreham-by-Sea, West Sussex BN43 5DA.
Tel: 01273 462994
Parham House & Gardens – Parham Park, Nr Pulborough,
West Sussex RH20 4HS. Tel: 01903 742021
The Priest House – North Lane, West Hoathly, West Sussex RH19 4PP.
Tel: 01342 810479
West Dean Gardens – The Edward James Foundation, Estate Office West Dean,
Chichester, West Sussex PO18 0QZ. Tel: 01243 818210
Worthing Museum & Art Gallery – Chapel Road, Worthing,
West Sussex BN11 1HP. Tel: 01903 239999

Warwickshire

Arbury Hall – Nuneaton, Warwickshire CV10 7PT. Tel: 02476 382804
Kenilworth Castle – Kenilworth, Warwickshire CV8 1NE. Tel: 01926 852078
Shakespeare Houses – The Shakespeare Centre, Henley Street, Stratford-upon-
Avon, Warwickshire CV37 6QW. Tel: 01789 204016

West Midlands

The Barber Institute of Fine Arts – University of Birmingham, Edgbaston,
Birmingham, West Midlands B15 2TS. Tel: 0121 414 7333
The Birmingham Botanical Gardens & Glasshouses – Westbourne Road,
Edgbaston, Birmingham, West Midlands B15 3TR. Tel: 0121 454 1860

Historic Houses, Castles & Gardens

We are pleased to feature over 140 places to visit during your stay at a Condé Nast Johansens Recommendation.
More information about these attractions, including opening times and entry fees, can be found on www.johansens.com

Worcestershire

Harvington Hall – Harvington, Kidderminster, Worcestershire DY10 4LR.
Tel: 01562 777846

Little Malvern Court – Nr Malvern, Worcestershire WR14 4JN.
Tel: 01684 892988

Witley Court and Gardens – Witley Court, Great Witley, Worcestershire WR6 6JT.

North Yorkshire

Castle Howard – Nr York, North Yorkshire YO60 7DA. Tel: 01653 648333

Duncombe Park – Helmsley, Ryedale, York, North Yorkshire YO62 5EB.
Tel: 01439 770213

Forbidden Corner – Tupgill Park Estate, Coverham, Nr Middleham,
North Yorkshire DL8 4TJ. Tel: 01969 640638

Fountains Abbey and Studley Royal Water Garden – Ripon Nr Harrogate,
North Yorkshire HG4 3DY. Tel: 01765 608888

Ripley Castle – Ripley Castle Estate, Harrogate, North Yorkshire HG3 3AY.
Tel: 01423 770152

Skipton Castle – Skipton, North Yorkshire BD23 1AW. Tel: 01756 792442

West Yorkshire

Bramham Park – The Estate Office, Bramham Park, Wetherby,
West Yorkshire LS23 6ND. Tel: 01937 846000

Bronte Parsonage Museum – Church Street, Haworth, West Yorkshire.
Tel: 01535 642323

N. Ireland

North Down Museum – Town Hall, Bangor, Down BT20 4BT, N. Ireland.
Tel: 02891 271200

Seaforde Gardens – Seaforde, Downpatrick, Down BT30 8PG, N. Ireland.
Tel: 028 4481 1225

Ireland

Bantry House & Gardens – Bantry, Cork, Ireland. Tel: 00 353 2 750 047

Blarney Castle , House and Gardens – Blarney, Co. Cork, Ireland.
Tel: 00 353 21 385252

Dunloe Castle Hotel Gardens – Gap of Dunloe, Beaufort, Killarney, Co Kerry,
Ireland. Tel: 00 353 64 44111

Kilmokea Country Manor and Gardens – Great Island, Campile, Wexford,
Ireland. Tel: 00 35351 388109

Lismore Castle Gardens & Art Gallery – Lismore, Waterford, Ireland.
Tel: 00 353 (0)5854424

Scotland

Ardwell Gardens – Ardwell House, Ardwell, Stranraer, Dumfries & Galloway
DG9 9LY. Tel: 01776 860 227

Auchinleck House – Ochiltree, North Ayrshire. Tel: 01628 825920

Balfour Castle – Shapinsay, Orkney KW17 2DY. Tel: 01856 711282

Bowhill House & Country Park – Bowhill, Selkirk, Scottish Borders TD7 5ET.
Tel: 01750 22204

Callendar House – Callendar Park, Falkirk FK1 1YR. Tel: 01324 503770

Castle Kennedy Gardens – The Estates Office, Rephad, Stranraer, Dumfries &
Galloway DG9 8BX. Tel: (01776) 702024

Drumlanrig Castle, Gardens & Country Park – Thornhill, Dumfriesshire,
Dumfries & Galloway DG3 4AQ. Tel: 01848 331555

Floors Castle – Kelso, Borders TD5 7SF. Tel: 01573 223333

Golden Grove – Llanasa, Nr Holywell, Flintshire CH8 9NA. Tel: 01745 854452

Inveraray Castle – Cherry Park, Inveraray, Highland PA32 8XF.
Tel: 01499 302 203

Kelburn Castle and Country Centre – Kelburn, Fairlie (Nr Largs),
Ayrshire KA29 0BE. Tel: 01475 568685

Manderston – Duns, Berwickshire, Scottish Borders TD11 3PP.
Tel: 01361 883 450

Newliston – Kirkliston, West Lothian EH29 9EB.
Tel: 0131 333 3231

Paxton House & Country Park – Paxton, Nr Berwick upon Tweed, Scottish
Borders TD15 1SZ. Tel: 01289 386291

Traquair House – Innerleithen, Peebles, Scottish Borders EH44 6PW.
Tel: 01896 830 323

Wales

Bodnant Garden – Tal Y Cafn, Conwy LL28 5RE. Tel: 01492 650460

Dolbelydr – Trefnant, Denbighshire. Tel: 01628 825920

Llanvihangel Court – Nr Abergavenny, Monmouthshire NP7 8DH.
Tel: 01873 890 217

Plas Brondanw Gardens – Llanfrothen, Nr Penrhyndeudraeth,
Gwynedd LL48 6ET. Tel: 01743 241181

St Davids Cathedral – The Deanery, The Close, St Davids,
Pembrokeshire SA62 6RH. Tel: 01437 720 199

Usk Castle – Castle House, Monmouth Rd, Usk, Monmouthshire NP15 1SD.
Tel: 01291 672563

France

Château de Chenonceau – 37150 Chenonceaux, France 37150, France.
Tel: 00 33 2 47 23 90 07

The Netherlands

Het Loo Palace National Museum – Koninklijk Park 1, NL–7315 JA Apeldoorn,
The Netherlands. Tel: 00 31 55 577 2400

Hotels, Europe & The Mediterranean

All the properties listed below can be found in our Recommended Hotels & Spas, Europe & The Mediterranean 2008 Guide.
More information on our portfolio of guides can be found on page 343.

Andorra

Sport Hotel Hermitage & Spa ....Soldeu ....+376 870 670

Austria

Palais Coburg Residenz.......................Vienna ....+43 1 518 180

Belgium

Firean Hotel ....Antwerp ....+32 3 237 02 60
Hotel Die Swaene ....Bruges ....+32 50 34 27 98
Romantik Hotel Manoir du Dragon ..Knokke~Heist............................+32 50 63 05 80
Grand Hotel Damier ....Kortrijk ....+32 56 22 15 47
Hostellerie Ter Driezen ....Turnhout ....+32 14 41 87 57

Croatia

Stancija Meneghetti ....Bale ....+385 52 528 816
Grand Villa Argentina........................Dubrovnik ....+385 20 44 0555

Czech Republic

Alchymist Grand Hotel and Spa ....Prague...+420 257 286 011
Aria Hotel Prague..............................Prague...+420 225 334 111
Bellagio Hotel Prague ....Prague...+420 221 778 999
Golden Well Hotel ....Prague...+420 257 011 213
The Iron Gate Hotel & Suites ....Prague...+420 225 777 777
Nosticova Residence ....Prague...+420 257 312 513
Hotel Nautilus ....Tábor..+420 380 900 900

Estonia

Ammende Villa ....Pärnu ....+372 44 73 888
The Three Sisters Hotel ....Tallinn ....+372 630 6300

France

Château d'Isenbourg ....Alsace~Lorraine.........................+33 3 89 78 58 50
Château de L'Ile ....Alsace~Lorraine.........................+33 3 88 66 85 00
Domaine de la Grange de Condé ......Alsace~Lorraine.........................+33 3 87 79 30 50
Hostellerie les Bas Rupts
  Le Chalet Fleuri ....Alsace~Lorraine.........................+33 3 29 63 09 25
Hôtel à la Cour d'Alsace.....................Alsace~Lorraine.........................+33 3 88 95 07 00
Hôtel Les Têtes ....Alsace~Lorraine.........................+33 3 89 24 43 43
Romantik Hôtel le Maréchal ....Alsace~Lorraine.........................+33 3 89 41 60 32
Château de Bonaban ....Brittany ....+33 2 99 58 24 50
Domaine de Bodeuc............................Brittany ....+33 2 99 90 89 63
Domaine de Rochevilaine ....Brittany ....+33 2 97 41 61 61
Hôtel et Spa de La Bretesche ....Brittany ....+33 2 51 76 86 96
Hôtel l'Agapa & Spa ....Brittany ....+33 2 96 49 01 10
Manoir de Kertalg ....Brittany ....+33 2 98 39 77 77
Ti al Lannec.......................................Brittany ....+33 2 96 15 01 01

Château Hôtel André Ziltener ....Burgandy
                                         - Franche~Comte..............+33 3 80 62 41 62
Abbaye de la Bussière ....Burgundy
                                         - Franche~Comté..............+33 3 80 49 02 29
Château de Gilly ....Burgundy
                                         - Franche~Comté..............+33 3 80 62 89 98
Château de Vault de Lugny ....Burgundy
                                         - Franche~Comté..............+33 3 86 34 07 86
Château les Roches ....Burgundy
                                         - Franche~Comté..............+33 3 80 84 32 71
Hostellerie des Monts de Vaux...........Burgundy
                                         - Franche~Comté..............+33 3 84 37 12 50
Château d'Etoges................................Champagne~Ardennes ....+33 3 26 59 30 08
Château de Fère ....Champagne~Ardennes ....+33 3 23 82 21 13
Domaine du Château de Barive.........Champagne~Ardennes ....+33 3 23 22 15 15
Le Moulin du Landion ....Champagne~Ardennes ....+33 3 25 27 92 17
Alain Llorca - Le Moulin de Mougins..Côte d'Azur ....+33 4 93 75 78 24

Château Eza ....Côte d'Azur...................+33 4 93 41 12 24
La Ferme d'Augustin ....Côte d'Azur ....+33 4 94 55 97 00
La Villa Mauresque ....Côte d'Azur ....+33 494 83 02 42
Le Bailli de Suffren ....Côte d'Azur ....+33 4 98 04 47 00
Le Mas d'Artigny & Spa ....Côte d'Azur ....+33 4 93 32 84 54
Château d'Artigny ....Loire Valley ....+33 2 47 34 30 30
Château de la Barre............................Loire Valley ....+33 2 43 35 00 17
Château de Pray ....Loire Valley ....+33 247 57 23 67
Domaine de Beauvois ....Loire Valley ....+33 2 47 55 50 11
Domaine de la Tortinière ....Loire Valley ....+33 2 47 34 35 00
Hostellerie des Hauts
  de Sainte~Maure ....Loire Valley ....+33 2 47 65 50 65
Le Choiseul ....Loire Valley ....+33 2 47 30 45 45
Le Manoir les Minimes ....Loire Valley ....+33 2 47 30 40 40
Le Prieuré...Loire Valley ....+33 2 41 67 90 14
Château de Floure ....Midi~Pyrénées ....+33 4 68 79 11 29
Hôtel Lous Grits ....Midi~Pyrénées ....+33 562 283 710
Relais Royal ....Midi~Pyrénées ....+33 5 61 60 19 19
Château la Chenevière ....Normandy ....+33 2 31 51 25 25
Château les Bruyères ....Normandy ....+33 2 31 32 22 45
Domaine Saint~Clair, Le Donjon........Normandy ....+33 2 35 27 08 23
Le Castel...Normandy ....+33 2 33 17 00 45
Manoir de la Poterie,
  Spa "Les Thermes" ....Normandy ....+33 2 31 88 10 40
Manoir de Mathan ....Normandy ....+33 2 31 22 21 73
Carlton Hôtel ....North - Picardy ....+33 3 20 13 33 13
Château de Cocove.............................North - Picardy ....+33 3 21 82 68 29
La Chartreuse du Val Saint~Esprit ....North - Picardy ....+33 3 21 62 80 00
La Howarderie ....North - Picardy ....+33 3 20 10 31 00

Hotels, Europe & The Mediterranean

All the properties listed below can be found in our Recommended Hotels & Spas, Europe & The Mediterranean 2008 Guide. More information on our portfolio of guides can be found on page 343.

Hospes Lancaster	Paris	+33 1 40 76 40 76
Hôtel Balzac	Paris	+33 1 44 35 18 00
Hôtel de Sers	Paris	+33 1 53 23 75 75
Hôtel du Petit Moulin	Paris	+33 1 42 74 10 10
Hôtel Duc de Saint~Simon	Paris	+33 1 44 39 20 20
Hôtel Duret	Paris	+33 1 45 00 42 60
Hôtel le Tourville	Paris	+33 1 47 05 62 62
Hôtel Opéra Richepanse	Paris	+33 1 42 60 36 00
Hôtel San Régis	Paris	+33 1 44 95 16 16
La Trémoille	Paris	+33 1 56 52 14 00
La Villa Maillot	Paris	+33 1 53 64 52 52
Le Sainte~Beuve	Paris	+33 1 45 48 20 07
Cazaudehore "La Forestière"	Paris Region	+33 1 30 61 64 64
Château d'Esclimont	Paris Region	+33 2 37 31 15 15
Hostellerie du Bas-Breau	Paris Region	+33 1 60 66 40 05
Le Manoir de Gressy	Paris Region	+33 1 60 26 68 00
Château de L'Yeuse	Poitou~Charentes	+33 5 45 36 82 60
Hôtel "Résidence de France"	Poitou~Charentes	+33 5 46 28 06 00
Hôtel de Toiras	Poitou~Charentes	+33 546 35 40 32
Relais de Saint~Preuil	Poitou~Charentes	+33 5 45 80 80 08
Bastide du Calalou	Provence	+33 4 94 70 17 91
Château de Massillan	Provence	+33 4 90 40 64 51
Château de Montcaud	Provence	+33 4 66 89 60 60
Château des Alpilles	Provence	+33 4 90 92 03 33
Domaine le Hameau des Baux	Provence	+33 4 90 54 10 30
L'Estelle en Camargue	Provence	+33 4 90 97 89 01
Le Mas de la Rose	Provence	+33 4 90 73 08 91
Le Spinaker	Provence	+33 4 66 53 36 37
Les Mas des Herbes Blanches	Provence	+33 4 90 05 79 79
Manoir de la Roseraie	Provence	+33 4 75 46 58 15
Chalet Hôtel La Marmotte	Rhône~Alpes	+33 4 50 75 80 33
Château de Bagnols	Rhône~Alpes	+33 4 74 71 40 00
Château de Coudrée	Rhône~Alpes	+33 4 50 72 62 33
Château de Divonne	Rhône~Alpes	+33 4 50 20 00 32
Domaine de Divonne	Rhône~Alpes	+33 4 50 40 34 34
Le Beau Rivage	Rhône~Alpes	+33 4 74 56 82 82
Le Fer à Cheval	Rhône~Alpes	+33 4 50 21 30 39
Château de Sanse	South West	+33 5 57 56 41 10
Château Le Mas de Montet	South West	+33 5 53 90 08 71
Hôtel du Palais	South West	+33 5 59 41 64 00
Le Relais du Château Franc Mayne	South West	+33 5 57 24 62 61
Château des Briottières	Western Loire	+33 2 41 42 00 02

Great Britain

Luton Hoo Hotel, Golf & Spa	Bedfordshire	+44 1582 734437
The French Horn	Berkshire	+44 1189 692 204
Soar Mill Cove Hotel	Devon	+44 1548 561 566
Ashdown Park Hotel	East Sussex	+44 1342 824 988
The Grand Hotel	East Sussex	+44 1323 412345
Rye Lodge	East Sussex	+44 1797 223838
Tylney Hall	Hampshire	+44 1256 764881
Jumeirah Carlton Tower	London	+44 20 7235 1234
Jumeirah Lowndes Hotel	London	+44 20 7823 1234
The Mayflower Hotel	London	+44 20 7370 0991
Twenty Nevern Square	London	+44 20 7565 9555
Hoar Cross Hall Spa Resort	Staffordshire	+44 1283 575671
Nailcote Hall	Warwickshire	+44 2476 466 174

Greece

Hotel Pentelikon	Athens	+30 2 10 62 30 650
Argentikon Luxury Suites	Chios	+30 227 10 33 111
Villa de Loulia	Corfu	+30 266 30 95 394
Elounda Gulf Villas & Suites	Crete	+30 28410 90300
Elounda Peninsula All Suite Hotel	Crete	+30 28410 68250

Paradise Island Villas	**Crete**	**+30 289 702 2893**
Pleiades Luxurious Villas	Crete	+30 28410 90450
St Nicolas Bay Resort Hotel & Villas	Crete	+30 2841 025041
Imaret	Kavala	+30 2510 620 151
Pavezzo Country Retreat	Lefkada	+30 26450 71782
Apanema	Mykonos	+30 22890 28590
Tharroe of Mykonos	Mykonos	+30 22890 27370
Nikos Takis Fashion Hotel	Rhodes	+30 22410 70773
Alexander's Boutique Hotel	Santorini	+30 22860 71818
Canaves Oia	Santorini	+30 22860 71453
Xenon Estate	Spetses	+30 22980 74120

Hungary

Allegro Hotel - Tihany Centrum	Tihany - Lake Balaton	+36 87 448 456

Italy

Furore Inn Resort & Spa	Campania	+39 089 830 4711
Hotel Villa Maria	Campania	+39 089 857255
Maison La Minervetta	Campania	+39 081 877 4455
Manzi Terme Hotel & Spa	Campania	+39 081994722
Hotel des Nations	Emilia Romagna	+39 0541 647 878
Hotel Posta (Historical Residence)	Emilia Romagna	+39 05 22 43 29 44
Hotel Villa Roncuzzi	Emilia Romagna	+39 0544 534776
Palazzo Dalla Rosa Prati	Emilia Romagna	+39 0521 386 429
Torre di San Martino		
- Historical Residence	Emilia Romagna	+39 0523 972002
Urban Hotel Design	Friuli Venezia	+39 040 302065
Buonanotte Garibaldi	Lazio	+390 658 330 733
Hotel dei Borgognoni	Lazio	+39 06 6994 1505
Hotel dei Consoli	Lazio	+39 0668 892 972
Hotel Fenix	Lazio	+39 06 8540 741
Hotel Villa Clementina	Lazio	+39 06 9986268
La Locanda della Chiocfciola	Lazio	+39 0761 402 734
La Posta Vecchia Hotel Spa	Lazio	+39 0699 49501
Relais Falisco	Lazio	+39 0761 54 98
Relais Le Torrette	Lazio	+39 0763 726009

Hotels, Europe & The Mediterranean

All the properties listed below can be found in our Recommended Hotels & Spas, Europe & The Mediterranean 2008 Guide. More information on our portfolio of guides can be found on page 343.

Villa Spalletti Trivelli ....Lazio ....+39 06 48907934

Abbadia San Giorgio

- Historical Residence ....Liguria ....+39 0185 491119

Grand Hotel Diana Majestic.................Liguria ....+39 0183 402 727

Grand Hotel Miramare.......................Liguria ....+39 0185 287013

Hotel Punta Est ....Liguria ....+39 019 600611

Hotel San Giorgio

- Portofino House ....Liguria ....+39 0185 26991

Hotel Vis à Vis............................Liguria ....+39 0185 42661

Bagni di Bormio Spa Resort ....Lombardy ....+39 0342 910131

Grand Hotel Gardone Riviera ....Lombardy ....+39 0365 20261

Grand Hotel Villa Serbelloni ....Lombardy ....+39 031 950 216450

Hotel Bellerive ....Lombardy ....+39 0365 520 410

Hotel de la Ville ....Lombardy ....+39 039 3942 1

I Due Roccoli Relais ....Lombardy ....+39 030 9822 977

L'Albereta ....Lombardy ....+39 030 7760 550

Petit Palais maison de charme ....Lombardy ....+39 02 584 891

THE PLACE

- Luxury serviced apartments ....Lombardy ....+39 02 76026633

Albergo L'Ostelliere ....Piemonte ....+39 0143 607 801

Foresteria dei Poderi Einaudi ....Piemonte ....+39 0173 70414

Hotel Cristallo ....Piemonte ....+39 0163 922 822

Hotel Pironi...............................Piemonte ....+39 0323 70624

Hotel Principi di Piemonte ....Piemonte ....+39 011 55151

Hotel Villa Aminta ....Piemonte ....+39 0323 933 818

Relais Il Borgo ....Piemonte ....+39 0141 921272

Villa dal Pozzo d'Annone ....Piemonte ....+39 0322 7255

Country House Cefalicchio ....Puglia ....+39 0883 662 736

Hotel Titano ....San Marino Republic.................+378 991007

Grand Hotel in Porto Cervo ....Sardinia ....+39 0789 91533

Tartheshotel..............................Sardinia ....+39 070 97 29000

Villa del Parco and Spa,
   Forte Village.....................Sardinia ....+39 070 92171

Villa Las Tronas ....Sardinia ....+39 079 981 818

Baia Taormina Grand Palace

   Hotels & Spa ....Sicily ....+39 0942 756292

Grand Hotel Arciduca......................Sicily ....+39 090 9812136

Grand Hotel Atlantis Bay..................Sicily ....+39 0942 618011

Grand Hotel Mazzarò Sea Palace .....Sicily ....+39 0942 612111

Hotel Signum..............................Sicily ....+39 090 9844222

Locanda Don Serafino ....Sicily ....+39 0932 220065

Palazzo Failla Hotel ....Sicily ....+39 0932 941059

Poggio del Sole Resort....................Sicily ....+39 0932 666 452

Therasia Resort ....Sicily ....+39 090 9852555

Castel Fragsburg ....Trentino - Alto Adige /
                            Dolomites ....+39 0473 244071

Du Lac et du Parc Grand Resort........Trentino - Alto Adige /
                            Dolomites ....+39 0464 566600

Hotel Gardena Grödnerhof ....Trentino - Alto Adige /
                            Dolomites ....+39 0471 796 315

Posthotel Cavallino Bianco ....Trentino - Alto Adige /
                            Dolomites ....+39 0471 613113

Romantik Hotel Art Hotel Cappella ..Trentino - Alto Adige /
                            Dolomites ....+39 0471 836183

Albergo Pietrasanta

- Palazzo Barsanti Bonetti ....Tuscany ....+39 0584 793 727

Albergo Villa Marta ....Tuscany ....+39 0583 37 01 01

Borgo La Bagnaia Resort,
   Spa and Events Venue ....Tuscany ....+39 0577 813000

Casa Howard Guest Houses

- Rome and Florence ....Tuscany ....+39 066 992 4555

Castello Banfi - Il Borgo ....Tuscany ....+39 0577 877 700

Country House Casa Cornacchi ....Tuscany ....+39 055 998229

Hotel Byron...............................Tuscany ....+39 0584 787 052

Hotel Plaza e de Russie ....Tuscany ....+39 0584 44449

Hotel Villa Ottone ....Tuscany ....+39 0565 933 042

Il Pellicano Hotel & Spa ....Tuscany ....+39 0564 858111

L'Andana ....Tuscany ....+39 0564 944 800

Lucignanello Bandini ....Tuscany ....+39 0577 803 068

Marignolle Relais & Charme ....Tuscany ....+39 055 228 6910

Monsignor Della Casa
   Country Resort.........................Tuscany ....+39 055 840 821

Pieve di Caminino
   (Historical Residence) ....Tuscany ....+39 0564 569 736

Relais la Suvera (Dimora Storica).......Tuscany ....+39 0577 960 300

Relais Piazza Signoria ....Tuscany ....+39 055 3987239

Relais Villa Belpoggio
   (Historical House) ....Tuscany ....+39 055 9694411

Residenza del Moro ....Tuscany ....+39 055 290884

Tombolo Talasso Resort ....Tuscany ....+39 0565 74530

Villa Bordoni ....Tuscany ....+39 055 884 0004

Villa le Piazzole ....Tuscany ....+39 055 223520

Villa Marsili ....Tuscany ....+39 0575 605 252

Villa Poggiano ....Tuscany ....+39 0578 758292

Abbazia San Faustino

- Luxury Country House ....Umbria ....+39 0720 1717

Castello di Petroia ....Umbria ....+39 075 92 02 87

I Casali di Monticchio ....Umbria ....+39 0763 62 83 65

L'Antico Forziere ....Umbria ....+39 075 972 4314

La Preghiera ....Umbria ....+39 075 9302428

Le Torri di Bagnara
   (Medieval Historical Residences) ....Umbria ....+39 075 579 2001

Relais Alla Corte del Sole................Umbria ....+39 075 9689 008

Relais Todini ....Umbria ....+39 075 887521

Romantik Hotel
   le Silve di Armenzano ....Umbria ....+39 075 801 9000

San Crispino Resort & Spa ....Umbria ....+39 075 804 3257

Hotel Jolanda Sport ....Valle d'Aosta.......................+39 0125 366 140

Mont Blanc Hotel Village ....Valle d'Aosta ....+39 0165 864 111

Ai Capitani Hotel ....Veneto ....+39 045 6400782

Albergo Quattro Fontane

- Residenza d'Epoca ....Veneto ....+39 041 526 0227

Ca Maria Adele ....Veneto ....+39 041 52 03 078

Hotels, Europe & The Mediterranean

All the properties listed below can be found in our Recommended Hotels & Spas, Europe & The Mediterranean 2008 Guide. More information on our portfolio of guides can be found on page 343.

Ca' Nigra Lagoon Resort	Veneto	+39 041 2750047
Ca' Sagredo Hotel	Veneto	+39 041 2413111
Charming House DD724	Veneto	+39 041 277 0262
Color Hotel	Veneto	+39 045 621 0857
Hotel Flora	Veneto	+39 041 52 05 844
Hotel Gabbia d'Oro (Historical Residence)	Veneto	+39 045 8003060
Hotel Giorgione	Veneto	+39 041 522 5810
Hotel Sant' Elena Venezia	Veneto	+39 041 27 17 811
Hotel Villa Ca' Sette	Veneto	+39 0424 383 350
Locanda San Verolo	Veneto	+39 045 720 09 30
Locanda San Vigilio	Veneto	+39 045 725 66 88
Londra Palace	Veneto	+39 041 5200533
Methis Hotel	Veneto	+39 049 872 5555
Novecento Boutique Hotel	Veneto	+39 041 24 13 765
Park Hotel Brasilia	Veneto	+39 0421 380851
Relais Duca di Dolle	Veneto	+39 0438 975 809
Relais la Magioca	Veneto	+39 045 600 0167

Latvia

TB Palace Hotel & Spa	Jūrmala	+371 714 7094
Hotel Bergs	Riga	+371 6777 0900

Lithuania

Grotthuss Hotel	Vilnius	+370 5 266 0322
The Narutis Hotel	Vilnius	+370 5 2122 894

Luxembourg

Hotel Saint~Nicolas	Remich	+35 226 663

The Netherlands

Ambassade Hotel	Amsterdam	+31 20 5550 222
Duin & Kruidberg Country Estate	Santpoort	+31 23 512 1800
Auberge de Campveerse Toren	Veere	+31 0118 501 291

Portugal

Quinta Jacintina	Almancil	+351 289 350 090
Ria Park Hotel & Spa	Almancil	+351 289 359 800
Casa do Terreiro do Poço	Borba	+351 917 256077
Albatroz Palace, Luxury Suites	Cascais	+351 21 484 73 80
Hotel Cascais Mirage	Cascais	+351 210 060 600
Quinta de San José	Ervedosa Do Douro	+351 254 420000
Hotel Palacio Estoril Hotel and Golf	Estoril	+351 21 468 0400
Convento do Espinheiro Heritage Hotel & Spa	Evora	+351 266 788 200
Quinta da Bela Vista	Funchal	+351 291 706 400
Quinta das Vistas Palace Gardens	Funchal	+351 291 750 000
Hotel Lusitano	Golegã	+351 249 979 170
As Janelas Verdes	Lisbon	+351 21 39 68 143
Heritage Av Liberdade	Lisbon	+351 213 404 040
Hotel Aviz	Lisbon	+351 210 402 000
Hotel Britania	Lisbon	+351 21 31 55 016
Casas do Côro	Marialva - Mêda	+351 91 755 2020
Vintage House	Pinhão	+351 254 730 230
Estalagem da Ponta do Sol	Ponta do Sol	+351 291 970 200
Hotel Quinta do Lago	Quinta do Lago - Almancil	+351 289 350 350
Convento de São Paulo	Redondo	+351 266 989 160

Slovenia

Hotel Golf Bled	**Bled**	**+386 4579 1700**

Spain

Barceló la Bobadilla	Andalucía	+34 958 32 18 61
Casa de los Bates	Andalucía	+34 958 349 495
Casa No 7	Andalucía	+34 954 221 581
Casa Romana Hotel Boutique	Andalucía	+34 954 915 170
Casa Viña de Alcantara	Andalucía	+34 956 393 010
Cortijo Soto Real	Andalucía	+34 955 869 200
El Ladrón de Agua	Andalucía	+34 958 21 50 40
El Molino de Santillán	Andalucía	+34 952 40 09 49
Fairplay Golf Hotel & Spa	Andalucía	+34 956 429100
Gran Hotel Elba Estepona & Thalasso Spa	Andalucía	+34 952 809 200
Hacienda Benazuza el Bulli Hotel	Andalucía	+34 955 70 33 44
Hacienda La Boticaria	Andalucía	+34 955 69 88 20
Hospes las Casas del Rey de Baeza	Andalucía	+34 954 561 496
Hospes Palacio de los Patos	Andalucía	+34 958 535 790
Hospes Palacio del Bailío	Andalucía	+34 957 498 993
Hotel Almenara	Andalucía	+34 956 58 20 00
Hotel Casa Morisca	Andalucía	+34 958 221 100
Hotel Cortijo Faín	Andalucía	+34 956 704 131
Hotel La Fuente del Sol	Andalucía	+34 95 12 39 823
Hotel La Viñuela	Andalucía	+34 952 519 193
Hotel Molina Lario	Andalucía	+34 952 06 002
Hotel Palacio de Los Granados	Andalucía	+34 955 905 344
Hotel Palacio de Santa Inés	Andalucía	+34 958 22 23 62
La Posada del Torcal	Andalucía	+34 952 03 11 77
Los Castaños	Andalucía	+34 952 180 778
Mikasa Suites Resort	Andalucía	+34 950 138 073
Palacio de los Navas	Andalucía	+34 958 21 57 60

Hotels, Europe & The Mediterranean

All the properties listed below can be found in our Recommended Hotels & Spas, Europe & The Mediterranean 2008 Guide. More information on our portfolio of guides can be found on page 343.

Palacio de San Benito	Andalucía	+34 954 88 33 36
Posada de Palacio	Andalucía	+34 956 36 4840
Santa Isabel la Real	Andalucía	+34 958 294 658
Hotel el Privilegio de Tena	Aragón	+34 974 487 206
Hotel La Cepada	Asturias	+34 985 84 94 45
Palacio de Cutre	Asturias	+34 985 70 80 72
Atzaró Agroturismo	Balearic Islands	+34 971 33 88 38
Blau Porto Petro Beach Resort & Spa	Balearic Islands	+34 971 648 282
Can Lluc	Balearic Islands	+34 971 198 673
Can Simoneta	Balearic Islands	+34 971 816 110
Cas Gasi	Balearic Islands	+34 971 197 700

Hospes Maricel	**Balearic Islands**	**+34 971 707 744**
Hotel Aimia	Balearic Islands	+34 971 631 200
Hotel Cala Sant Vicenç	Balearic Islands	+34 971 53 02 50
Hotel Dalt Murada	Balearic Islands	+34 971 425 300
Hotel Hacienda Na Xamena	Balearic Islands	+34 971 334 500
Hotel La Moraleja	Balearic Islands	+34 971 534 010
Hotel Migjorn	Balearic Islands	+34 971 650 668
Hotel Tres	Balearic Islands	+34 971 717 333
Palacio Ca Sa Galesa	Balearic Islands	+34 971 715 400
Read's Hotel & Vespasian Spa	Balearic Islands	+34 971 14 02 61
Son Brull Hotel & Spa	Balearic Islands	+34 971 53 53 53
Valldemossa Hotel & Restaurant	Balearic Islands	+34 971 61 26 26
Abama	Canary Islands	+34 902 105 600
Hotel Elba Palace Golf	Canary Islands	+34 928 16 39 22
Hotel Jardín Tropical	Canary Islands	+34 922 74 60 00
Hotel las Madrigueras	Canary Islands	+34 922 77 78 18
Jardín de la Paz	Canary Islands	+34 922 578 818
Kempinski Atlantis Bahía Real	Canary Islands	+34 928 53 64 44
Princesa Yaiza Suite Hotel Resort	Canary Islands	+34 928 519 222
Posada Los Nogales	Cantabria	+34 942 589 222
Castillo de Buen Amor	Castilla y León	+34 923 355 002
Hacienda Zorita	Castilla y León	+34 923 129 400
Hotel Rector	Castilla y León	+34 923 21 84 82
Posada de la Casa del Abad de Ampudia	Castilla y León	+34 979 768 008
Finca Canturias	Castilla~La Mancha	+34 925 59 41 08
Hotel Palacio de la Serna	Castilla~La Mancha	+34 926 842413
Can Bonastre Wine Resort	Cataluña	+34 91 772 87 67
Dolce Sitges Hotel	Cataluña	+34 938 109 000
El Convent Begur	Cataluña	+34 972 62 30 91
Gallery Hotel	Cataluña	+34 934 15 99 11
Grand Hotel Central	Cataluña	+34 93 295 79 00
Hospes Villa Paulita	Cataluña	+34 972 884 662
Hotel Casa Fuster	Cataluña	+34 93 255 30 00

Hotel Claris	Cataluña	+34 93 487 62 62
Hotel Cram	Cataluña	+34 93 216 77 00
Hotel Duquesa de Cardona	Cataluña	+34 93 268 90 90
Hotel Gran Derby	Cataluña	+34 93 445 2544
Hotel Granados 83	Cataluña	+34 93 492 96 70
Hotel Omm	Cataluña	+34 93 445 40 00
Hotel Rigat Park & Spa Beach Hotel	Cataluña	+34 972 36 52 00
Hotel Santa Marta	Cataluña	+34 972 364 904
Le Meridien Ra Beach Hotel & Spa	Cataluña	+34 977 694 200
Mas Passamaner	Cataluña	+34 977 766 333
Romantic Villa - Hotel Vistabella	Cataluña	+34 972 25 62 00
San Sebastian Playa Hotel	Cataluña	+34 93 894 86 76
Casa Palacio Conde de la Corte	Extremadura	+34 924 563 311
Antiguo Convento	Madrid	+34 91 632 22 20
Gran Meliá Fénix	Madrid	+34 91 431 67 00
Hospes Madrid	Madrid	+34 902 254 255
Hotel Orfila	Madrid	+34 91 702 77 70
Hotel Quinta de los Cedros	Madrid	+34 91 515 2200
Hotel Urban	Madrid	+34 91 787 77 70
Hotel Villa Real	Madrid	+34 914 20 37 67
Hotel Etxegana	País Vasco	+34 946 338 448
Casa Lehmi	Valencia	+34 96 588 4018
Hospes Amérigo	Valencia	+34 965 14 65 70
Hospes Palau de la Mar	Valencia	+34 96 316 2884
Hotel Marisol Park	Valencia	+34 965875700
Hotel Mont Sant	Valencia	+34 962 27 50 81
Hotel Neptuno	Valencia	+34 963 567 777
Hotel Sidi Saler & Spa	Valencia	+34 961 61 04 11
Hotel Sidi San Juan & Spa	Valencia	+34 96 516 13 00
Hotel Termas Marinas el Palasiet	Valencia	+34 964 300 250
Ibb Masia de Lacy	Valencia	+34 96 144 0567
Mas de Canicattí	Valencia	+34 96 165 05 34
Torre la Mina	Valencia	+34 964 57 1746

Switzerland

Park Hotel Weggis	Weggis	+41 41 392 05 05
Alden Hotel Splügenschloss	Zurich	+41 44 289 99 99

Turkey

The Marmara Antalya	Antalya	+90 242 249 36 00
Tuvana Residence	Antalya	+90 242 247 60 15
Sungate Port Royal Deluxe Resort Hotel	Antalya - Kemer	+90 242 824 9750
Turkiz Hotel Thalasso Centre & Marina	Antalya - Kemer	+90 242 8144100
Divan Bodrum Palmira	Bodrum	+90 252 377 5601
The Marmara Bodrum	Bodrum	+90 252 313 8130
Oyster Residence	Fethiye - Ölüdeniz	+90 252 617 0765
Cappadocia Cave Suites	Göreme - Cappadocia	+90 384 271 2800
A'jia Hotel	Istanbul	+90 216 413 9300
The Marmara Istanbul	Istanbul	+90 212 251 4696
The Marmara Pera	Istanbul	+90 212 251 4646
Sumahan On The Water	Istanbul	+90 216 422 8000
Villa Mahal	Kalkan	+90 242 844 32 68
Richmond Nua Wellness - Spa	Sapanca - Adapazarı	+90 264 582 2100

Hotels - The Americas

Properties listed below can be found in our Recommended Hotels, Inns, Resorts & Spas - The Americas, Atlantic, Caribbean & Pacific 2008 Guide. More information on our portfolio of guides can be found on page 247.

Recommendations in Canada

CANADA - BRITISH COLUMBIA (SALT SPRING ISLAND)

Hastings House Country Estate

160 Upper Ganges Road, Salt Spring Island, British Columbia V8K 2S2

Tel: +1 250 537 2362
www.johansens.com/hastingshouse

CANADA - BRITISH COLUMBIA (SOOKE)

Sooke Harbour House

1528 Whiffen Spit Road, Sooke, British Columbia V0S 1N0

Tel: +1 250 642 3421
www.johansens.com/sookeharbour

CANADA - BRITISH COLUMBIA (VANCOUVER)

Pan Pacific Vancouver

300-999 Canada Place, Vancouver, British Columbia V6C 3B5

Tel: +1 604 662 8111
www.johansens.com/panpacific

CANADA - BRITISH COLUMBIA (VANCOUVER)

The Sutton Place Hotel Vancouver

845 Burrard Street, Vancouver, British Columbia V6Z 2K6

Tel: +1 604 682 5511
www.johansens.com/suttonplacebc

CANADA - BRITISH COLUMBIA (TOFINO)

Wickaninnish Inn

Osprey Lane at Chesterman Beach, Tofino, British Columbia V0R 2Z0

Tel: +1 250 725 3100
www.johansens.com/wickaninnish

CANADA - BRITISH COLUMBIA (VANCOUVER)

Wedgewood Hotel & Spa

845 Hornby Street, Vancouver, British Columbia V6Z 1V1

Tel: +1 604 689 7777
www.johansens.com/wedgewoodbc

CANADA - BRITISH COLUMBIA (VICTORIA)

Brentwood Bay Lodge

849 Verdier Avenue, Victoria, British Columbia V8M 1C5

Tel: +1 250 544 2079
www.johansens.com/brentwood

CANADA - BRITISH COLUMBIA (VICTORIA)

Fairholme Manor

638 Rockland Place, Victoria, British Columbia V8S 3R2

Tel: +1 250 598 3240
www.johansens.com/fairholme

CANADA - BRITISH COLUMBIA (VICTORIA)

Villa Marco Polo Inn

1524 Shasta Place, Victoria, British Columbia V8S 1X9

Tel: +1 250 370 1524
www.johansens.com/villamarcopolo

CANADA - BRITISH COLUMBIA (WHISTLER)

Adara Hotel

4122 Village Green, Whistler, British Columbia V0N 1B4

Tel: +1 604 905 4009
www.johansens.com/adara

CANADA - NEW BRUNSWICK (ST. ANDREWS BY-THE-SEA)

Kingsbrae Arms

219 King Street, St. Andrews By-The-Sea, New Brunswick E5B 1Y1

Tel: +1 506 529 1897
www.johansens.com/kingsbraearms

CANADA - ONTARIO (NIAGARA-ON-THE-LAKE)

Riverbend Inn & Vineyard

16104 Niagara River Parkway, Niagara-on-the-Lake, Ontario L0S 1J0

Tel: +1 905 468 8866
www.johansens.com/riverbend

CANADA - ONTARIO (TORONTO)

Windsor Arms

18 St. Thomas Street, Toronto, Ontario M5S 3E7

Tel: +1 416 971 9666
www.johansens.com/windsorarms

CANADA - QUÉBEC (LA MALBAIE)

La Pinsonnière

124 Saint-Raphaël, La Malbaie, Québec G5A 1X9

Tel: +1 418 665 4431
www.johansens.com/lapinsonniere

CANADA - QUÉBEC (MONT-TREMBLANT)

Hôtel Quintessence

3004 chemin de la chapelle, Mont-Tremblant, Québec J8E 1E1

Tel: +1 819 425 3400
www.johansens.com/quintessence

Hotels - The Americas

Properties listed below can be found in our Recommended Hotels, Inns, Resorts & Spas - The Americas, Atlantic, Caribbean & Pacific 2008 Guide.
More information on our portfolio of guides can be found on page 247.

CANADA - QUÉBEC (MONTRÉAL)

Hôtel Nelligan

106 rue Saint-Paul Ouest, Montréal, Québec H2Y 1Z3

Tel: +1 514 788 2040
www.johansens.com/nelligan

CANADA - QUÉBEC (MONTRÉAL)

Le Place d'Armes Hôtel & Suites

55 rue Saint-Jacques Ouest, Montréal, Québec H2Y 3X2

Tel: +1 514 842 1887
www.johansens.com/hotelplacedarmes

Recommendations in Mexico

MEXICO - BAJA CALIFORNIA NORTE (TECATE)

Rancho La Puerta

Tecate, Baja California Norte

Tel: +1 877 440 7778
www.johansens.com/rancholapuerta

MEXICO - BAJA CALIFORNIA SUR (CABO SAN LUCAS)

Esperanza

Km. 7 Carretera Transpeninsular, Punta Ballena, Cabo San Lucas, Baja California Sur 23410

Tel: +52 624 145 6400
www.johansens.com/esperanza

MEXICO - BAJA CALIFORNIA SUR (LOS CABOS)

Marquis Los Cabos Beach Resort & Spa

Lote 74, Km. 21.5 Carretera Transpeninsular, Fraccionamiento Cabo Real, Los Cabos, Baja California Sur 23400

Tel: +52 624 144 2000
www.johansens.com/marquisloscabos

MEXICO - BAJA CALIFORNIA SUR (SAN JOSÉ DEL CABO)

Casa Del Mar Spa Resort

KM 19.5 Carretera Transpeninsular, San José del Cabo, Baja California Sur 23400

Tel: +52 624 145 7700
www.johansens.com/casadelmar

MEXICO - BAJA CALIFORNIA SUR (SAN JOSÉ DEL CABO)

Casa Natalia

Blvd. Mijares 4, San José Del Cabo, Baja California Sur 23400

Tel: +52 624 146 7100
www.johansens.com/casanatalia

MEXICO - COLIMA (COLIMA)

Hacienda de San Antonio

Municipio de Comala, Colima, Colima 28450

Tel: +52 312 316 0300
www.johansens.com/sanantonio

MEXICO - DISTRITO FEDERAL (MEXICO CITY)

Casa Vieja

Eugenio Sue 45 (Colonia Polanco), Mexico Distrito Federal 11560

Tel: +52 55 52 82 0067
www.johansens.com/casavieja

MEXICO - GUANAJUATO (GUANAJUATO)

Quinta Las Acacias

Paseo de la Presa 168, Guanajuato, Guanajuato 36000

Tel: +52 473 731 1517
www.johansens.com/acacias

MEXICO - JALISCO (COSTA ALEGRE)

El Tamarindo Beach & Golf Resort

Km 7.5 Highway 200, Carretera Barra de Navidad - Puerto Vallarta, Cihuatlan, Jalisco 48970

Tel: +52 315 351 5031 ext. 204
www.johansens.com/eltamarindo

MEXICO - JALISCO (COSTA ALEGRE / MANZANILLO)

Cuixmala

Costa Cuixmala, Carretera Melaque - Puerto Vallarta Km 46.2, La Huerta, Jalisco 48893

Tel: +52 315 351 0044
www.johansens.com/cuixmala

MEXICO - JALISCO (PUERTO VALLARTA)

Casa Velas Hotel Boutique

Pelicanos 311, Fracc. Marina Vallarta, Puerto Vallarta, Jalisco 48354

Tel: +52 322 226 6688
www.johansens.com/casavelas

MEXICO - JALISCO (PUERTA VALLARTA / COSTA ALEGRE)

Las Alamandas Resort

Carretera Barra de Navidad - Puerto Vallarta km 83.5, Col. Quemaro, Jalisco 48850

Tel: +52 322 285 5500
www.johansens.com/lasalamandas

MEXICO - MICHOACÁN (MORELIA)

Hotel Los Juaninos

Morelos Sur 39, Centro, Morelia, Michoacán 58000

Tel: +52 443 312 00 36
www.johansens.com/juaninos

Hotels - The Americas

Properties listed below can be found in our Recommended Hotels, Inns, Resorts & Spas - The Americas, Atlantic, Caribbean & Pacific 2008 Guide. More information on our portfolio of guides can be found on page 247.

MEXICO - MICHOACÁN (MORELIA)

Hotel Virrey de Mendoza

Av. Madero Pte. 310, Centro Histórico, Morelia, Michoacán 58000

Tel: +52 44 33 12 06 33
www.johansens.com/hotelvirrey

MEXICO - MICHOACÁN (MORELIA)

Villa Montaña Hotel & Spa

Patzimba 201, Vista Bella, Morelia, Michoacán 58090

Tel: +52 443 314 02 31
www.johansens.com/montana

MEXICO - NAYARIT (NUEVO VALLARTA)

Grand Velas All Suites & Spa Resort

Av. Cocoteros 98 Sur, Nuevo Vallarta, Nayarit 63735

Tel: +52 322 226 8000
www.johansens.com/grandvelas

MEXICO - OAXACA (OAXACA)

Casa Oaxaca

Calle García Vigil 407, Centro, Oaxaca, Oaxaca 68000

Tel: +52 951 514 4173
www.johansens.com/oaxaca

MEXICO - OAXACA (OAXACA)

Hotel la Provincia

Porfirio Diaz #108 Centro Historico, Oaxaca, Oaxaca 68000, Mexico

Tel: +52 951 51 40999
www.johansens.com/hotellaprovicia

MEXICO - PUEBLA (CHOLULA)

La Quinta Luna

3 sur 702, San Pedro Cholula, Puebla 72760

Tel: +52 222 247 8915
www.johansens.com/quintaluna

MEXICO - QUINTANA ROO (ISLA MUJERES)

Casa De Los Sueños

Lote 9A y 9B, A 200 MTS de Garrafon, Fracc Turquesa, Isla Mujeres, Quintana Roo 77400

Tel: +52 998 877 0651
www.johansens.com/lossuenos

MEXICO - QUINTANA ROO (PUERTO MORELOS)

Ceiba del Mar Spa Resort

Costera Norte Lte. 1, S.M. 10, MZ. 26, Puerto Morelos, Quintana Roo 77580

Tel: +52 998 872 8060
www.johansens.com/ceibademar

MEXICO - QUINTANA ROO (TULUM)

Casa Nalum

Sian Ka'an Biosphere Reserve, Quintana Roo

Tel: +52 19991 639 510
www.johansens.com/casanalum

MEXICO - YUCATÁN (MÉRIDA)

Hacienda Xcanatun - Casa de Piedra

Carretera Mérida - Progreso, Km 12, Mérida, Yucatán 97302

Tel: +52 999 941 0273
www.johansens.com/xcanatun

Recommendations in U.S.A

U.S.A. - ALABAMA (PISGAH)

Lodge on Gorham's Bluff

101 Gorham Drive, Pisgah, Alabama 35765

Tel: +1 256 451 8439
www.johansens.com/gorhamsbluff

U.S.A. - ARIZONA (GREER)

Hidden Meadow Ranch

620 Country Road 1325, Greer, Arizona 85927

Tel: +1 928 333 1000
www.johansens.com/hiddenmeadow

U.S.A. - ARIZONA (PARADISE VALLEY / SCOTTSDALE)

Sanctuary on Camelback Mountain

5700 East McDonald Drive, Scottsdale, Arizona 85253

Tel: +1 480 948 2100
www.johansens.com/sanctuarycamelback

U.S.A. - ARIZONA (SEDONA)

Sedona Rouge Hotel & Spa

2250 West Highway 89A, Sedona, Arizona 86336

Tel: +1 928 203 4111
www.johansens.com/sedonarouge

U.S.A. - ARIZONA (TUCSON)

Arizona Inn

2200 East Elm Street, Tucson, Arizona 85719

Tel: +1 520 325 1541
www.johansens.com/arizonainn

Hotels - The Americas

Properties listed below can be found in our Recommended Hotels, Inns, Resorts & Spas - The Americas, Atlantic, Caribbean & Pacific 2008 Guide. More information on our portfolio of guides can be found on page 247.

U.S.A. - ARIZONA (TUCSON)

Tanque Verde Ranch

14301 East Speedway Boulevard, Tucson, Arizona 85748

Tel: +1 520 296 6275
www.johansens.com/tanqueverde

U.S.A. - ARIZONA (WICKENBURG)

Rancho de los Caballeros

1551 South Vulture Mine Road, Wickenburg, Arizona 85390

Tel: +1 928 684 5484
www.johansens.com/caballeros

U.S.A. - CALIFORNIA (CARMEL-BY-THE-SEA)

L'Auberge Carmel

Monte Verde at Seventh, Carmel-by-the-Sea, California 93921

Tel: +1 831 624 8578
www.johansens.com/laubergecarmel

U.S.A. - CALIFORNIA (CARMEL-BY-THE-SEA)

Tradewinds Carmel

Mission Street at Third Avenue, Carmel-by-the-Sea, California 93921

Tel: +1 831 624 2776
www.johansens.com/tradewinds

U.S.A. - CALIFORNIA (CARMEL VALLEY)

Bernardus Lodge

415 Carmel Valley Road, Carmel Valley, California 93924

Tel: +1 831 658 3400
www.johansens.com/bernardus

U.S.A. - CALIFORNIA (BIG SUR)

Post Ranch Inn

Highway 1, P.O. Box 219, Big Sur, California 93920

Tel: +1 831 667 2200
www.johansens.com/postranchinn

U.S.A. - CALIFORNIA (BIG SUR)

Ventana Inn and Spa

Highway 1, Big Sur, California 93920

Tel: +1 831 667 2331
www.johansens.com/ventana

U.S.A. - CALIFORNIA (EUREKA)

The Carter House Inns

301 L Street, Eureka, California 95501

Tel: +1 707 444 8062
www.johansens.com/carterhouse

U.S.A. - CALIFORNIA (GLEN ELLEN)

The Gaige House

13540 Arnold Drive, Glen Ellen, California 95442

Tel: +1 707 935 0237
www.johansens.com/gaige

U.S.A. - CALIFORNIA (HEALDSBURG)

The Grape Leaf Inn

539 Johnson Street, Healdsburg, California 95448

Tel: +1 707 433 8140
www.johansens.com/grapeleaf

U.S.A. - CALIFORNIA (HEALDSBURG)

Hotel Healdsburg

25 Matheson St, Healdsburg, California 95448

Tel: +1 707 431 2800
www.johansens.com/healdsburg

U.S.A. - CALIFORNIA (INDIAN WELLS)

Miramonte Resort and Spa

45-000 Indian Wells Lane, Indian Wells, California 92210

Tel: +1 760 341 2200
www.johansens.com/miramonte

U.S.A. - CALIFORNIA (KENWOOD)

The Kenwood Inn and Spa

10400 Sonoma Highway, Kenwood, California 95452

Tel: +1 707 833 1293
www.johansens.com/kenwoodinn

U.S.A. - CALIFORNIA (LA JOLLA)

Estancia La Jolla Hotel & Spa

9700 North Torrey Pines Road, La Jolla, California 92037

Tel: +1 858 550 1000
www.johansens.com/estancialajolla

U.S.A. - CALIFORNIA (LITTLE RIVER)

Stevenswood Spa Resort

8211 North Highway 1, Little River, CALIFORNIA 95456

Tel: +1 800 421 2810
www.johansens.com/stevenswood

U.S.A. - CALIFORNIA (LOS ANGELES)

Hotel Bel-Air

701 Stone Canyon Road, Los Angeles, California 90077

Tel: +1 310 472 1211
www.johansens.com/belair

Hotels - The Americas

Properties listed below can be found in our Recommended Hotels, Inns, Resorts & Spas - The Americas, Atlantic, Caribbean & Pacific 2008 Guide. More information on our portfolio of guides can be found on page 247.

U.S.A. - CALIFORNIA (MENDOCINO)

The Stanford Inn By The Sea

Coast Highway One & Comptche-Ukiah Road, Mendocino, California 95460

Tel: +1 707 937 5615
www.johansens.com/stanford

U.S.A. - CALIFORNIA (MILL VALLEY)

Mill Valley Inn

165 Throckmorton Avenue, Mill Valley, California 94941

Tel: +1 415 389 6608
www.johansens.com/millvalleyinn

U.S.A. - CALIFORNIA (MONTEREY)

Old Monterey Inn

500 Martin Street, Monterey, California 93940

Tel: +1 831 375 8284
www.johansens.com/oldmontereyinn

U.S.A. - CALIFORNIA (NAPA)

1801 First Inn

1801 First Street, Napa, California 94559

Tel: +1 707 224 3739
www.johansens.com/1801inn

U.S.A. - CALIFORNIA (NAPA)

Milliken Creek Inn & Spa

1815 Silverado Trail, Napa, California 94558

Tel: +1 707 255 1197
www.johansens.com/milliken

U.S.A. - CALIFORNIA (NEWPORT BEACH)

The Island Hotel Newport Beach

690 Newport Center Drive, Newport Beach, California 92660

Tel: +1 949 759 0808
www.johansens.com/newportbeach

U.S.A. - CALIFORNIA (OAKHURST)

Château du Sureau & Spa

48688 Victoria Lane, Oakhurst, California 93644

Tel: +1 559 683 6860
www.johansens.com/chateausureau

U.S.A. - CALIFORNIA (RANCHO SANTA FE)

The Inn at Rancho Santa Fe

5951 Linea del Cielo, Rancho Santa Fe, California 92067

Tel: +1 858 756 1131
www.johansens.com/ranchosantafe

U.S.A. - CALIFORNIA (SAN DIEGO)

Tower23 Hotel

4551 Ocean Blvd., San Diego, California 92109

Tel: +1 858 270 2323
www.johansens.com/tower23

U.S.A. - CALIFORNIA (SAN FRANCISCO)

The Union Street Inn

2229 Union Street, San Francisco, California 94123

Tel: +1 415 346 0424
www.johansens.com/unionstreetsf

U.S.A. - CALIFORNIA (SAN FRANCISCO BAY AREA)

Inn Above Tide

30 El Portal, Sausalito, California 94965

Tel: +1 415 332 9535
www.johansens.com/innabovetide

U.S.A. - CALIFORNIA (SANTA BARBARA)

Harbor View Inn

28 West Cabrillo Boulevard, Santa Barbara, California 93101

Tel: +1 805 963 0780
www.johansens.com/harborview

U.S.A. - CALIFORNIA (SANTA YNEZ)

The Santa Ynez Inn

3627 Sagunto Street, Santa Ynez, California 93460-0628

Tel: +1 805 688 5588
www.johansens.com/santaynez

U.S.A. - CALIFORNIA (SONOMA)

Ledson Hotel & Harmony Lounge

480 First Street East, Sonoma, California 95476

Tel: +1 707 996 9779
www.johansens.com/ledsonhotel

U.S.A. - CALIFORNIA (ST. HELENA)

Meadowood

900 Meadowood Lane, St. Helena, California 94574

Tel: +1 707 963 3646
www.johansens.com/meadowood

U.S.A. - COLORADO (BOULDER)

The Bradley Boulder Inn

2040 16th Street, Boulder, Colorado 80302

Tel: +1 303 545 5200
www.johansens.com/bradleyboulderinn

Hotels - The Americas

Properties listed below can be found in our Recommended Hotels, Inns, Resorts & Spas - The Americas, Atlantic, Caribbean & Pacific 2008 Guide. More information on our portfolio of guides can be found on page 247.

U.S.A. - COLORADO (CRAWFORD)

Smith Fork Ranch

45362 Needlerock Road, Crawford, Colorado 81415

Tel: +1 970 921 3454
www.johansens.com/smithfork

U.S.A. - COLORADO (TELLURIDE)

The Hotel Telluride

199 North Cornet Street, Telluride, Colorado 81435

Tel: +1 970 369 1188
www.johansens.com/telluride

U.S.A. - COLORADO (DENVER)

Castle Marne Bed & Breakfast Inn

1572 Race Street, Denver, Colorado 80206

Tel: +1 303 331 0621
www.johansens.com/castlemarne

U.S.A. - COLORADO (VAIL)

The Tivoli Lodge at Vail

386 Hanson Ranch Road, Vail, Colorado 81657

Tel: +1 970 476 5615
www.johansens.com/tivoli

U.S.A. - COLORADO (DENVER)

Hotel Monaco

1717 Champa Street at 17th, Denver, Colorado 80202

Tel: +1 303 296 1717
www.johansens.com/monaco

U.S.A. - COLORADO (VAIL)

Vail Mountain Lodge & Spa

352 East Meadow Drive, Vail, Colorado 81657

Tel: +1 970 476 0700
www.johansens.com/vailmountain

U.S.A. - COLORADO (ESTES PARK)

Taharaa Mountain Lodge

3110 So. St. Vrain, Estes Park, Colorado 80517

Tel: +1 970 577 0098
www.johansens.com/taharaa

U.S.A. - CONNECTICUT (GREENWICH)

Delamar Greenwich Harbor

500 Steamboat Road, Greenwich, Connecticut 06830

Tel: +1 203 661 9800
www.johansens.com/delamar

U.S.A. - COLORADO (MANITOU SPRINGS)

The Cliff House at Pikes Peak

306 Cañon Avenue, Manitou Springs, Colorado 80829

Tel: +1 719 685 3000
www.johansens.com/thecliffhouse

U.S.A. - CONNECTICUT (WESTPORT)

The Inn at National Hall

2 Post Road West, Westport, Connecticut 06880

Tel: +1 203 221 1351
www.johansens.com/nationalhall

U.S.A. - COLORADO (MONTROSE)

Elk Mountain Resort

97 Elk Walk, Montrose, Colorado 81401

Tel: +1 970 252 4900
www.johansens.com/elkmountain

U.S.A. - DELAWARE (REHOBOTH BEACH)

The Bellmoor

Six Christian Street, Rehoboth Beach, Delaware 19971

Tel: +1 302 227 5800
www.johansens.com/thebellmoor

U.S.A. - COLORADO (STEAMBOAT SPRINGS)

Vista Verde Guest Ranch

P.O. Box 770465, Steamboat Springs, Colorado 80477

Tel: +1 970 879 3858
www.johansens.com/vistaverderanch

U.S.A. - DELAWARE (REHOBOTH BEACH)

Boardwalk Plaza Hotel

Olive Avenue & The Boardwalk, Rehoboth Beach, Delaware 19971

Tel: +1 302 227 7169
www.johansens.com/boardwalkplaza

U.S.A. - COLORADO (TELLURIDE)

Fairmont Heritage Place Franz Klammer Lodge

567 Mountain Village Boulevard, Telluride, Colorado 81436

Tel: +1 970 728 4239
www.johansens.com/fairmont

U.S.A. - DELAWARE (WILMINGTON)

Inn at Montchanin Village

Route 100 & Kirk Road, Montchanin, Delaware 19710

Tel: +1 302 888 2133
www.johansens.com/montchanin

Hotels - The Americas

Properties listed below can be found in our Recommended Hotels, Inns, Resorts & Spas - The Americas, Atlantic, Caribbean & Pacific 2008 Guide. More information on our portfolio of guides can be found on page 247.

U.S.A. - DISTRICT OF COLUMBIA (WASHINGTON)

The Hay-Adams

Sixteenth & H. Streets N.W., Washington D.C. 20006

Tel: +1 202 638 6600
www.johansens.com/hayadams

U.S.A. - FLORIDA (MIAMI BEACH)

The Setai Hotel & Resort

2001 Collins Ave., Miami Beach, Florida 33139, U.S.A.

Tel: +1 305 520 6000
www.johansens.com/setai

U.S.A. - FLORIDA (COCONUT GROVE)

Grove Isle Hotel & Spa

Four Grove Isle Drive, Coconut Grove, Florida 33133

Tel: +1 305 858 8300
www.johansens.com/groveisle

U.S.A. - FLORIDA (MIAMI BEACH)

Casa Tua

1700 James Avenue, Miami Beach, Florida 33139

Tel: +1 305 673 0973
www.johansens.com/casatua

U.S.A. - FLORIDA (FISHER ISLAND)

Fisher Island Hotel & Resort

One Fisher Island Drive, Fisher Island, Florida 33109

Tel: +1 305 535 6000
www.johansens.com/fisherisland

U.S.A. - FLORIDA (NAPLES)

LaPlaya Beach & Golf Resort

9891 Gulf Shore Drive, Naples, Florida 34108

Tel: +1 239 597 3123
www.johansens.com/laplaya

U.S.A. - FLORIDA (JUPITER BEACH)

Jupiter Beach Resort & Spa

5 North A1A, Jupiter, Florida 33477-5190

Tel: +1 561 746 2511
www.johansens.com/jupiterbeachresort

U.S.A. - FLORIDA (SANTA ROSA BEACH)

WaterColor Inn and Resort

34 Goldenrod Circle, Santa Rosa Beach, Florida 32459

Tel: +1 850 534 5000
www.johansens.com/watercolor

U.S.A. - FLORIDA (KEY WEST)

Ocean Key Resort

Zero Duval Street, Key West, Florida 33040

Tel: +1 305 296 7701
www.johansens.com/oceankey

U.S.A. - FLORIDA (ST. PETE BEACH)

Don CeSar Beach Resort

3400 Gulf Boulevard, St. Pete Beach, Florida 33706

Tel: +1 727 360 1881
www.johansens.com/doncesar

U.S.A. - FLORIDA (KEY WEST)

Simonton Court Historic Inn & Cottages

320 Simonton Street, Key West, Florida 33040

Tel: +1 305 294 6386
www.johansens.com/simontoncourt

U.S.A. - GEORGIA (ADAIRSVILLE)

Barnsley Gardens Resort

597 Barnsley Gardens Road, Adairsville, Georgia 30103

Tel: +1 770 773 7480
www.johansens.com/barnsleygardens

U.S.A. - FLORIDA (KEY WEST)

Sunset Key Guest Cottages

245 Front Street, Key West, Florida 33040

Tel: +1 305 292 5300
www.johansens.com/sunsetkey

U.S.A. - GEORGIA (CUMBERLAND ISLAND)

Greyfield Inn

Cumberland Island, Georgia

Tel: +1 904 261 6408
www.johansens.com/greyfieldinn

U.S.A. - FLORIDA (MIAMI BEACH)

Hotel Victor

1144 Ocean Drive, Miami Beach, Florida 33139

Tel: +1 305 428 1234
www.johansens.com/hotelvictor

U.S.A. - GEORGIA (MADISON)

The James Madison Inn

260 West Washington Street, Madison, Georgia 30650

Tel: +1 706 342 7040
www.johansens.com/jamesmadison

Hotels - The Americas

Properties listed below can be found in our Recommended Hotels, Inns, Resorts & Spas - The Americas, Atlantic, Caribbean & Pacific 2008 Guide.
More information on our portfolio of guides can be found on page 247.

U.S.A. - GEORGIA (SAVANNAH)

The Gastonian

220 East Gaston Street, Savannah, Georgia 31401

Tel: +1 912 232 2869
www.johansens.com/gastonian

U.S.A. - HAWAII (BIG ISLAND)

The Palms Cliff House

28-3514 Mamalahoa Highway 19, P.O. Box 189, Honomu, Hawaii 96728-0189

Tel: +1 808 963 6076
www.johansens.com/palmscliff

U.S.A. - HAWAII (MAUI)

Hotel Hana-Maui and Honua Spa

5031 Hana Highway, Hana, Maui, Hawaii 96713

Tel: +1 808 248 8211
www.johansens.com/hanamaui

U.S.A. - HAWAII (BIG ISLAND)

Shipman House

131 Ka'iulani Street, Hilo, Hawaii 96720

Tel: +1 808 934 8002
www.johansens.com/shipman

U.S.A. - IDAHO (KETCHUM)

Knob Hill Inn

960 North Main Street, P.O. Box 800, Ketchum, Idaho 83340

Tel: +1 208 726 8010
www.johansens.com/knobhillinn

U.S.A. - KANSAS (LAWRENCE)

The Eldridge

701 Massachusetts, Lawrence, Kansas 66044

Tel: +1 785 749 5011
www.johansens.com/eldridge

U.S.A. - LOUISIANA (NEW ORLEANS)

Hotel Maison de Ville

727 Rue Toulouse, New Orleans, Louisiana 70130

Tel: +1 504 561 5858
www.johansens.com/maisondeville

U.S.A. - LOUISIANA (NEW ORLEANS)

The Lafayette Hotel

600 St. Charles Avenue, New Orleans, Louisiana 70130

Tel: +1 504 524 4441
www.johansens.com/lafayette

U.S.A. - LOUISIANA (NEW ORLEANS)

The St. James Hotel

330 Magazine Street, New Orleans, Louisiana 70130

Tel: +1 504 304 4000
www.johansens.com/stjamesno

U.S.A. - MAINE (GREENVILLE)

The Lodge At Moosehead Lake

368 Lily Bay Road, P.O. Box 1167, Greenville, Maine 04441

Tel: +1 207 695 4400
www.johansens.com/lodgeatmooseheadlake

U.S.A. - MAINE (KENNEBUNKPORT)

The White Barn Inn

37 Beach Avenue, Kennebunkport, Maine 04043

Tel: +1 207 967 2321
www.johansens.com/whitebarninn

U.S.A. - MAINE (PORTLAND)

Portland Harbor Hotel

468 Fore Street, Portland, Maine 04101

Tel: +1 207 775 9090
www.johansens.com/portlandharbor

U.S.A. - MARYLAND (FROSTBURG)

Savage River Lodge

1600 Mt. Aetna Road, Frostburg, Maryland 21532

Tel: +1 301 689 3200
www.johansens.com/savageriver

U.S.A. - MASSACHUSETTS (BOSTON)

The Charles Street Inn

94 Charles Street, Boston, Massachusetts 02114

Tel: +1 617 314 8900
www.johansens.com/charlesstreetinn

U.S.A. - MASSACHUSETTS (BOSTON)

Fifteen Beacon

15 Beacon Street, Boston, Massachusetts 2108

Tel: +1 617 670 1500
www.johansens.com/fifteenbeacon

U.S.A. - MASSACHUSETTS (BOSTON)

Hotel Commonwealth

500 Commonwealth Avenue, Boston, Massachusetts 02215

Tel: +1 617 933 5000
www.johansens.com/commonwealth

Hotels - The Americas

Properties listed below can be found in our Recommended Hotels, Inns, Resorts & Spas - The Americas, Atlantic, Caribbean & Pacific 2008 Guide. More information on our portfolio of guides can be found on page 247.

U.S.A. - MASSACHUSETTS (BOSTON)

The Lenox

61 Exeter Street at Boylston, Boston, Massachusetts 02116

Tel: +1 617 536 5300
www.johansens.com/lenox

U.S.A. - MASSACHUSETTS (BOSTON)

The Liberty Hotel

215 Charles Street, Boston, Massachusetts 02114

Tel: +1 617 224 4000
www.johansens.com/liberty

U.S.A. - MASSACHUSETTS (CAPE COD)

Wequassett Resort and Golf Club

On Pleasant Bay, Chatham, Cape Cod, Massachusetts 02633

Tel: +1 508 432 5400
www.johansens.com/wequassett

U.S.A. - MASSACHUSETTS (CAPE COD)

The Crowne Pointe Historic Inn & Spa

82 Bradford Street, Provincetown, Cape Cod, Massachusetts 02657

Tel: +1 508 487 6767
www.johansens.com/crownepointe

U.S.A. - MASSACHUSETTS (IPSWICH)

The Inn at Castle Hill

280 Argilla Road, Ipswich, Massachusetts 01938

Tel: +1 978 412 2555
www.johansens.com/castlehill

U.S.A. - MASSACHUSETTS (LENOX)

Blantyre

16 Blantyre Road, P.O. Box 995, Lenox, Massachusetts 01240

Tel: +1 413 637 3556
www.johansens.com/blantyre

U.S.A. - MASSACHUSETTS (LENOX)

Cranwell Resort, Spa & Golf Club

55 Lee Road, Route 20, Lenox, Massachusetts 01240

Tel: +1 413 637 1364
www.johansens.com/cranwell

U.S.A. - MASSACHUSETTS (MARTHA'S VINEYARD)

The Charlotte Inn

27 South Summer Street, Edgartown, Massachusetts 02539

Tel: +1 508 627 4151
www.johansens.com/charlotte

U.S.A. - MASSACHUSETTS (MARTHA'S VINEYARD)

Winnetu Oceanside Resort at South Beach

31 Dunes Road, Edgartown, Massachusetts 02539

Tel: +1 508 310 1733
www.johansens.com/winnetu

U.S.A. - MISSISSIPPI (JACKSON)

Fairview Inn & Restaurant

734 Fairview Street, Jackson, Mississippi 39202

Tel: +1 601 948 3429
www.johansens.com/fairviewinn

U.S.A. - MISSISSIPPI (NATCHEZ)

Monmouth Plantation

36 Melrose Avenue, Natchez, Mississippi 39120

Tel: +1 601 442 5852
www.johansens.com/monmouthplantation

U.S.A. - MISSISSIPPI (NESBIT)

Bonne Terre Country Inn

4715 Church Road West, Nesbit, Mississippi 38651

Tel: +1 662 781 5100
www.johansens.com/bonneterre

U.S.A. - MISSOURI (KANSAS CITY)

The Raphael Hotel

325 Ward Parkway, Kansas City, Missouri 64112

Tel: +1 816 756 3800
www.johansens.com/raphael

U.S.A. - MISSOURI (RIDGEDALE)

Big Cedar Lodge

612 Devil's Pool Road, Ridgedale, Missouri 65739

Tel: +1 417 335 2777
www.johansens.com/bigcedar

U.S.A. - MONTANA (BIG SKY)

The Big EZ Lodge

7000 Beaver Creek Road, Big Sky, Montana 59716

Tel: +1 406 995 7000
www.johansens.com/bigez

U.S.A. - MONTANA (DARBY)

Triple Creek Ranch

5551 West Fork Road, Darby, Montana 59829

Tel: +1 406 821 4600
www.johansens.com/triplecreek

Hotels - The Americas

Properties listed below can be found in our Recommended Hotels, Inns, Resorts & Spas - The Americas, Atlantic, Caribbean & Pacific 2008 Guide. More information on our portfolio of guides can be found on page 247.

U.S.A. - NEW HAMPSHIRE (WHITEFIELD / WHITE MOUNTAINS)

Mountain View Grand Resort & Spa

Mountain View Road, Whitefield, New Hampshire 03598

Tel: +1 603 837 2100

www.johansens.com/mountainview

U.S.A. - NEW MEXICO (ESPAÑOLA)

Rancho de San Juan

P.O. Box 4140, Highway 285, Española, New Mexico 87533

Tel: +1 505 753 6818

www.johansens.com/ranchosanjuan

U.S.A. - NEW MEXICO (SANTA FE)

The Bishop's Lodge Resort & Spa

1297 Bishop's Lodge Road, Santa Fe, New Mexico 87501

Tel: +1 505 983 6377

www.johansens.com/bishopslodge

U.S.A. - NEW MEXICO (TAOS)

El Monte Sagrado Living Resort & Spa

317 Kit Carson Road, Taos, New Mexico 87571

Tel: +1 505 758 3502

www.johansens.com/elmontesagrado

U.S.A. - NEW YORK (BUFFALO)

The Mansion on Delaware Avenue

414 Delaware Avenue, Buffalo, New York 14202

Tel: +1 716 886 3300

www.johansens.com/mansionondelaware

U.S.A. - NEW YORK (EAST AURORA)

The Roycroft Inn

40 South Grove Street, East Aurora, New York 14052

Tel: +1 716 652 5552

www.johansens.com/roycroftinn

U.S.A. - NEW YORK (HUNTINGTON)

OHEKA Castle Hotel & Estate

135 West Gate Drive, Huntington, New York 11743

Tel: +1 631 659 1400

www.johansens.com/oheka

U.S.A. - NEW YORK (LAKE PLACID)

Mirror Lake Inn Resort & Spa

77 Mirror Lake Drive, Lake Placid, New York

Tel: +1 518 523 2544

www.johansens.com/mirrorlake

U.S.A. - NEW YORK (LAKE PLACID)

Whiteface Lodge

7 Whiteface Inn Lane, Lake Placid, New York 12946

Tel: +1 518 523 0500

www.johansens.com/whiteface

U.S.A. - NEW YORK (NEW YORK CITY)

Hotel Plaza Athénée

37 East 64th Street, New York City, New York 10021

Tel: +1 212 734 9100

www.johansens.com/athenee

U.S.A. - NEW YORK (NEW YORK CITY)

The Inn at Irving Place

56 Irving Place, New York, New York City 10003

Tel: +1 212 533 4600

www.johansens.com/irvingplace

U.S.A. - NEW YORK (NEW YORK CITY)

Jumeirah Essex House

160 Central Park South, New York City, New York 10019

Tel: +1 212 247 0300

www.johansens.com/essexhouse

U.S.A. - NEW YORK (TARRYTOWN)

Castle On The Hudson

400 Benedict Avenue, Tarrytown, New York 10591

Tel: +1 914 631 1980

www.johansens.com/hudson

U.S.A. - NEW YORK (VERONA)

The Lodge at Turning Stone

5218 Patrick Road, Verona, New York 13478

Tel: +1 315 361 8525

www.johansens.com/turningstone

U.S.A. - NEW YORK/LONG ISLAND (EAST HAMPTON)

The Baker House 1650

181 Main Street, East Hampton, New York 11937

Tel: +1 631 324 4081

www.johansens.com/bakerhouse

U.S.A. - NEW YORK/LONG ISLAND (EAST HAMPTON)

The Mill House Inn

31 North Main Street, East Hampton, New York 11937

Tel: +1 631 324 9766

www.johansens.com/millhouse

Hotels - The Americas

Properties listed below can be found in our Recommended Hotels, Inns, Resorts & Spas - The Americas, Atlantic, Caribbean & Pacific 2008 Guide. More information on our portfolio of guides can be found on page 247.

U.S.A. - NEW YORK/LONG ISLAND (SOUTHAMPTON)

1708 House

126 Main Street, Southampton, New York 11968

Tel: +1 631 287 1708
www.johansens.com/1708house

U.S.A. - NORTH CAROLINA (NEW BERN)

The Aerie Inn

509 Pollock Street, New Bern, North Carolina 28562

Tel: +1 252 636 5553
www.johansens.com/aerieinn

U.S.A. - NORTH CAROLINA (ASHEVILLE)

Haywood Park Hotel

One Battery Park Avenue, Asheville, North Carolina 28801

Tel: +1 828 252 2522
www.johansens.com/haywoodpark

U.S.A. - NORTH CAROLINA (RALEIGH - DURHAM)

The Siena Hotel

1505 E. Franklin Street, Chapel Hill, North Carolina 27514

Tel: +1 919 929 4000
www.johansens.com/siena

U.S.A. - NORTH CAROLINA (ASHEVILLE)

Inn on Biltmore Estate

One Antler Hill Road, Asheville, North Carolina 28803

Tel: +1 828 225 1600
www.johansens.com/biltmore

U.S.A. - OKLAHOMA (OKLAHOMA CITY)

Colcord Hotel

15 North Robinson, Oklahoma City, Oklahoma 73102

Tel: +1 405 601 4300
www.johansens.com/colcord

U.S.A. - NORTH CAROLINA (BLOWING ROCK)

Gideon Ridge Inn

202 Gideon Ridge Road, Blowing Rock, North Carolina 28605

Tel: +1 828 295 3644
www.johansens.com/gideonridge

U.S.A. - OKLAHOMA (TULSA)

Hotel Ambassador

1324 South Main Street, Tulsa, Oklahoma 74119

Tel: +1 918 587 8200
www.johansens.com/ambassador

U.S.A. - NORTH CAROLINA (CHARLOTTE)

Ballantyne Resort

10000 Ballantyne Commons Parkway, Charlotte, North Carolina 28277

Tel: +1 704 248 4000
www.johansens.com/ballantyneresort

U.S.A. - OREGON (PORTLAND)

The Heathman Hotel

1001 S.W. Broadway, Portland, Oregon 97205

Tel: +1 503 241 4100
www.johansens.com/heathman

U.S.A. - NORTH CAROLINA (DUCK)

The Sanderling Resort & Spa

1461 Duck Road, Duck, North Carolina 27949

Tel: +1 252 261 4111
www.johansens.com/sanderling

U.S.A. - OREGON (PORTLAND)

The Benson Hotel

309 Southwest Broadway, Portland, Oregon 97205

Tel: +1 503 228 2000
www.johansens.com/benson

U.S.A. - NORTH CAROLINA (HIGHLANDS)

Inn at Half Mile Farm

P.O. Box 2769, 214 Half Mile Drive, Highlands, North Carolina 28741

Tel: +1 828 526 8170
www.johansens.com/halfmilefarm

U.S.A. - OREGON (EUGENE)

The Campbell House

252 Pearl Street, Eugene, Oregon 97401

Tel: +1 541 343 1119
www.johansens.com/campbell

U.S.A. - NORTH CAROLINA (HIGHLANDS)

Old Edwards Inn and Spa

445 Main Street, Highlands, North Carolina 28741

Tel: +1 828 526 8008
www.johansens.com/oldedwards

U.S.A. - PENNSYLVANIA (BRADFORD)

Glendorn

1000 Glendorn Drive, Bradford, Pennsylvania 16701

Tel: +1 814 362 6511
www.johansens.com/glendorn

Hotels - The Americas

Properties listed below can be found in our Recommended Hotels, Inns, Resorts & Spas - The Americas, Atlantic, Caribbean & Pacific 2008 Guide. More information on our portfolio of guides can be found on page 247.

U.S.A. - PENNSYLVANIA (HERSHEY)

The Hershey Hotel & Spa

100 Hotel Road, Hershey, Pennsylvania 17033

Tel: +1 717 533 2171
www.johansens.com/hershey

U.S.A. - PENNSYLVANIA (NEW HOPE)

The Inn at Bowman's Hill

518 Lurgan Road, New Hope, Pennsylvania 18938

Tel: +1 215 862 8090
www.johansens.com/bowmanshill

U.S.A. - PENNSYLVANIA (PHILADELPHIA)

Rittenhouse 1715, A Boutique Hotel

1715 Rittenhouse Square, Philadelphia, Pennsylvania 19103

Tel: +1 215 546 6500
www.johansens.com/rittenhouse

U.S.A. - PENNSYLVANIA (SKYTOP)

Skytop Lodge

One Skytop, Skytop, Pennsylvania 18357

Tel: +1 570 595 7401
www.johansens.com/skytop

U.S.A. - RHODE ISLAND (NEWPORT)

Chanler at Cliff Walk

117 Memorial Boulevard, Newport, Rhode Island 02840

Tel: +1 401 847 1300
www.johansens.com/chanler

U.S.A. - RHODE ISLAND (NEWPORT)

La Farge Perry House

24 Kay Street, Newport, Rhode Island 02840

Tel: +1 401 847 2223
www.johansens.com/lafargeperry

U.S.A. - RHODE ISLAND (PROVIDENCE)

Hotel Providence

311 Westminster Street, Providence, Rhode Island 02903

Tel: +1 401 861 8000
www.johansens.com/providence

U.S.A. - SOUTH CAROLINA (BLUFFTON)

The Inn at Palmetto Bluff

476 Mount Pelia Road, Bluffton, South Carolina 29910

Tel: +1 843 706 6500
www.johansens.com/palmettobluff

U.S.A. - SOUTH CAROLINA (CHARLESTON)

The Boardwalk Inn at Wild Dunes Resort

5757 Palm Boulevard, Isle of Palms, South Carolina 29451

Tel: +1 843 886 6000
www.johansens.com/boardwalk

U.S.A. - SOUTH CAROLINA (CHARLESTON)

Charleston Harbor Resort & Marina

20 Patriots Point Road, Charleston, South Carolina 29464

Tel: +1 843 856 0028
www.johansens.com/charlestonharbor

U.S.A. - SOUTH CAROLINA (CHARLESTON)

Woodlands Resort & Inn

125 Parsons Road, Summerville, South Carolina 29483

Tel: +1 843 875 2600
www.johansens.com/woodlandssc

U.S.A. - SOUTH CAROLINA (KIAWAH ISLAND)

The Sanctuary at Kiawah Island Golf Resort

One Sanctuary Beach Drive, Kiawah Island, South Carolina 29455

Tel: +1 843 768 6000
www.johansens.com/sanctuary

U.S.A. - SOUTH CAROLINA (MYRTLE BEACH)

Marina Inn at Grande Dunes

8121 Amalfi Place, Myrtle Beach, South Carolina 29572

Tel: +1 843 913 1333
www.johansens.com/marinainn

U.S.A. - SOUTH CAROLINA (TRAVELERS REST)

La Bastide

10 Road Of Vines, Travelers Rest, South Carolina 29210

Tel: +1 864 836 8463
www.johansens.com/labastide

U.S.A. - TENNESSEE (MEMPHIS)

Madison Hotel Memphis

79 Madison Avenue, Memphis, Tennessee 38103

Tel: +1 901 333 1200
www.johansens.com/madisonmemphis

U.S.A. - TENNESSEE (NASHVILLE)

The Hermitage Hotel

231 Sixth Avenue North, Nashville, Tennessee 37219

Tel: +1 615 244 3121
www.johansens.com/hermitagetn

Hotels - The Americas

Properties listed below can be found in our Recommended Hotels, Inns, Resorts & Spas - The Americas, Atlantic, Caribbean & Pacific 2008 Guide. More information on our portfolio of guides can be found on page 247.

U.S.A. - TEXAS (AUSTIN)

The Mansion at Judges' Hill

1900 Rio Grande, Austin, Texas 78705

Tel: +1 512 495 1800
www.johansens.com/judgeshill

U.S.A. - TEXAS (GRANBURY)

The Inn on Lake Granbury

205 West Doyle Street, Granbury, Texas 76048

Tel: +1 817 573 0046
www.johansens.com/lakegranbury

U.S.A. - TEXAS (HOUSTON)

Hotel Granduca

1080 Uptown Park Boulevard, Houston, Texas 77056

Tel: +1 713 418 1000
www.johansens.com/granduca

U.S.A. - TEXAS (HOUSTON)

Hotel ICON

220 Main, Houston, Texas 77002

Tel: +1 713 224 4266
www.johansens.com/hotelicon

U.S.A. - UTAH (MOAB)

Sorrel River Ranch Resort & Spa

Mile 17 Scenic Byway 128, H.C. 64 BOX 4000, Moab, Utah 84532

Tel: +1 435 259 4642
www.johansens.com/sorrelriver

U.S.A. - UTAH (SUNDANCE)

Sundance Resort

RR#3 Box A-1, Sundance, Utah 84604

Tel: +1 801 225 4107
www.johansens.com/sundance

U.S.A. - VERMONT (LUDLOW/OKEMO)

Castle Hill Resort & Spa

Jct. Routes 103 and 131, Cavendish, Vermont 05142

Tel: +1 802 226 7361
www.johansens.com/castlehillvt

U.S.A. - VERMONT (WARREN)

The Pitcher Inn

275 Main Street, P.O. Box 347, Warren, Vermont 05674

Tel: +1 802 496 6350
www.johansens.com/pitcherinn

U.S.A. - VERMONT (WOODSTOCK)

The Jackson House Inn

114-3 Senior Lane, Woodstock, Vermont 05091

Tel: +1 802 457 2065
www.johansens.com/jacksonhouse

U.S.A. - VIRGINIA (ABINGDON)

The Martha Washington Inn

150 West Main Street, Abingdon, Virginia 24210

Tel: +1 276 628 3161
www.johansens.com/themartha

U.S.A. - VIRGINIA (CHARLOTTESVILLE)

Boar's Head Inn

200 Ednam Drive, Charlottesville, Virginia 22903

Tel: +1 434 972 2232
www.johansens.com/boarsheadusa

U.S.A. - VIRGINIA (GLOUCESTER)

The Inn at Warner Hall

4750 Warner Hall Road, Gloucester, Virginia 23061

Tel: +1 804 695 9565
www.johansens.com/warnerhall

U.S.A. - VIRGINIA (IRVINGTON)

Hope and Glory Inn

65 Tavern Road, Irvington, Virginia 22480

Tel: +1 804 438 6053
www.johansens.com/hopeandglory

U.S.A. - VIRGINIA (MIDDLEBURG)

The Goodstone Inn & Estate

36205 Snake Hill Road, Middleburg, Virginia 20117

Tel: +1 540 687 4645
www.johansens.com/goodstoneinn

U.S.A. - VIRGINIA (STAUNTON)

Frederick House

28 North New Street, Staunton, Virginia 24401

Tel: + 1 540 885 4220
www.johansens.com/frederickhouse

U.S.A. - VIRGINIA (WASHINGTON METROPOLITAN AREA)

Morrison House

116 South Alfred Street, Alexandria, Virginia 22314

Tel: +1 703 838 8000
www.johansens.com/morrisonhouse

Hotels - The Americas

Properties listed below can be found in our Recommended Hotels, Inns, Resorts & Spas - The Americas, Atlantic, Caribbean & Pacific 2008 Guide. More information on our portfolio of guides can be found on page 247.

U.S.A. - VIRGINIA (WILLIAMSBURG)

Wedmore Place

5810 Wessex Hundred, Williamsburg, Virginia 23185

Tel: +1 757 476 5885
www.johansens.com/wedmore

U.S.A. - WYOMING (GRAND TETON NATIONAL PARK)

Jenny Lake Lodge

Inner Park Loop Road, Grand Teton National Park, Wyoming 83013

Tel: +1 307 543 3300
www.johansens.com/jennylake

U.S.A. - WASHINGTON (BELLEVUE)

The Bellevue Club Hotel

11200 S.E. 6th Street, Bellevue, Washington 98004

Tel: +1 425 455 1616
www.johansens.com/bellevue

Recommendations in Central America

U.S.A. - WASHINGTON (BELLINGHAM)

The Chrysalis Inn and Spa

804 10th Street, Bellingham, Washington 98225

Tel: +1 360 756 1005
www.johansens.com/chrysalis

BELIZE - AMBERGRIS CAYE (SAN PEDRO)

Victoria House

P.O. Box 22, San Pedro, Ambergris Caye

Tel: +501 226 2067
www.johansens.com/victoriahouse

U.S.A. - WASHINGTON (SEATTLE)

Hotel Ändra

2000 Fourth Avenue, Seattle, Washington 98121

Tel: +1 206 448 8600
www.johansens.com/hotelandra

BELIZE - CAYO (SAN IGNACIO)

The Lodge at Chaa Creek

P.O. Box 53, San Ignacio, Cayo

Tel: +501 824 2037
www.johansens.com/chaacreek

U.S.A. - WASHINGTON (SPOKANE)

The Davenport Hotel and Tower

10 South Post Street, Spokane, Washington 99201

Tel: +1 509 455 8888
www.johansens.com/davenport

COSTA RICA - ALAJUELA (BAJOS DEL TORO)

El Silencio Lodge & Spa

Bajos del Toro, Alajuela

Tel: +506 291 3044
www.johansens.com/elsilencio

U.S.A. - WASHINGTON (WINTHROP)

Sun Mountain Lodge

P.O. Box 1,000, Winthrop, Washington 98862

Tel: +1 509 996 2211
www.johansens.com/sunmountain

COSTA RICA - ALAJUELA (LA FORTUNA DE SAN CARLOS)

Tabacón Grand Spa Thermal Resort

La Fortuna de San Carlos, Arenal

Tel: +506 519 1900
www.johansens.com/tabacon

U.S.A. - WASHINGTON (WOODINVILLE)

The Herbfarm

14590 North East 145th Street, Woodinville, Washington 98072

Tel: +1 425 485 5300
www.johansens.com/herbfarm

COSTA RICA - GUANACASTE (ISLITA)

Hotel Punta Islita

Guanacaste

Tel: +506 231 6122
www.johansens.com/hotelpuntaislita

U.S.A. - WYOMING (CHEYENNE)

Nagle Warren Mansion

222 East 17Th Street, Cheyenne, Wyoming 82001

Tel: +1 307 637 3333
www.johansens.com/naglewarrenmansion

COSTA RICA - GUANACASTE (PLAYA CONCHAL)

Paradisus Playa Conchal

Bahía Brasilito, Playa Conchal, Santa Cruz, Guanacaste

Tel: +506 654 4123
www.johansens.com/paradisusplayaconchal

Hotels - The Americas

Properties listed below can be found in our Recommended Hotels, Inns, Resorts & Spas - The Americas, Atlantic, Caribbean & Pacific 2008 Guide. More information on our portfolio of guides can be found on page 247.

COSTA RICA - OSA PENISULA (PUERTO JIMENEZ)

Lapa Rios Eco Lodge

Puerto Jimenez, Osa Penisula

Tel: +506 735 5130
www.johansens.com/laparios

COSTA RICA - PUNTARENAS (MANUEL ANTONIO)

Gaia Hotel & Reserve

Km 2.7 Carretera Quepos, Manuel Antonio

Tel: +506 777 9797
www.johansens.com/gaiahr

GUATEMALA - ANTIGUA GUATEMALA

Filadelfia Coffee Resort & Spa

150 meters North of the San Felipe Chapel, Antigua Guatemala

Tel: +502 7728 0800
www.johansens.com/filadelfia

HONDURAS - ATLÁNTIDA (LA CEIBA)

The Lodge at Pico Bonito

A. P. 710, La Ceiba, Atlántida, C. P. 31101

Tel: +504 440 0388
www.johansens.com/picobonito

Recommendations in South America

ARGENTINA - BUENOS AIRES (CIUDAD DE BUENOS AIRES)

1555 Malabia House

Malabia 1555, C1414DME Ciudad de Buenos Aires, Buenos Aires

Tel: +54 11 4832 3345
www.johansens.com/malabiahouse

ARGENTINA - BUENOS AIRES (CIUDAD DE BUENOS AIRES)

Home Buenos Aires

Honduras 5860, Ciudad de Buenos Aires, Buenos Aires 1414

Tel: +54 11 4778 1008
www.johansens.com/homebuenosaires

ARGENTINA - BUENOS AIRES (CIUDAD DE BUENOS AIRES)

LoiSuites Recoleta Hotel

Vicente López 1955 – C1128ACC, Ciudad de Buenos Aires, Buenos Aires

Tel: +54 11 5777 8950
www.johansens.com/loisuites

ARGENTINA - BUENOS AIRES (CIUDAD DE BUENOS AIRES)

Moreno Hotel Buenos Aires

Moreno 376, Ciudad de Buenos Aires, Buenos Aires C1091AAH

Tel: +54 11 6091 2000
www.johansens.com/moreno

ARGENTINA - NEUQUÉN (VILLA LA ANGOSTURA)

Correntoso Lake & River Hotel

Av. Siete Lagos 4505, Villa La Angostura, Patagonia

Tel: +54 11 4803 0030
www.johansens.com/correntoso

ARGENTINA - NEUQUÉN (VILLA LA ANGOSTURA)

Hotel Las Balsas

Bahía Las Balsas s/n, Villa La Angostura, Neuquén 8407

Tel: +54 2944 494308
www.johansens.com/lasbalsas

ARGENTINA - RIO NEGRO (SAN CARLOS BARILOCHE)

Isla Victoria Lodge

Isla Victoria, Parque Nacional Nahuel Huapi, C.C. 26 (R8401AKU)

Tel: +54 43 94 96 05
www.johansens.com/islavictoria

ARGENTINA - SANTA CRUZ (EL CALAFATE)

Los Sauces Casa Patagónica

Los Gauchos 1352/70, CP9405, El Calafate, Santa Cruz

Tel: +54 2902 495854
www.johansens.com/lossauces

BRAZIL - ALAGOAS (SÃO MIGUEL DOS MILAGRES)

Pousada do Toque

Rua Felisberto de Ataide, Povoado do Toque, São Miguel dos Milagres, 57940-000 Alagoas

Tel: +55 82 3295 1127
www.johansens.com/pousadadotoque

BRAZIL - BAHIA (ARRAIAL D'ÁJUDA)

Maitei Hotel

Estrada do Mucugê, 475, Arraial D'Ájuda, Porto Seguro, Bahia 45816-000

Tel: +55 73 3575 3877
www.johansens.com/maitei

BRAZIL - BAHIA (CORUMBAU)

Fazenda São Francisco

Ponta do Corumbau s/n, Prado, Bahia

Tel: +55 11 3078 4411
www.johansens.com/fazenda

Hotels - The Americas

Properties listed below can be found in our Recommended Hotels, Inns, Resorts & Spas - The Americas, Atlantic, Caribbean & Pacific 2008 Guide. More information on our portfolio of guides can be found on page 247.

BRAZIL - BAHIA (CORUMBAU)

Tauana

Corumbau, Prado, Bahia

Tel: +55 73 3668 5172
www.johansens.com/tauana

BRAZIL - BAHIA (CORUMBAU)

Vila Naiá - Paralelo 17°

Ponta do Corumbau s/n, Corumbau, Prado, Bahia

Tel: +55 73 3573 1006
www.johansens.com/vilanaia

BRAZIL - BAHIA (ITACARÉ)

Txai Resort

Rod. Ilhéus-Itacaré km 48, Itacaré, Bahia 45530-000

Tel: +55 73 2101 5000
www.johansens.com/txairesort

BRAZIL - BAHIA (MARAU)

Kiaroa Eco-Luxury Resort

Loteamento da Costa, área SD6, Distrito de barra grande, Municipio de Maraú, Bahia, CEp 45 520-000

Tel: +55 71 3272 1320
www.johansens.com/kiaroa

BRAZIL - BAHIA (PRAIA DO FORTE)

Praia do Forte EcoResort & Thalasso Spa

Avenida do Farol, Praia do Forte - Mata de São João, Bahia

Tel: +55 71 36 76 40 00
www.johansens.com/praiadoforte

BRAZIL - BAHIA (TRANCOSO)

Estrela d'Agua

Estrada Arraial d'Ajuda, Trancoso S/N, Trancoso Porto Seguro, Bahia 45818-000

Tel: +55 73 3668 1030
www.johansens.com/estreladagua

BRAZIL - BAHIA (TRANCOSO)

Etnia Pousada and Boutique

Trancoso, Bahia 45818-000

Tel: +55 73 3668 1137
www.johansens.com/etnia

BRAZIL - MINAS GERAIS (TIRADENTES)

Pousada dos Inconfidentes

Rua João Rodrigues Sobrinho 91, 36325-000, Tiradentes, Minas Gerais

Tel: +55 32 3355 2135
www.johansens.com/inconfidentes

BRAZIL - MINAS GERAIS (TIRADENTES)

Solar da Ponte

Praça das Mercês S/N, Tiradentes, Minas Gerais 36325-000

Tel: +55 32 33 55 12 55
www.johansens.com/solardaponte

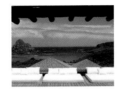

BRAZIL - PERNAMBUCO (FERNANDO DE NORONHA)

Pousada Maravilha

Rodovia BR-363, s/n, Sueste, Ilha de Fernando de Noronha, Pernambuco 53990-000

Tel: +55 81 3619 0028
www.johansens.com/maravilha

BRAZIL - PERNAMBUCO (PORTO DE GALINHAS)

Nannai Beach Resort

Rodovia PE-09, acesso à Muro Alto, Km 3, Ipojuca, Pernambuco 55590-000

Tel: +55 81 3552 0100
www.johansens.com/nannaibeach

BRAZIL - RIO DE JANEIRO (ANGRA DOS REIS)

Sítio do Lobo

Ponta do Lobo, Ilha Grande, Angra dos Reis, Rio de Janeiro

Tel: +55 21 2227 4138
www.johansens.com/sitiodolobo

BRAZIL - RIO DE JANEIRO (BÚZIOS)

Casas Brancas Boutique-Hotel & Spa

Alto do Humaitá 10, Armação dos Búzios, Rio de Janeiro 28950-000

Tel: +55 22 2623 1458
www.johansens.com/casasbrancas

BRAZIL - RIO DE JANEIRO (BÚZIOS)

Pérola Búzios Design Hotel

Av. José Bento Ribeiro Dantas, 222, Armação dos Búzios, Rio de Janeiro 28950-000

Tel: +55 22 2620 8507
www.johansens.com/perolabuzios

BRAZIL - RIO DE JANEIRO (BÚZIOS)

Portobay Glenzhaus

Rua dos Coqueiros, 10, Armação dos Búzios, Rio de Janeiro 28950-000

Tel: +55 22 2623 2823
www.johansens.com/glenzhaus

BRAZIL - RIO DE JANEIRO (PETRÓPOLIS)

Parador Santarém Marina

Estrada Correia da Veiga, 96, Petrópolis, Rio de Janeiro 25745-260

Tel: +55 24 2222 9933
www.johansens.com/paradorsantarem

Hotels - The Americas

Properties listed below can be found in our Recommended Hotels, Inns, Resorts & Spas - The Americas, Atlantic, Caribbean & Pacific 2008 Guide. More information on our portfolio of guides can be found on page 247.

BRAZIL - RIO DE JANEIRO (PETRÓPOLIS)

Solar do Império

Koeler Avenue, 376- Centro, Petrópolis, Rio de Janeiro

Tel: +55 24 2103 3000
www.johansens.com/solardoimperio

BRAZIL - RIO DE JANEIRO (PETRÓPOLIS)

Tankamana EcoResort

Estrada Júlio Cápua, S/N Vale Do Cuiabá, Itaipava - Petrópolis, Rio De Janeiro 25745-050

Tel: +55 24 2222 9181
www.johansens.com/tankamana

BRAZIL - RIO DE JANEIRO (RIO DE JANEIRO)

Hotel Marina All Suites

Av. Delfim Moreira, 696, Praia do Leblon, Rio de Janeiro 22441-000

Tel: +55 21 2172 1001
www.johansens.com/marinaallsuites

BRAZIL - RIO GRANDE DO NORTE (PRAIA DA PIPA)

Toca da Coruja

Av. Baia dos Golfinhos, 464, Praia da Pipa, Tibau do Sul, Rio Grande do Norte 59178-000

Tel: +55 84 3246 2226
www.johansens.com/rocadacoruja

BRAZIL - RIO GRANDE DO SUL (GRAMADO)

Estalagem St. Hubertus

Rua Carrieri, 974, Gramado, Rio Grande do Sul 95670-000, Brazil

Tel: +55 54 3286 1273
www.johansens.com/sthubertus

BRAZIL - RIO GRANDE DO SUL (GRAMADO)

Kurotel

Rua Nações Unidas 533, P.O. Box 65, Gramado, Rio Grande do Sul 95670-000

Tel: +55 54 3295 9393
www.johansens.com/kurotel

BRAZIL - RIO GRANDE DO SUL (SÃO FRANCISCO DE PAULA)

Pousada Do Engenho

Rua Odon Cavalcante, 330, São Francisco de Paula 95400-000, Rio Grande do Sul

Tel: +55 54 3244 1270
www.johansens.com/pousadadoengenho

BRAZIL - SANTA CATARINA (GOVERNADOR CELSO RAMOS)

Ponta dos Ganchos

Rua Eupídio Alves do Nascimento, 104, Governador Celso Ramos, Santa Catarina 88190-000

Tel: +55 48 3262 5000
www.johansens.com/pontadosganchos

BRAZIL - SANTA CATARINA (PALHOÇA)

Ilha do Papagaio

Ilha do Papagaio, Palhoça, Santa Catarina 88131-970

Tel: +55 48 3286 1242
www.johansens.com/ilhadopapagaio

BRAZIL - SANTA CATARINA (PRAIA DO ROSA)

Pousada Solar Mirador

Estrada Geral do Rosa s/n, Praia do Rosa, Imbituba, Santa Catarina 88780-000

Tel: +55 48 3355 6144
www.johansens.com/solarmirador

BRAZIL - SANTA CATARINA (PRAIA DO ROSA)

Quinta do Bucanero

Estrada Geral do Rosa s/n, Praia do Rosa, Imbituba, Santa Catarina 88780-000

Tel: +55 48 3355 6056
www.johansens.com/bucanero

BRAZIL - SÃO PAULO (CAMPOS DO JORDÃO)

Hotel Frontenac

Av. Dr. Paulo Ribas, 295 Capivari, Campos do Jordão 12460-000

Tel: +55 12 3669 1000
www.johansens.com/frontenac

BRAZIL - SÃO PAULO (ILHABELA)

DPNY Beach Hotel Boutique

Av. Pacheco do Nascimento, 7668, Praia do Curral, Ilhabela, São Paulo 11630-000

Tel: +55 12 3894 2121
www.johansens.com/dpnybeach

BRAZIL - SÃO PAULO (MAIRIPORÃ)

Spa Unique Garden

Estrada Laramara, 3500, Mairiporã, São Paulo 07600-970

Tel: +55 11 4486 8700
www.johansens.com/uniquegarden

BRAZIL - SÃO PAULO (SÃO PAULO)

Hotel Unique

Av. Brigadeiro Luis Antonio, 4.700, São Paulo, São Paulo 01402-002

Tel: +55 11 3055 4710
www.johansens.com/hotelunique

CHILE - PATAGONIA (PUERTO GUADAL)

Hacienda Tres Lagos

Carretera Austral Sur Km 274, Localidad Lago Negro, Puerto Guadal, Patagonia

Tel: +56 2 333 4122
www.johansens.com/treslagos

Hotels - The Americas, Atlantic & Caribbean

All the properties listed below can be found in our Recommended Hotels, Inns, Resorts & Spas - The Americas, Atlantic, Caribbean & Pacific 2008
Details of this Guide and others in our portfolio can be found on page 343.

CHILE - ARAUCANIA (PUCON)

Hotel Antumalal

Carretera Pucon - Villarica Highway at km 2 from
Pucon, Pucon, Araucania

Tel: +56 45 441 011
www.johansens.com/antumalal

CHILE - SANTIAGO (SAN FELIPE)

Termas de Jahuel Hotel & Spa

Jahuel, San Felipe, Santiago

Tel: +56 2 411 1720
www.johansens.com/jahuel

CHILE - ARAUCANÍA (VILLARRICA)

Villarrica Park Lake Hotel

Camino a Villarrica km.13, Araucanía, Villarrica

Tel: +56 2 207 7070
www.johansens.com/villarrica

PERU - LIMA PROVINCIAS (YAUYOS)

Refugios Del Peru - Viñak Reichraming

Santiago de Viñak, Yauyos, Lima

Tel: +51 1 421 6952
www.johansens.com/refugiosdelperu

Recommendations in the Atlantic

ATLANTIC - BAHAMAS (ANDROS)

Kamalame Cay

Staniard Creek, Andros

Tel: +1 242 368 6281
www.johansens.com/kamalamecay

ATLANTIC - BAHAMAS (GRAND BAHAMA ISLAND)

Old Bahama Bay at Ginn Sur Mer

West End, Grand Bahama Island

Tel: +1 242 350 6500
www.johansens.com/oldbahamabay

ATLANTIC - BAHAMAS (HARBOUR ISLAND)

Pink Sands

Chapel Street, Harbour Island

Tel: +1 242 333 2030
www.johansens.com/pinksands

ATLANTIC - BERMUDA (HAMILTON)

Rosedon Hotel

P.O. Box Hm 290, Hamilton Hmax

Tel: +1 441 295 1640
www.johansens.com/rosedonhotel

ATLANTIC - BERMUDA (HAMILTON)

Waterloo House

P.O. Box H.M. 333, Hamilton H.M. B.X.

Tel: +1 441 295 4480
www.johansens.com/waterloohouse

ATLANTIC - BERMUDA (PAGET)

Horizons and Cottages

33 South Shore Road, Paget, P.G. 04

Tel: +1 441 236 0048
www.johansens.com/horizonscottages

ATLANTIC - BERMUDA (SOMERSET)

Cambridge Beaches Resort & Spa

Kings Point, Somerset

Tel: +1 441 234 0331
www.johansens.com/cambridgebeaches

ATLANTIC - BERMUDA (SOUTHAMPTON)

The Reefs

56 South Shore Road, Southampton

Tel: +1 441 238 0222
www.johansens.com/thereefs

Recommendations in the Caribbean

CARIBBEAN - ANGUILLA (RENDEZVOUS BAY)

CuisinArt Resort & Spa

P.O. Box 2000, Rendezvous Bay

Tel: +1 264 498 2000
www.johansens.com/cuisinartresort

CARIBBEAN - ANTIGUA (ST. JOHN'S)

Blue Waters

P.O. Box 257, St. John's

Tel: +44 870 360 1245
www.johansens.com/bluewaters

Hotels - Caribbean

All the properties listed below can be found in our Recommended Hotels, Inns, Resorts & Spas - The Americas, Atlantic, Caribbean & Pacific 2008
Details of this Guide and others in our portfolio can be found on page 343.

CARIBBEAN - ANTIGUA (ST. JOHN'S)

Curtain Bluff

P.O. Box 288, St. John's

Tel: +1 268 462 8400
www.johansens.com/curtainbluff

CARIBBEAN - BARBUDA (PALMETTO POINT)

The Beach House

Palmetto Point

Tel: +1 516 767 3057
www.johansens.com/beachbarbuda

CARIBBEAN - ANTIGUA (ST. JOHN'S)

Galley Bay

Five Islands, St. John's

Tel: +1 954 481 8787
www.johansens.com/galleybay

CARIBBEAN - BRITISH VIRGIN ISLANDS (PETER ISLAND)

Peter Island Resort

Peter Island

Tel: +1 770 476 9988
www.johansens.com/peterislandresort

CARIBBEAN - ANTIGUA (ST. JOHN'S)

The Verandah

Indian Town Road, St. John's

Tel: +1 268 460 5000
www.johansens.com/verandah

CARIBBEAN - BRITISH VIRGIN ISLANDS (PETER ISLAND)

The Villas at Peter Island

Peter Island

Tel: +1 770 476 9988
www.johansens.com/villaspeterisland

CARIBBEAN - ANTIGUA (ST. MARY'S)

Carlisle Bay

Old Road, St. Mary's

Tel: +1 268 484 0000
www.johansens.com/carlislebay

CARIBBEAN - BRITISH VIRGIN ISLANDS (VIRGIN GORDA)

Biras Creek Resort

North Sound, Virgin Gorda

Tel: +1 310 440 4225
www.johansens.com/birascreek

CARIBBEAN - BARBADOS (CHRIST CHURCH)

Little Arches

Enterprise Beach Road, Christ Church

Tel: +1 246 420 4689
www.johansens.com/littlearches

CARIBBEAN - CURAÇAO (WILLEMSTAD)

Avila Hotel on the beach

Penstraat 130, Willemstad

Tel: +599 9 461 4377
www.johansens.com/avilabeach

CARIBBEAN - BARBADOS (ST. JAMES)

Coral Reef Club

St. James

Tel: +1 246 422 2372
www.johansens.com/coralreefclub

CARIBBEAN - DOMINICAN REPUBLIC (PUERTO PLATA)

Casa Colonial Beach & Spa

P.O. Box 22, Puerto Plata

Tel: +1 809 320 3232
www.johansens.com/casacolonial

CARIBBEAN - BARBADOS (ST. JAMES)

The Sandpiper

Holetown, St. James

Tel: +1 246 422 2251
www.johansens.com/sandpiper

CARIBBEAN - GRENADA (ST. GEORGE'S)

Spice Island Beach Resort

Grand Anse Beach, St. George's

Tel: +1 473 444 4423/4258
www.johansens.com/spiceisland

CARIBBEAN - BARBADOS (ST. PETER)

Cobblers Cove

Speightstown, St. Peter

Tel: +1 246 422 2291
www.johansens.com/cobblerscove

CARIBBEAN - JAMAICA (MONTEGO BAY)

Half Moon

Rose Hall, Montego Bay

Tel: +1 876 953 2211
www.johansens.com/halfmoon

All the properties listed below can be found in our Recommended Hotels, Inns, Resorts & Spas - The Americas, Atlantic, Caribbean & Pacific 2008
Details of this Guide and others in our portfolio can be found on page 343.

CARIBBEAN - JAMAICA (MONTEGO BAY)

Round Hill Hotel and Villas

P.O. Box 64, Montego Bay

Tel: +1 876 956 7050
www.johansens.com/roundhill

CARIBBEAN - ST. KITTS & NEVIS (NEVIS)

Montpelier Plantation Inn

P.O. Box 474, Nevis

Tel: +1 869 469 3462
www.johansens.com/montpelierplantation

CARIBBEAN - JAMAICA (MONTEGO BAY)

Tryall Club

P.O. Box 1206, Montego Bay

Tel: +1 876 956 5660
www.johansens.com/tryallclub

CARIBBEAN - ST. LUCIA (SOUFRIÈRE)

Anse Chastanet

Soufrière

Tel: +1 758 459 7000
www.johansens.com/ansechastanet

CARIBBEAN - JAMAICA (OCHO RIOS)

Royal Plantation

Main Street , P.O. Box 2, Ocho Rios, St. Ann

Tel: +1 876 974 5601
www.johansens.com/royalplantation

CARIBBEAN - ST. LUCIA (SOUFRIÈRE)

Jade Mountain at Anse Chastanet

Soufrière

Tel: +1 758 459 4000
www.johansens.com/jademountain

CARIBBEAN - PUERTO RICO (OLD SAN JUAN)

Chateau Cervantes

Recinto Sur, Old San Juan

Tel: +1 787 724 7722
www.johansens.com/cervantes

CARIBBEAN - ST. LUCIA (SOUFRIÈRE)

Ladera Resort

Soufrière

Tel: +1 758 459 7323
www.johansens.com/ladera

CARIBBEAN - PUERTO RICO (RINCON)

Horned Dorset Primavera

Apartado 1132, Rincón, 00677

Tel: +1 787 823 4030
www.johansens.com/horneddorset

CARIBBEAN - ST. MARTIN (BAIE LONGUE)

La Samanna

P.O. Box 4077, 97064

Tel: +590 590 87 64 00
www.johansens.com/lasamanna

CARIBBEAN - SAINT-BARTHÉLEMY (ANSE DE TOINY)

Le Toiny

Anse de Toiny, 97133

Tel: +590 590 27 88 88
www.johansens.com/letoiny

CARIBBEAN - THE GRENADINES (MUSTIQUE)

Firefly

Mustique Island

Tel: +1 784 488 8414
www.johansens.com/firefly

CARIBBEAN - SAINT-BARTHÉLEMY (GRAND CUL DE SAC)

Hotel Guanahani & Spa

Grand Cul de Sac, 97133

Tel: +590 590 27 66 60
www.johansens.com/guanahani

CARIBBEAN - THE GRENADINES (PALM ISLAND)

Palm Island

Tel: +1 954 481 8787
www.johansens.com/palmisland

CARIBBEAN - SAINT-BARTHÉLEMY (GRAND CUL DE SAC)

Le Sereno

Grand Cul de Sac

Tel: +590 590 298 300
www.johansens.com/lesereno

CARIBBEAN - TURKS & CAICOS (GRACE BAY BEACH)

Grace Bay Club

P.O. Box 128, Providenciales

Tel: +1 649 946 5050
www.johansens.com/gracebayclub

Hotels - Caribbean & Pacific

All the properties listed below can be found in our Recommended Hotels, Inns, Resorts & Spas - The Americas, Atlantic, Caribbean & Pacific 2008 Details of this Guide and others in our portfolio can be found on page 343.

CARIBBEAN - TURKS & CAICOS (PARROT CAY)

Parrot Cay

P.O. Box 164, Providenciales

Tel: +1 649 946 7788
www.johansens.com/parrotcay

CARIBBEAN - TURKS & CAICOS (POINT GRACE)

Point Grace

P.O. Box 700, Providenciales

Tel: +1 649 946 5096
www.johansens.com/pointgrace

CARIBBEAN - TURKS & CAICOS (GRACE BAY BEACH)

The Somerset on Grace Bay

Princess Drive, Providenciales

Tel: +1 649 946 5900
www.johansens.com/somersetgracebay

CARIBBEAN - TURKS & CAICOS (WEST GRACE BAY BEACH)

Turks & Caicos Club

West Grace Bay Beach, P.O. Box 687, Providenciales

Tel: +1 649 946 5800
www.johansens.com/turksandcaicos

CARIBBEAN - TURKS & CAICOS (GRACE BAY BEACH)

The Regent Palms

P.O. Box 681, Grace Bay, Providenciales

Tel: +1 649 946 8666
www.johansens.com/regentpalms

Recommendations in the Pacific

PACIFIC - FIJI ISLANDS (LABASA)

Nukubati Island, Great Sea Reef, Fiji

P.O. Box 1928, Labasa

Tel: +61 2 93888 196
www.johansens.com/nukubati

PACIFIC - FIJI ISLANDS (LAUTOKA)

Blue Lagoon Cruises

183 Vitogo Parade, Lautoka

Tel: +679 6661 622
www.johansens.com/bluelagooncruises

PACIFIC - FIJI ISLANDS (QAMEA ISLAND)

Qamea Resort & Spa

P.A. Matei, Tavenui

Tel: +679 888 0220
www.johansens.com/qamea

PACIFIC - FIJI ISLANDS (SAVUSAVU)

Jean-Michel Cousteau Fiji Islands Resort

Lesiaceva Point, SavuSavu

Tel: +1 415 788 5794
www.johansens.com/jean-michelcousteau

PACIFIC - FIJI ISLANDS (SIGATOKA)

Myola Plantation

P.O. Box 638, Sigatoka

Tel: +679 652 1084
www.johansens.com/myola

PACIFIC - FIJI ISLANDS (UGAGA ISLAND)

Royal Davui

P.O. Box 3171, Lami

Tel: +679 336 1624
www.johansens.com/royaldavui

PACIFIC - FIJI ISLANDS (YAQETA ISLAND)

Navutu Stars Resort

P.O. Box 1838, Lautoka

Tel: +679 664 0553 and +679 664 0554
www.johansens.com/navutustars

PACIFIC - FIJI ISLANDS (YASAWA ISLAND)

Yasawa Island Resort

P.O. Box 10128, Nadi Airport, Nadi

Tel: +679 672 2266
www.johansens.com/yasawaisland

The International Mark of Excellence

For further information, hotel search, gift certificates, online bookshop and special offers visit:

www.johansens.com

Annually Inspected for the Independent Traveler

Individuality Matters to our Partnership

We recognise that every client is individual and has particular legal requirements.

Our approach

We seek to anticipate your legal needs by understanding your business and by developing a close working relationship with you.

We aim to reduce the burden of the legal aspects of decision making, enabling you to maximize opportunities whilst limiting your business, financial and legal risks.

We structure our services with a view to saving expensive management time, thereby producing cost effective decision making.

Our expertise

Since the firm was founded over 50 years ago, we have developed an acknowledged expertise in the areas of corporate & commercial law, litigation, property, employment and franchising law. We also have a leading reputation as legal advisors in the media and hotels sectors. For personal matters, we also have a dedicated Private Client Group which provides a comprehensive and complementary range of services to the individual and their families.

We take pride in watching our clients' businesses grow and assisting them in that process wherever we can.

For more information about how we can help you or your business visit www.gdlaw.co.uk or contact Belinda Copland bcopland@gdlaw.co.uk tel: +44 (0)20 7404 0606

GOODMAN DERRICK LLP

Condé Nast Johansens Preferred Legal Partner

Index by Property

Index by Property

Index by Property/Location

Index by Location

London

England

A

B

Index by Location

Index by Location

Index by Location

North West England

SCOTLAND

Berwick-Upon-Tweed

Northumberland National Park

Carlisle

Lake District National Park

Windermere

Kendal

Yorkshire Dales National Park

Isle of Man

Douglas

Skipton

Barrow-in-Furness

Fleetwood

Blackpool

Preston

Southport

Bolton

Wigan

Manchester

Liverpool

WALES

© Lovell Johns Limited, Oxford

North East England

Berwick-Upon-Tweed

Alnwick

Newcastle
Newcastle

Middlesbrough

Teeside

Durham

North York Moors
National Park

Thirsk

Dales
Park

Skipton

Harrogate

York

Leeds
Bradford

Halifax

Hull

Wakefield

Huddersfield

Doncaster

ster

Sheffield

A1

A98

A697

106

108

A1

A697

A1068

A1

A696

A69

A68

A692

A693

A691

A690

A19

A167

A1(M)

A688

A689

A68

A66

153

A1

154
155

156
108

A1(M)

A168

A59

A658

A6068

A65

A61

A59

A64

157

158

A171

A172

A170

A64

A166

A165

A163

A1079

A1079

A1035

A614

A63

A63

A164

A15

A180

A46

A16

A15

A6

A158

A57

A631

A631

A57

92

A623

A616

A628

A638

A628

M1

M18

A1(M)

A19

A1

A1041

M62

M18

M180

A15

160

M62

M67

50

159

A59

Skipton

A59

Teeside

235

© Lovell Johns Limited, Oxford

Central England

Peak District National park

Manchester
Liverpool
Liverpool
Manchester
Chester
Whitchurch
WALES
Shrewsbury
Ludlow
Hereford
Ross-on-Wye
WALES
Gloucester
Cheltenham
Cirencester
Worcester
Kidderminster
Bridgnorth
Wolverhampton
Birmingham
Birmingham
Stoke
Buxton
Sheffield
Chesterfield
Derby
East Midlands
Nottingham
Leicester
Grantham
Kettering
Northampton
Milton Keynes
Stratford-upon-Avon
Oxford
Doncaster

Eastern England

Louth

Lincoln

Cromer

King's Lynn

The Broads

Norwich

Great Yarmouth

Peterborough

Thetford

Newmarket

Bury St Edmunds

Cambridge

Ipswich

Felixstowe

Bishop's Stortford

Stansted

Colchester

Luton

Chelmsford

© Lovell Johns Limited, Oxford

Channel Islands & South West England

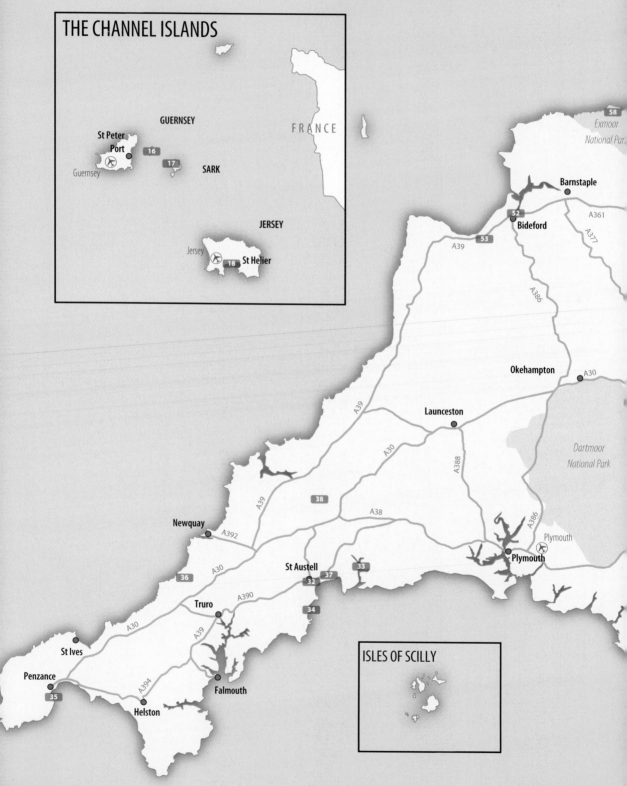

WALES

THE CHANNEL ISLANDS

FRANCE

GUERNSEY

St Peter Port
Guernsey
16
17
SARK

JERSEY

Jersey
St Helier
18

Exmoor National Park

58

Barnstaple

52
Bideford
53
A39
A361
A377

A386

Okehampton
A30

Launceston

A39

Dartmoor National Park

A30
A388
A386

38

Newquay
A392
A38
Plymouth
Plymouth

A39

A30
36

St Austell
33
32
37

Truro
A390
34

A30
A394
A39

St Ives

Penzance
35

Helston
Falmouth

ISLES OF SCILLY

WALES

Bristol

Bristol

Bath

Warminster

Exmoor
National Park

Taunton

Yeovil

Blandford
Forum

Exeter

Bridport

Dorchester

Bourne

Bournem

Weymouth

Torquay

Kingsbridge

Southern England

© Lovell Johns Limited, Oxford

South East England

Felixstowe

Colchester

Stansted

Hertford

Chelmsford

Sheerness

Ramsgate

Dartford

GREATER
LONDON

City

Maidstone

Canterbury

Gatwick

Tonbridge

Ashford

Dover

East
Grinstead

Royal
Tunbridge
Wells

Folkestone

Uckfield

Brighton

Hastings

Newhaven

Eastbourne

© Lovell Johns Limited, Oxford

241

Ireland

SCOTLA

Coleraine

City of Derry
Londonderry
A37
A2
A26
A44
A6
A29
M2
A36
Larne
N14
N15
M2
A505
Belfast
Belfast
A32
A5
A4
A29
M1
A1
A20
N15
A4
Armagh
A28
A7
N16
Newry
A24
Ballina
Sligo
N17
N5
N4
Cavan
N2
Dundalk
N17
Knock International
N5
N3
M1
Longford
N1
Drogheda
N2
M1
Galway
N17
164
Dublin
N6
Athlone
M4
Dublin
N7
Dun Laoghaire
N18
N7
N7
N11
Shannon
N9
Shannon
N7
Limerick
N8
Kilkenny
N24
N9
N21
Tralee
163
N10
N30
N24
Wexford
N20
6N
N25
162
Killarney
Waterford
N22
N25
Kenmare
Cork
Cork

W

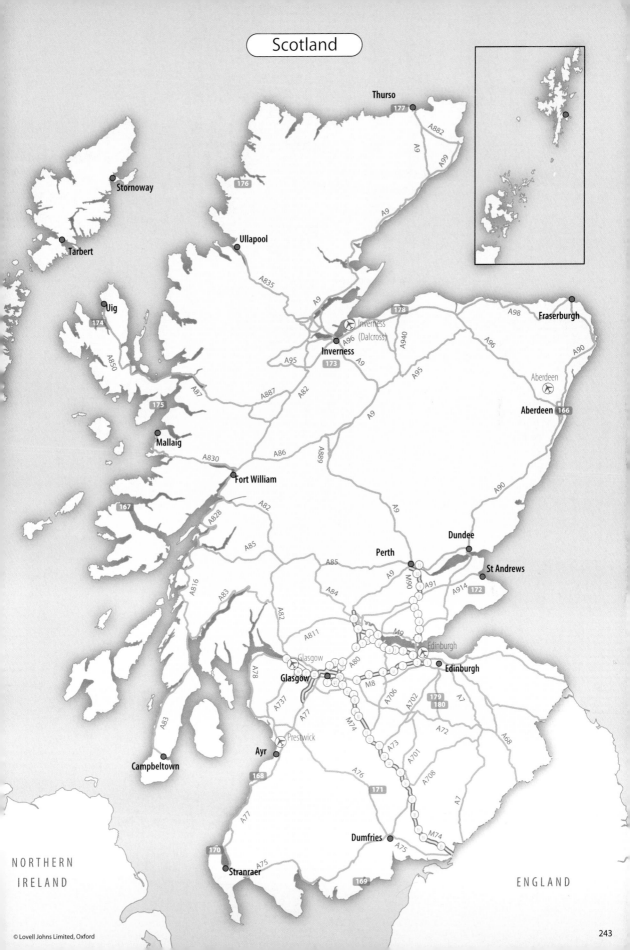

Scotland

Thurso | 177
A882
A9
A99

Stornoway

Tarbert

176

Ullapool

A835
A9

Uig
174
A850
A87
175

Inverness (Dalcross)
A96
Inverness | 173
A95
A887
A82
A940
A96
A98
Fraserburgh
A90
Aberdeen
A95
A9
Aberdeen | 166

Mallaig
A86
A889

A830
Fort William

167
A828
A82
A85
A9
A90

A816
A83
A82
A85
Perth
A85
A9
M90
A91
A914 | 172
Dundee
St Andrews

A811
M9
Edinburgh

Glasgow
A80
M8
Edinburgh
A706
A702
179
180
A7
A72
A68

A78
A737
A77
M74
A73
A701
A708
A7

Prestwick
Ayr
168
A76
171
A701

Campbeltown

A77
A76

Dumfries
A75
M74

Stranraer
A75
170
169

NORTHERN
IRELAND

ENGLAND

© Lovell Johns Limited, Oxford

243

Wales

Holyhead

A55

184 Llandudno

A55

A5

A55

A470

Caernarfon

A487

A5

183

A494

Wrexham

A483

A525

Snowdonia National Park

A5

A494

124

A470

A470

A458

A483

187 Dolgellau

186

A487

A470

A489

ENGLAND

A470

A487

A44

A470

Aberystwyth

A470

A44

A483

A487

A483

A44

185

A487

A483

A470

Brecon

A438

Fishguard

A40

A483

A470

190

A479

Carmarthen

A40

191

188

182

A48

A40

A470

A40

Brecon Beacons National Park

A477

A483

Abergavenny

Pembroke

A40

A465

A449

189

Swansea

M4

A470

M4

Cardiff

Cardiff

192

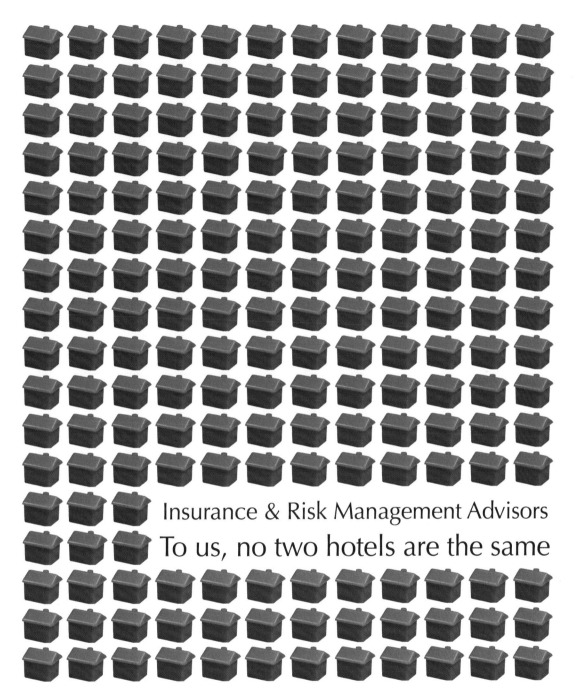

Insurance & Risk Management Advisors

To us, no two hotels are the same

+44 151 243 0287

Johansens@jltgroup.com

Insurance | Experience | Excellence

Preferred insurance partner of Condé Nast Johansens

JARDINE LLOYD THOMPSON

Leisure

Treat your hotel business as well as you treat your guests.

Avon Data Systems is a world class provider of hotel management systems. We have been developing hospitality software for over 20 years and have a proven track record in increasing the efficiency of each and every department of the hotel.

Today, our latest generation of software is up and running in hundreds of hotels throughout the UK and across the globe. In independent hotels and hotel groups of every size and combination, it enables owners, managers and staff to take control of business, fast, leaving you more time to spend looking after your guests.

PMS • Conference and Banqueting • EPOS
• Real Time Internet Reservations

To find out how to maximise
the efficiency of your hotel
(and your time) call:

+44 (0)117 910 9166

sales@avondata.co.uk

www.avondata.co.uk

avon data systems
hospitality solutions

Avon Data Systems Ltd,
Unit 2 Vincent Court,
89 Soundwell Road, Staple Hill,
Bristol, BS16 4QR United Kingdom

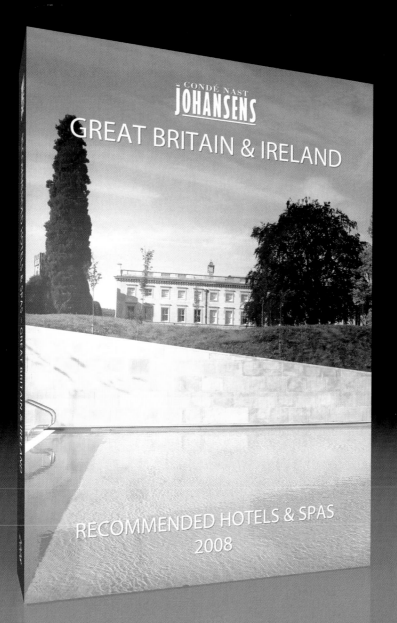

Tell us about your stay

Following your stay in a Condé Nast Johansens Recommendation, please spare a moment to complete this Guest Survey Report. This is an important source of information for Condé Nast Johansens, in order to maintain the highest standards for our Recommendations and to support our team of Inspectors. It is also the prime source of nominations for Condé Nast Johansens Awards for Excellence, which are held annually and include properties from all over the world that represent the finest standards and best value for money in luxury, independent travel.

1. Your details

Your name: ....

Your address: ....

Postcode: ....

Country: ....

E-mail: ....

Telephone: ....

Please tick if you would like to receive information or offers from The Condé Nast Publications Ltd by telephone ☐ or SMS ☐ or E-mail ☐ . Please tick if you would like to receive information or offers from other selected companies by telephone ☐ or SMS ☐ or E-mail ☐ . Please tick this box if you prefer not to receive direct mail from The Condé Nast Publications Ltd ☐ and other reputable companies ☐

2. Hotel details

Name of hotel: ....

Country: ....

Date of visit: .... Room No: ....

3. Reason for your visit

○ Leisure   ○ Business   ○ Meeting   ○ Restaurant

4. Any other comments

....

....

....

....

If you wish to make additional comments, please write separately to the Publisher, Condé Nast Johansens Ltd, 6-8 Old Bond Street, London W1S 4PH, Great Britain

5. Your rating of the hotel

Please tick one box in each category below (as applicable)

	EXCELLENT	GOOD	DISAPPOINTING	POOR
Bedrooms				
Comfort	○	○	○	○
Amenities	○	○	○	○
Bathroom	○	○	○	○
Public Areas				
Inside	○	○	○	○
Outdoor	○	○	○	○
Housekeeping				
Cleanliness	○	○	○	○
Maintenance	○	○	○	○
Service				
Check in/out	○	○	○	○
Professionalism	○	○	○	○
Friendliness	○	○	○	○
Dining	○	○	○	○
Internet Facilities				
Bedrooms	○	○	○	○
Public Areas	○	○	○	○
Ambience	○	○	○	○
Value for Money	○	○	○	○
Food and drink				
Breakfast	○	○	○	○
Lunch	○	○	○	○
Dinner	○	○	○	○
Choice of dishes	○	○	○	○
Wine List	○	○	○	○
Did The Hotel Meet Your Expectations?	○	○	○	○

I most liked: ....

I least liked: ....

My favourite member of staff: ....

Please fax your completed survey to +44 (0)207 152 3566 or go to www.johansens.com where you can complete the survey online